CONTRACT LAW AND THEORY

D1613954

ASPEN TREATISE SERIES

CONTRACT LAW AND THEORY

ERIC A. POSNER

Kirkland & Ellis Professor of Law
The University of Chicago Law School

Wolters Kluwer
Law & Business

Copyright © 2011 CCH Incorporated.

Published by Wolters Kluwer Law & Business in New York.

Wolters Kluwer Law & Business serves customers worldwide with CCH, Aspen Publishers, and Kluwer Law International products. (www.wolterskluwerlb.com)

No part of this publication may be reproduced or transmitted in any form or by any means, electronic or mechanical, including photocopy, recording, or utilized by any information storage or retrieval system, without written permission from the publisher. For information about permissions or to request permissions online, visit us at www.wolterskluwerlb.com, or a written request may be faxed to our permissions department at 212-771-0803.

To contact Customer Service, e-mail customer.service@wolterskluwer.com, call 1-800-234-1660, fax 1-800-901-9075, or mail correspondence to:

Wolters Kluwer Law & Business
Attn: Order Department
PO Box 990
Frederick, MD 21705

Printed in the United States of America.

1 2 3 4 5 6 7 8 9 0

ISBN 978-1-4548-1071-1

Library of Congress Cataloging-in-Publication Data

Posner, Eric A.
      Contract law and theory / Eric A. Posner.
        p. cm. — (Aspen treatise series)
      ISBN 978-1-4548-1071-1 (alk. paper)
    1. Contracts–United States.   I. Title.

KF801.P67 2011

346.7302—dc23

                                        2011037456

About Wolters Kluwer Law & Business

Wolters Kluwer Law & Business is a leading global provider of intelligent information and digital solutions for legal and business professionals in key specialty areas, and respected educational resources for professors and law students. Wolters Kluwer Law & Business connects legal and business professionals as well as those in the education market with timely, specialized authoritative content and information-enabled solutions to support success through productivity, accuracy and mobility.

Serving customers worldwide, Wolters Kluwer Law & Business products include those under the Aspen Publishers, CCH, Kluwer Law International, Loislaw, Best Case, ftwilliam.com and MediRegs family of products.

CCH products have been a trusted resource since 1913, and are highly regarded resources for legal, securities, antitrust and trade regulation, government contracting, banking, pension, payroll, employment and labor, and healthcare reimbursement and compliance professionals.

Aspen Publishers products provide essential information to attorneys, business professionals and law students. Written by preeminent authorities, the product line offers analytical and practical information in a range of specialty practice areas from securities law and intellectual property to mergers and acquisitions and pension/benefits. Aspen's trusted legal education resources provide professors and students with high-quality, up-to-date and effective resources for successful instruction and study in all areas of the law.

Kluwer Law International products provide the global business community with reliable international legal information in English. Legal practitioners, corporate counsel and business executives around the world rely on Kluwer Law journals, looseleafs, books, and electronic products for comprehensive information in many areas of international legal practice.

Loislaw is a comprehensive online legal research product providing legal content to law firm practitioners of various specializations. Loislaw provides attorneys with the ability to quickly and efficiently find the necessary legal information they need, when and where they need it, by facilitating access to primary law as well as state-specific law, records, forms and treatises.

Best Case Solutions is the leading bankruptcy software product to the bankruptcy industry. It provides software and workflow tools to flawlessly streamline petition preparation and the electronic filing process, while timely incorporating ever-changing court requirements.

ftwilliam.com offers employee benefits professionals the highest quality plan documents (retirement, welfare and non-qualified) and government forms (5500/PBGC, 1099 and IRS) software at highly competitive prices.

MediRegs products provide integrated health care compliance content and software solutions for professionals in healthcare, higher education and life sciences, including professionals in accounting, law and consulting.

Wolters Kluwer Law & Business, a division of Wolters Kluwer, is headquartered in New York. Wolters Kluwer is a market-leading global information services company focused on professionals.

Summary of Contents

Contents

Contents

Acknowledgments

I thank Mitu Gulati for providing me with comments on the manuscript, James Kraehenbuehl and Greg Pesce for helpful research assistance, and the Microsoft Fund and the Russell Baker Scholars Fund at the University of Chicago Law School for financial assistance. I also gratefully thank generations of students, from 1995 to 2011, who helped me refine my ideas about contract law.

Chapter *1*

Introduction

§1.1   Note to Students

Contract law is a set of rules related to the social practice of promising. Promises are important because they are the devices that people use to commit themselves to take actions in the future. All of commerce and much else depends on this capacity to commit. Indeed, contracting, promising, and committing are just aspects of cooperation, which is the key to social, economic, and political life. Contract law is a broad subject; mastery of it will help you understand many other areas of law in which contractual ideas operate — including bankruptcy law, commercial law, secured transactions, corporate law, securities law, and even family law, constitutional law, criminal law, and administrative law.

Moral philosophers have pondered the basic questions about private and social cooperation for centuries, but the modern way of thinking about contract law is heavily influenced by economics. According to this approach, people are rational and enter into contracts in order to cooperate with each other. In a cooperative relationship, both sides of the transaction expect to do better than if each acted alone. But unexpected events can arise that make the deal a bad one for one party or the other. In a perfect world, the parties would design a contract that took account of all possible future contingencies. Such a contract would specify each party's obligations under alternative future states of the world, excusing the party from performing when the cost of performance is high or the benefit is low. Because the world is not perfect — because the cost of transacting is high — contracts do not anticipate all future states of the world. When a dispute arises, the court's job is to interpret the contract in such a way as to maximize the value of the transaction for the parties. One can understand much of contract law from this deceptively simple starting point.

The book reflects my thinking about contract law, as it has evolved over many years, in response to reading cases and scholarship, and occasional practice. It is intended as a textbook; thus, it is light on citations. In its emphasis on theory, the book differs from traditional treatises and student guides. But in its attempt to apply that theory to a wide range of doctrines — most of those taught in the first-year contracts course — the book differs from existing theoretical work on contract law. The philosophy of this book is that one can learn contract law only if one can understand the theoretical considerations that inform it. Students need to understand not only the "what" of the doctrine, but the "why" — why one rule rather than another makes sense from the standpoint of policy. A grasp of theory makes learning the rules a great deal easier. In the process of learning a rule, the lesson takes deeper hold if the student can understand the relationship between that rule and other rules within the overall structure of contract law.

In the interest of expository simplicity, the descriptions of the law will often be general, and no attempt will be made, except when stated, to account for differences across jurisdictions. Students who seek a more fine-grained description of contract law should consult treatises.[1]

§1.2 How to Use This Book

Contract law has few natural joints; thus, the organization of the field into intelligible chunks will vary from book to book. Compare, for example, the table of contents for the Restatement of Contracts and those for any casebook. We can easily separate off remedies, and everyone does that. But then things become more difficult. It is tempting to distinguish "contract formation," "contract enforcement," and "contract interpretation," but it turns out that these concepts overlap. Some casebooks separate out the consideration doctrine and promissory estoppel as "grounds for enforcing promises," but these rules determine what contracts can be formed, akin to the offer-acceptance doctrines. Conditions are usually put in their own section, but they can be understood as rules for interpreting and enforcing contracts. Learning contracts in this way is like learning a

---

[1] For example, E. Allan Farnsworth, Contracts (4th ed. 2004); Joseph M. Perillo & John D. Calamari, Calamari and Perillo on Contracts (6th ed. 2009). Brian A. Blum, Contracts: Examples and Explanations (4th ed. 2007), and Marvin A. Chirelstein, Concepts and Case Analysis in the Law of Contracts (6th ed. 2010), are lucid introductions to contract law for students. Students who seek an introduction to the economic analysis of contract law should consult Steven Shavell, Foundations of the Economic Analysis of Law chs. 13-16 (2004); Robert Cooter & Thomas Ulen, Law and Economics ch. 7 (6th ed. 2011); Richard A. Posner, Economic Analysis of Law ch. 4 (5th ed. 1998). These books contain further citations to the literature.

language by first memorizing nouns, then verbs, then adjectives. But there is no alternative: ideas that interconnect must be introduced in a linear fashion. In classes, instructors can overcome this problem by briefly anticipating at various stages concepts that will be explained in greater detail later in the course. For books, the reader must be prepared to jump around and rely heavily on the index.

Classes focus heavily on the case method. Students read little stories composed by judges and, with the help of the instructor, learn to see how courts develop and apply doctrine. In this book, I take a different approach, one that relies more on the paradigm of the textbook than on that of the casebook. Chapter 2 is the linchpin. Like a textbook treatment of biology or economics, it lays out the rules of contract law by beginning with the simplest ideas and gradually explaining their complexities. The approach taken in Chapter 2 differs from the way classes are taught, and has no parallel, so it may be disorienting for some students. But I believe that introducing a conceptual framework that students can work from as they go through the course will make learning easier.

The remaining chapters discuss doctrine more directly, and follow an organization that is similar to that of most casebooks. Although I discuss some cases, I continue the textbook approach that emphasizes analysis rather than narrative. The last two chapters address issues that are sometimes ignored and sometimes addressed in an ad hoc fashion in contracts classes, but are rarely a formal part of the syllabus.

Chapter *2*

Building Blocks

§2.1   What Is Contract Law About?

The word "contract" is used in many ways, but let us start with a rough definition, to be qualified below: a "contract" is a legal relationship between two or more parties, each of whom is required to yield or transfer legal entitlements for the benefit of the other (or others). The purpose of a contract is to facilitate the exchange of money, goods, and services.

Let us unpack some of these ideas. When lawyers talk about contracts, they mean legal relationships, not the underlying exchanges to which those relationships refer. If X agrees to buy Y's house for a certain amount of money, they might say that they have a contract; but until the exchange is reduced to writing, and other formalities are met, the law holds that no

contract exists. If no contract exists, X and Y might have no legal obligations to each other, though they may have moral obligations to each other;
or, if they do have legal obligations, these obligations do not arise from
the existence of a contract, but from other areas of the law, such as the
law of restitution.

A contract almost always involves each person giving up something;
usually, there is a "transfer" in the metaphorical if not the literal sense.
The canonical example is the sale of goods. Seller gives up her ownership
interest in these goods and receives in return the right to Buyer's cash.
Buyer gives up his ownership of the cash and receives in return the right
to Seller's goods. But virtually anything can be the subject of a contract. X
drives his car into Y, injuring her severely. She now has a tort claim, even
if she has not yet sued; Y, as Seller, can sell that tort claim to X in return
for cash. There is a transfer of a sort here, but one could just as easily say
that Y gave up a tort claim rather than "transferring" it to X, who after all
cannot do anything with it.

Contracts almost always involve a detriment to each side. When Uncle
promises Nephew $100 if Nephew refrains from smoking, there is a
detriment — a legal detriment in the sense that each gives up a right (and
it makes no difference if Nephew's health improves as a result of not smok-
ing or if Uncle's moral character improves as a result of having $100 less).[1]
The detriment must be real, not formal. If Uncle promises Nephew $100 if
Nephew promises not to jump off the top of Mount Everest, there is no
contract. The parties are pretending that there is a detriment, but a detriment counts only if the promisor could gain from having the legal right
that is given up. Thus, the original exchange of promises is probably not a
contract if Nephew is a nonsmoker who would never be tempted to smoke,
and this is believed by both parties.

This ambiguity appears also in the charitable giving cases. Donor
promises $1 million to College; College states that it will hang a plaque
with Donor's name. Is this a contract? On the one hand, we would not
say that Donor has paid College $1 million in return for the hanging of the
plaque. That's a contract, but it would be denied by everyone involved. On
the other hand, there is a detriment on each side; and morally, Donor
would have a right to object if College refused to hang the plaque,
and College would have the right to object if Donor never delivered the
cash. Still, a moral obligation is not the same as a legal obligation. Gifts
followed by tangible expressions of gratitude are not contracts, even
though they are sometimes enforced as though they were, and maybe
should be. We will discuss these issues in more detail under the topic of
consideration.

---

[1] This example is based on the facts of Hamer v. Sidway, 27 N.E. 256 (N.Y. 1891).

Contract law is a part of the common law, which was, and continues to be, created by judges rather than by legislatures. The best and most reliable source of contract law is therefore the cases. But judges decide cases differently over time, and judges in different states sometimes decide cases differently, so when we refer to "contract law" we implicitly generalize from many different contract laws. Academics, lawyers, and judges have attempted to derive the "general principles" from the cases and incorporate them in the Restatement (Second) of Contracts. This reference work can be a helpful starting point for teaching and research, but many of the rules are stated at too high a level of generality to be useful. The states have also enacted a Uniform Commercial Code (U.C.C.); its second article applies to sales of goods. Thus, one must keep in mind that the common law rules apply to all contracts *except* sales of goods. The U.C.C. is a statute that has been enacted in the states, but courts often interpret it with the common law in mind.[2] This has caused interpretations of the U.C.C. to diverge among the states. The law of contract taught in most law schools is thus a kind of made-up pidgin or Esperanto; it would be impossible to teach all the different laws of the different states. One learns law school contract law in the same way that one learns a standard version of a foreign language in a language class and does not focus on each dialect.

§2.2   The Elements of Contract

All contracts are different but all share some basic elements. It is easiest to start out with an example. Suppose that Seller and Buyer enter a contract providing that Seller will supply a widget[3] to Buyer at some future date X, and that Buyer will pay Seller $P upon delivery.

If you prefer more concreteness, suppose that Buyer values (V) the widget at $100 (Buyer would be willing to pay up to $100 for the widget); the Seller's cost (C) is $50; and they agree on a price (P) of $75. We can distinguish the following elements.

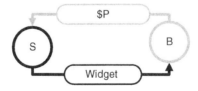

---

[2] Louisiana, however, has not enacted article 2.

[3] A "widget" is any object; like property law's "Blackacre," it permits an author to avoid the tiresome task of thinking up an example.

Benefit. Each party obtains an expected benefit from the contract. Seller obtains P; Buyer obtains a widget valued at V.

Cost. Each party incurs an expected cost. Seller loses the widget; Buyer loses P. Seller values the widget at C, which might also be thought of as the cost of production, so seller loses C.

Net benefit. Each party expects to obtain a net benefit from the contract — that is, the benefit minus the cost. Seller obtains the price minus her cost (P – C). Buyer obtains the value of the widget (that is, the amount at which she values the widget) minus the price (V – P). In the numerical terms of the example, that amounts to $25 for each.

Reliance/investment. Suppose that Buyer plans to install the widget in his factory, and could spend $20 in adjusting the factory in advance of delivery. This investment increases the value of the widget for Buyer and is sometimes referred to as a "reliance expenditure." Buyer would make this investment only if he thought that the $20 investment would increase the value of the widget by a sufficient amount of money. So if V = 100 without the investment, the investment costs 20, and V = 130 with the investment, Buyer will make the investment, putting aside time value, risk, and the like. The reason is that 130 – 20 = 110 > 100.

Similarly, Seller might make an investment that reduces her cost. Suppose that the widget is custom made, and Seller could reduce her costs by investing in an adjustment in her assembly line. If C = 50 without the investment, the investment costs $10, and C = 30 with the investment, then Seller will invest. The reason is that 30 + 10 = 40 < 50.

Efficiency. As a starting point, a contract is efficient if Buyer values the performance (the widget, in our example) at an amount higher than what it costs Seller. Another way of putting this is that the contract creates a surplus, or is jointly value maximizing. In our example, Seller and Buyer should enter the contract if V > C, and not otherwise. The contract is efficient even if the parties do not make an investment (100 > 50, creating a surplus of 50), but the parties do better if they both make investments.

The fact that a potential contract will make both parties better off does not mean that the two parties will necessarily enter it. Bargaining can break down for numerous reasons. The parties may fight over the contractual surplus. Seller wants a high price (up to $100, what Buyer would be willing to pay), while Buyer wants a low price (down to $50, the Seller's cost of production). If they haggle long enough, the value of the surplus will be eaten away as a result of wasted time and effort. Thus, if the surplus is not high, they might refrain from attempting to enter the transaction in the first place.[4]

---

[4] In economic models, the result depends on "asymmetric information": one or both parties know their own valuations but do not know the other party's valuations. Bluffing, delaying, and so forth are ways of signaling that one values the transaction relatively little, and so will not enter it unless the price is high (for Seller) or low (for Buyer).

Price, again. When Seller and Buyer negotiate their contract, they will choose a price, P. The price must be between V and C. Seller would not accept a price less than her cost, and Buyer would not pay more for the performance than she values it. Where exactly between V and C the price lies depends on the parties' relative bargaining power.

In a competitive market, sellers have no bargaining power. If Seller offers a widget at a price greater than C, Buyer can simply go elsewhere and find a seller who offers a lower price. Note that C here would cover the seller's cost of capital, salaries, and the rest. Thus, in a competitive market, $P = C$.[5]

Seller could also have all the bargaining power (be a monopolist). If Buyer wants the widget, he must buy from Seller. If Seller knows or can reliably estimate Buyer's valuation (meaning that Seller can price-discriminate), V, then Seller can make a take-it-or-leave-it offer at just under V, or, for simplicity, $P = V$.

In all other cases, P will lie between C and V — in the middle if the parties have equal bargaining power. Bargaining power is a function of outside opportunities, skill, information, sophistication, and the like — all issues that we will return to later in the book.

Note also that, in reality, P could lie below C or above V. This could happen simply if one party makes a mistake or is coerced by the other. Again, we will address these issues later.

Performance or breach. Every (bilateral) contractual relationship proceeds in two stages: entry and performance.[6] When the time for performance arrives, the promisor may not want to perform. Why not? In the simplest cases, a party might believe that the benefits of breach are greater than the benefits of performance.

Consider an example where Seller promises to deliver a widget at price P. Buyer will pay P upon delivery. Assume that the contract was premised on the assumption that $V > P > C$, as discussed above.

In this case, there is only one reason why Seller would breach, namely, it turns out that $P < C$, the price she receives is lower than her cost. Of course, Seller expected that $P > C$, or she would have not made the contract in the first place. But various contingencies can arise that result in C increasing. We can roughly divide them in two categories.

First, Seller's cost of production, delivery, and other necessities rises above P. For example, Seller normally manufactures widgets out of tin, which was cheap at the time of contracting. But the price of tin rose between the time of contracting and the time of performance, and so Seller's total cost, C, rises as well.

---

[5] Actually, marginal cost.

[6] In unilateral contracts, the stages are compressed, as at least one party accepts the offer (forming the contract) at the same time that she performs. See Section 2.4.

Second, Seller discovers that someone else will buy the widget promised to Buyer for a higher price. It may be that the market price of widgets rose between the time of contracting and the time of performance; but even without a market, it may be that Seller is approached by a desperate new buyer who is willing to pay a high price for the widget, a price higher than P.

Economists treat both of these contingencies as roughly the same. In the second case, they say Seller's "opportunity cost" has increased — because performance of the contract deprives Seller of the opportunity to obtain a higher return by selling to the new buyer at the higher price.[7] Thus, in both cases, Seller's cost, C, has risen.

There are other reasons Seller might want to breach. Suppose that she mistakenly entered the contract thinking that she would make money, but in fact she made a miscalculation. So when it comes time to perform, or even before, she discovers that the benefit (the price) is less than the cost. We will discuss these cases when we reach the doctrine of mistake. A seller might also breach, or at least threaten to breach, in an effort to force Buyer to revise the terms of the contract in favor of the seller — agreeing to a higher price, for example. We will discuss this case when we reach the doctrine of duress.

Finally, we should mention that Buyer's reasons for breach are mirror images of Seller's. Buyer might want to breach because his valuation (V) of the widget falls between contract entry and time for performance, or because she can get the same widget for a lower price from another seller, or because she mistakenly entered a contract with negative net benefits, or because she hopes to coerce Seller into giving her a better deal.

§2.3   Formalities

Contract law is shot through with formalities — rules that condition enforcement of a contract on the parties having engaged in certain actions that do not necessarily directly contribute to the value of the contract. Formalities are absolutely necessary, but at the same time they have a bad reputation, especially among academics. This odd state of affairs deserves an explanation, and a brief digression.

Our digression takes us to the law of bequests. Standard doctrine tells us that a person (the testator) is allowed to bequeath his property to anyone he chooses, and the law will respect the testator's intentions — but

---

[7] To understand the concept of opportunity cost, think of yourself choosing among stations on a radio dial. As you listen to station X, it may occur to you that although you prefer X to silence, you prefer station Y to X, depending on what is playing on Y. Not listening to Y is the opportunity cost of listening to X.

only if the testator observes the correct formalities. Typically, a testator will need to put his will in writing and have the writing signed by witnesses. If the testator does not comply with the formalities, the property is distributed according to a legal formula, usually split among immediate relatives. This all seems very natural, but of course these rules are formalities. We could imagine an alternative universe where the law, rather than requiring formality, simply took a guess at the testator's intention when it is not clearly expressed.

But this alternative universe is not attractive. A given person might frequently change his mind about how his property should be disposed of. Today, he wants it split among his devoted children; tomorrow, all of it to the child who calls him every week and none to the ingrate who won't produce grandchildren; the next day, to orphans in Haiti; the day after, to the ASPCA; and again, back to the children, or a child, or a trust fund for the family pet. This codger's opinions might be communicated to interested parties, who do not quite agree on what he said when it comes time for probate; or might be left on undated scraps of paper; or might be inferred (or not) from his behavior toward various relatives, interested parties, charities, and others.

The key point is that if we believe that the testator's wishes should be respected, then we are driven to an all-things-considered judgment about what his wishes most likely were, but this quickly can lead to a chaos of speculative inquiry. It is better to have a simple rule; but it should be understood that simple rules can trip up those who do not know about them, and those who do not have the time or money to comply with them, such as the testator who changes his mind — really, and not in passing — just minutes before he dies.

The formalities question is often put in terms of rules versus standards. A rule, like a formality, instructs the decisionmaker to ignore information that would be relevant to the resolution of a dispute in a world of zero decision costs. A standard instructs the decisionmaker to take into account this information. The recurring example is the speed limit. The simple rule — drive less than, say, 60 miles per hour — is easy to enforce: the car is moving either more or less than 60 miles per hour. The rule directs the decisionmaker to ignore potentially exculpating factors — for example, that the driver faces an emergency, the driver is experienced and skilled, the road is empty, and the weather is good — and also factors that indicate the driver should drive more slowly, such as hazardous conditions. Thus, the rule necessarily introduces "error costs" against a baseline of socially optimal behavior: drivers will drive 60 when they should drive more than 60 because of an emergency and less than 60 because of hazardous driving conditions. A standard — such as "drive reasonably" or "drive carefully" — would allow the decisionmaker to take account of these factors. But even a conscientious decisionmaker could apply the standard badly — so that drivers end up driving too fast or slow relative to the social optimum — and then people would have trouble predicting the legal consequences of their actions. Standards, then, produce "error costs." The law contains many rules and standards, and many overlap and apply to the same behavior. Generally speaking, drivers must obey speed limits and comply with standards such as laws that prohibit negligent or reckless driving. Rules, like formalities (which are just a type of rule), are better when decision costs are high and error costs are low; standards are better in the reverse case.[8]

Now let us return to contract law. Everything we have said applies here as well. Consider two parties, Seller and Buyer, negotiating over the sale of a widget. From the moment they meet to the moment that Buyer departs with the expectation of receiving the widget at some future date, there is a continuous stream of interaction: discussions, exchanges of memos, side conversations between subordinates and lawyers, promises and withdrawals of promises, offers and counter-offers. At some point, the parties believe that they have a deal: this might come at the end of their interactions but it might also come well before the end of their interactions, with subsequent discussion devoted to ironing out unimportant details or addressing possible future projects or wholly irrelevant topics. Knowing when (and if) the parties reach a deal is of great importance. They might converse for quite a long time and never reach a deal, in which case there is no contract. Even if they do reach a deal, much depends on whether the contract is entered early or later in the stream of discussion. If earlier, then subsequent exchanges of promises are not part of the contract: they might be new contracts or contract modifications or legally meaningless gobbledygook. If later, then earlier exchanges of promises might be part of the contract; whether they are depends on the parol evidence rule and other matters we will discuss later.

Doctrine tells us that a contract is formed when mutual assent occurs. This is, in fact, an extreme simplification, but we will explore why in Chapter 3. For now, the relevant question is, How does the court know when mutual assent occurs? One possibility is for the courts to make an all-things-considered best guess. Such an approach has virtues, but it creates a risk of judicial error — just as in the case of the testator. Another possibility is for the courts to apply rules: a contract exists when the parties have jumped through certain hoops. Contract law has opted for a confusing jumble of the two approaches, as we will see. But for now we focus on the rules, or formalities.

---

[8] For a discussion in a contracts case, see MindGames, Inc. v. Western Pub. Co., 218 F.3d 652 (7th Cir. 2000).

Consider, as an easy example, the Statute of Frauds, which says that certain types of contracts are enforceable only if they are in writing.[9] This rule, like all formalities (and indeed all rules), trades off decision costs and error costs. The rule makes it easier for courts to determine whether a contract exists: if it is not in writing it does not exist. But the rule results in some contracts that really do have mutual assent not being enforced. If the parties neglected to put their contract in writing, or if they chose not to do so in order to avoid drafting costs, then they are out of luck. Formalities make sense when decision costs would otherwise be high, so long as they do not result in error costs being too high as well. We will see more such examples throughout this book.

The formality is a type of rule. Ordinary rules, like the speed limit, direct people to curb their behavior in some way — driving slowly rather than driving fast. Formalities, unlike rules, require parties to engage in some gratuitous conduct that they would otherwise not engage in — for example, writing down a contract when the parties would otherwise agree orally, or obtaining the signatures of two witnesses on a will. It is because the extra bit of behavior has no substantive purpose that it can serve as a signal to the court that the parties seek to form a legal relationship. There would be no other reason for it. And yet a burdensome formality — one that required people to don clown suits in order to enter a contract, for example — would be excessively costly. So formalities track behavior, but not too much, with the result that it can be ambiguous whether people complied with the formality in order to signal a legal relationship or for some other reason. Thus, parties might write down a contract in order to create a record of their transaction, not to make it legally enforceable.

Formalities also arise naturally in daily life; they are not always enforced by the law. In contracting, the handshake is a ubiquitous formality. It means, "We have a deal." Note that the handshake is gratuitous. You could certainly negotiate a contract without shaking hands. But it's very gratuitousness allows it to be a signal that a deal is done. There would be no reason to shake hands — unless you sustain an erotic charge from the sensation of palm to palm — except to signal that each side has committed itself to follow through on the project that has been negotiated.

---

[9] See Restatement (Second) of Contracts §131 (1981):

> Unless additional requirements are prescribed by the particular statute, a contract within the Statute of Frauds is enforceable if it is evidenced by any writing, signed by or on behalf of the party to be charged, which
>
> > (a) reasonably identifies the subject matter of the contract,
> > (b) is sufficient to indicate that a contract with respect thereto has been made between the parties or offered by the signer to the other party, and
> > (c) states with reasonable certainty the essential terms of the unperformed promises in the contract.

§2.4   Unilateral and Bilateral Contracts

Bilateral contracts involve an exchange of promises; unilateral contracts involve an exchange of a promise for a performance. Unilateral contracts often involve rewards but they need not.[10]

Consider some examples. A standard sales contract is usually bilateral: Buyer promises to pay upon delivery, Seller promises to deliver in the future. Or consider a construction contract: Builder promises to construct a building, Owner of the property promises to make a series of progress payments.

As an example of a unilateral contract, consider the following poster: "$50 reward if you find my lost parakeet. Responds to the name 'Alphonse.'" This contract is formed only when the sought-after act is performed. If I return the parakeet, I have a contractual right to your $50. If I do not, I do not. I cannot accept your offer by making a return promise to find the parakeet.

Unilateral contracts are not always broadcast to the world in this way. Suppose the parakeet owner says to a particular person, "If you find my parakeet, I'll give you $50." Now only this particular person can form a contract with the owner, and the only way for him to do so is by finding the parakeet.

Unilateral contracts have advantages and disadvantages for both parties, relative to a bilateral contract. Because the party that performs — the promisee — does not make a commitment in advance, he can change his mind and not perform should he prefer to do so. By the same token, the promisor can withdraw her promise if the promisee has not yet performed.

Let us put this point more formally. Suppose you have lost your cat and want to motivate others to find the cat. You could put up posters saying, "$50 to anyone who finds Goneril and returns her to me unharmed." Here, you are offering to enter a unilateral contract, and anyone can accept and perform that contract by finding and returning Goneril. The advantage for you is that many people might be motivated by the prospect of reward to search for Goneril, but you have to pay only the person who finds her.

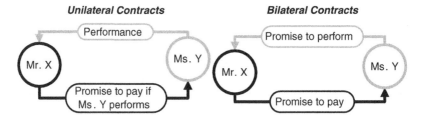

<hr />

[10] The Restatement abandons the unilateral/bilateral terminology (see Restatement (Second) of Contracts §1, cmt. f (1981)), but courts have not.

The disadvantage for you is that people who might otherwise be inclined to put some effort into finding your cat might not like the idea that they will be unpaid if they do not find her. So the alternative is to enter into a bilateral contract with one or more people: "In return for $10, you will spend one hour looking for Salome." The attraction of this contract is that one or more promisees are assured of payment. On the other hand, you might have no assurance that they will do their work. So you might enter bilateral contracts with numerous people, plus offer a reward for whoever finds the cat.

All else equal, however, the unilateral contract puts more risk on the promisee than a bilateral contract does. Risk is not free, and the promisor will have to pay more to persuade others to accept. In Sections 3.9 and 3.10, we will see why this matters.

§2.5   Conditions versus Promises

Compare the following contracts:

1. Buyer promises to pay Seller $100 and Seller promises to deliver a widget.
2. Buyer will pay Seller $100 conditional on Seller delivering a widget.
3. Seller will deliver a widget conditional on Buyer paying $100.
4. Seller will sell to Buyer a widget for $100.

These contracts might all seem identical, specifying the exchange of a widget and $100. The truth is more complex. Let us start with contract 1. A court might construe this contract as follows. If Buyer fails to pay $100, Seller must nonetheless deliver the widget. She can sue Buyer for $100. Similarly, if Seller fails to deliver, Buyer must pay $100 and can sue for the value of the widget. If the market price is $120, Buyer is entitled to damages of $120. If the court does construe the contract in this way (but it may not, as we will see), then we say that each party has made a promise, and each party can sue on the other's promise.

Consider now contract 2. If Seller does not deliver the widget, then we say that a condition of Buyer's performance has not been satisfied. Buyer did not make an absolute promise (as he might have in contract 1); he has made a conditional promise. The condition just indicates an if-then statement: if Seller delivers, then Buyer has an obligation to pay. If Seller fails to deliver, Buyer has no such obligation. As a consequence, if Seller fails to deliver, Buyer can withhold payment and sue for expectation damages — $20, if the market price of the widget is $120.

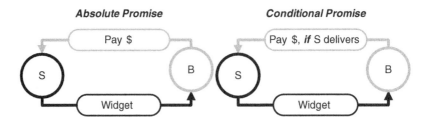

The difference between an "absolute" or unconditional promise and a conditional promise is just that the promisor need not perform if the condition is not satisfied.[11] Conditions shift risk from the promisor to the promisee. The advantage of the conditional promise for Buyer is that if Seller is judgment-proof (for example, she goes bankrupt), Buyer does not lose his $100. There is, of course, a correlative disadvantage for Seller: she loses the opportunity to escape liability through judgment-proofness and, as we will see in Section 7.3, may well forfeit something of considerable value.

We can quickly dispose of contracts 3 and 4. Contract 3 is like contract 2, except this time Seller's obligation to perform is conditional and Buyer's is absolute. This means that Seller need not perform if Buyer fails to prepay. Contract 4 is ambiguous: it is not clear whether the promises are supposed to be conditional or absolute. Courts tend in such cases to interpret the promises as conditional in the following sense. If one party is supposed to go first, then the other party's obligation is conditional on the first party performing. If performance is supposed to be simultaneous, then each party's obligation is conditional only on the prospect of the other party performing — say, by tendering or by giving assurances. And, indeed, a court might interpret contract 1 in the same way. We discuss these rules in Sections 7.3 and 7.4.

§2.6 Buyer and Seller

I have talked as though the buyer and the seller are in asymmetrical positions. In fact, their relationship is symmetrical. To see why, imagine that two people are negotiating a trade of a cow and a pig. The question might be which of many cows or pigs will be traded, what quality, and so on; but all of this can be put into terms of "cow units" and "pig units." The cow owner wants as many pig units as possible for a cow; the pig owner wants as many cow units as possible for a pig. Now who is the buyer and

---

[11] See Restatement (Second) of Contracts §224 (1981) ("A condition is an event, not certain to occur, which must occur, unless its non-occurrence is excused, before performance under a contract becomes due.").

who is the seller? If we take cow units as the medium of exchange (as the "money"), the seller is the pig owner, who wants as many cow units (like dollars) as possible, and the buyer is the cow owner, who wants as low a "price" (in cow units) as possible. If we take pig units as the medium of exchange, the seller is the cow owner and the buyer is the pig owner. Neither pig units nor cow units are more natural as units of exchange, however, so we cannot, in the abstract, call one party a buyer and one party a seller. Each party is both.

Now, suppose that the two people are negotiating a trade of some gold coins for a cow. Our first impulse is to say that the owner of the coins is the buyer. But suppose that the owner of gold coins wants to trade them for cash. Our impulse now is to call the owner of gold coins the seller. But why should the owner of the gold coins be called the buyer when dealing with the cow owner, but the seller when dealing with the cash owner? The answer is that our intuition drives us to call the party with the more negotiable goods the buyer. "Negotiable" roughly means "transferable": negotiable goods (like dollars) are easily transferred because they are small, light, durable, standardized, and recognized as stores of value. Gold coins are more money-like or negotiable than cows, so the gold coin owner is the buyer; but gold coins are less money-like than, well, money, so the gold coin owner is the seller. The reason the gold coins are less money-like than money is that it may take some expertise to value the gold coins in dollars, whereas it takes no expertise to value a dollar in dollars. A dollar is worth a dollar.

In ordinary sales transactions, the seller is the party that takes money for goods, and the buyer is the party that pays money for goods. In other transactions, involving the sale of services, for example, we can use the same terms, though they seem more metaphorical. A lawyer sells legal services and a client buys them; a doctor sells medical services and the patient buys them. A contractor sells construction services and the owner buys them; a baseball team sells "performances" and the fans buy them.

The common law tends not to make too much of the identity of a party with a complaint. Both a seller and a buyer can argue that a contract should be rescinded because of mistake or of an excessively high liquidated damages clause. But, in practice, the common law favors the buyer, and this is especially clear in the Uniform Commercial Code, which provides different rules for buyers and sellers even though the general principles of contract law — that, for example, expectation damages give the benefit of the bargain to the victim of breach — apply equally.[12] A buyer is more likely

---

[12] The U.C.C. also has different rules for transactions involving merchants. Merchants will be held to higher standards when they transact with consumers, see, e.g., U.C.C. §2-314, which governs implied warranties, because of their greater sophistication, which permits them to trick and manipulate (some) consumers. Transactions between merchants are sometimes governed by more flexible rules because merchants are better able to protect

to escape a contract because the seller withheld information about the quality of the goods, than a seller is in the mirror case, where the buyer failed to disclose information that he has about the goods. All the various implied warranty doctrines apply to the seller, not to the buyer. The unconscionability doctrine is almost always applied in the buyer's favor, not the seller's.

There is a simple reason for this pattern: goods (and services) are complicated, money is not. The seller almost always has a great deal of information about the product that she sells or the services that she provides. Most sellers are businesses and they are specialists. And even ordinary people, when they sell used cars or goods at a garage sale, will usually know more about their goods than the buyer does, just because the sellers have possessed them for a time. So buyers enter transactions at a disadvantage, and they have no corresponding advantage because what they offer is just money, which sellers understand as well as buyers.

This explains the greater solicitude in the law for buyers than for sellers. This is just a general pattern, of course, and there are many exceptions. Commercial buyers are often just as sophisticated as commercial sellers, and know as much about the goods in question, especially when they are fungible, or can be easily inspected. And we run into cases from time to time where sophisticated real estate speculators snap up land owned by unsophisticated farmers or ranchers. Where the pattern does not thus hold, deviations in judicial practice occur, as we will see.

§2.7 The Goal of a Contract (Herein, the Hold-up Problem)

Why do parties enter contracts? The answer is that each party believes that it will gain by exchanging goods or services in a manner that *extends over time*.

Seller has an apple orchard. As much as she likes apples, she does not want to keep the thousands that she grows. Even if she eats an apple a day, or a hundred apples a day, she will have many thousands sitting around, and they will eventually rot. We can quickly see that even if Seller loves the taste of apples, and would, if she did not own the orchard, happily pay as much as $1 to purchase an apple at a grocery store so that she can eat an apple a day, she would not pay that much, given that she owns the orchard. Indeed, with thousands of apples that are about to rot, Seller would not pay any amount of money for additional apples. What she would

---

themselves from sharp practices. See U.C.C. §2-205 (firm offers without consideration), id. §2-207(2) (acceptances that vary from offers).

like to do is sell the marginal apples for cash, which she can then use to buy things she wants and needs.

If Seller, the orchard owner, values her apples very little, there are many buyers who value them a lot. These buyers like the taste of apples and would be willing to pay (say) 50 cents to purchase an apple at a roadside stand at Seller's orchard. Supermarkets are also willing to pay for the apples, which they will then resell to buyers not interested in driving to the orchard.

Take, then, Seller, who values one of her many apples at (say) 2 cents, and a particular Buyer, who is willing to pay 50 cents, and there is room for a deal. If the parties agree on a price between 2 and 50 cents, then both are better off, by their own lights, than they would be without the deal. It is in this simple sense that a contract, involving as it does an exchange, makes the two parties involved better off.

The time element of contracts is a bit more subtle. The legal system contains sufficient resources to allow the parties to make the exchange without ever relying on contract law. The parties agree on a price of 5 cents. Buyer hands a nickel to Seller and Seller hands an apple to Buyer. If Seller were to take the nickel and refuse to hand over the apple, Buyer could sue Seller for unjust enrichment or conversion (that is, theft). If Buyer took an apple without paying, Seller could likewise sue Buyer for conversion. If the apple turned out to be wormy or the nickel to be counterfeit, similar tort or restitution claims could be brought. We can call their transaction a "contract" or just an "exchange" or "deal"; it doesn't really matter. But the focus of contract law is slightly different: normally a contract involves behavior extending through time.

Suppose that Buyer does not have a nickel on him, and so the parties agree that Buyer will take the apple today and will send Seller the nickel in a week. Or suppose that Seller has run out of apples, and so the parties agree that Buyer will pay today, and Seller will ship an apple to Buyer in a week. Or suppose that the parties agree that no transfers will occur today, but in a week Seller will ship an apple to Buyer, and when Buyer receives the apple he will wire 5 cents to Seller. In all of these cases, we can speak more naturally of promising, and hence we enter the domain of contract. The first two examples involve unilateral contracts — a promise for a performance today. The last example involves a bilateral contract — a promise for a promise. Contract law is all about interpreting and enforcing promises, and so it usually does not have much to say about the simple exchange described in the previous paragraph.

So in understanding why parties enter contracts, it is not enough to recognize that two people can jointly benefit from an exchange. The question is why it is useful to exchange goods, services, and money over time, such that a promise — a commitment to engage in some future behavior — becomes necessary.

There are two answers to this question. First, it is highly important to be able to transfer wealth across time, and this cannot easily be done without promising. Individuals generally invest in their own education early in life while earning little or no income, enter their most prosperous years midway through life, and then retire and earn no income at all toward the end of life. To maintain a more or less constant standard of living, one must borrow early in life, save in the middle of life, and live off savings at the end of life. When one borrows, one promises to pay the creditor principal and interest in the future; and when one saves, one receives a promise from the borrower (often a bank) that one will be paid principal and interest in the future. It is simply impossible to make these intertemporal deals without promising, and contract law ensures that these promises are kept. A similar point can be made about insurance and other financial instruments, and we will return to them in due course.

Second, many if not most transactions involve an investment or reliance element that is of great significance. Suppose our seller receives a request from a particular buyer, a wholesaler of specialty foods, who wants Seller to grow a rare specimen of apple for which there is no general demand. Seller can set aside an area of land to plant the special apple trees, but only if she can be sure that Buyer will in fact buy these apples — as she will otherwise not be able to sell apples from those trees on the market at a price that compensates her for the expense. Seller's adjustment of her operations is an "investment" of resources for the sake of a higher expected return, but Seller will make this investment only if Buyer will commit to buy the apples at the high price Seller needs. If she cannot obtain that commitment, then Buyer might change his mind, or hold out for a lower price — one that does not cover the investment — by threatening not to buy. Anticipating such behavior, Seller will not agree to make the investment, at least unless she can get Buyer to commit. The normal way for Buyer to commit is by making a legally enforceable contract.

The second problem is called "hold-up" — Buyer holds up Seller by threatening not to take the apples unless Seller lowers the price — and we will encounter it again.

§2.8   The Design of a Contract

Most law books on contracts underemphasize the design of contracts, yet the design of contracts is an inescapable feature of the law. To see why, consider the following examples.

1. The owner of a fledgling dot-com company hires a software engineer for a one-year term. The worker will be paid a nominal hourly

wage — just enough to cover food and rent — plus a stock option package. As it turns out, the stock of the company plummets, and the stock option is worthless.

2. Instead of the stock options, the dot-com owner says that he will give a fat bonus to the worker if his performance is satisfactory. At the end of the year, the bonus is denied because the worker's performance is unsatisfactory.

3. The owner of a farm hires a worker, gives him room and board, and offers him $5000 at the end of the year, but only if the worker stays for the full term. The worker leaves a month early (or is fired a month early) and is denied the payment.[13]

These cases differ along a number of dimensions, but let's start by noting that students usually disapprove of the result in the third case and are more tolerant of the first two. Whether the worker voluntarily leaves early or is fired, he ought to be paid for the amount of work he has performed on the farm. But though the conclusion may be correct (it depends on factors to be canvassed below), it is too hasty. It is too hasty because the exigencies of contract design produce contract terms that, at first sight, might seem odd or clearly exploitative, when in fact there is an innocent explanation.

Suppose that farm owners invest a fair amount of money training their workers during the first eight months of the year, then recover the cost of the investment only during the last four months of year. If the worker leaves after eight months, he can obtain a high-paying job at another farm — high-paying because the second owner values the training that the worker received at the first farm. Clearly, the first owner cannot remain in business if workers obtain training from him at below cost, then go elsewhere before he recovers his investment in the form of the valuable work output of those workers. So he backloads compensation: rather than pay the worker a fixed monthly amount, he provides the minimum throughout the period, then delivers the large $5000 payment at the end of the year. The worker, anticipating the payment, does not leave the first owner for the second, who will of course not pay as much.

If courts refused to enforce this contract, then owners would have to find some other way to deal with opportunistic workers: use different sorts of contracts maybe, but probably hire fewer workers and pay them less, while cutting back on production. This is not a desirable result.

One response to this argument is that, in the absence of judicial oversight, the employer can extract work from the worker, then fire him the

---

[13] See Britton v. Turner, 6 N.H. 481 (1834).

day before the end of the term (or drive him to quit by treating him intolerably) in order to avoid making the payment. The right response of the court is not to invalidate the contract, but to ensure that only opportunistic workers are denied payment.

This argument assumes that courts are able to distinguish opportunistic and non-opportunistic behavior — that is, the lazy employee from the industrious employee. One might doubt whether courts can do this. Indeed, if courts could do this, then one would see "just cause" terms in every employment contract; instead, most contracts are at will, including the sorts of contracts that we are discussing. Employers do not want courts looking over their shoulders. What protects workers from employment opportunism? Maybe nothing (but then why would employees take the job in the first place?), or maybe the employer's desire to maintain a reputation for fairness among existing and future employees.

This argument can be taken too far. Courts routinely impose general good faith obligations on parties in contractual relations, and good faith can be understood to ban the same type of opportunism. But most of the time, the concept of good faith has little application in the cases, which are decided on other grounds.[14] Courts remain hesitant about looking over parties' shoulders and finding good faith obligations that are not clearly rooted in the text or in evidence of customary behavior.

Look now at the dot-com examples. The first example is less troubling because the employee has stock options. Unless the employer engages in sophisticated fraud (for example, by diverting corporate profits into his pocket), he cannot opportunistically deny the employee a share of the profits. Indeed, the employer and employee share an interest in maximizing profits. The second example is more like the farm example; here the employer could act opportunistically. Yet I doubt that we worry too much about this. The employee is sophisticated, the practice is familiar, and without knowing more about the farm economy one might conclude the same for the farm example.

Some people might think that courts should review the discharge in either case. Unlike the case of the profit sharing plan, the other two contracts give the employer the ability to mistreat the employee. The worker joins the firm only if he trusts the employer to give him the bonus if he deserves it. If the worker does a good job and the employer withholds the bonus, we feel outrage. Surely a court should prevent this injustice.

To analyze this argument, let us start with two questions. Why didn't the contract contain a term that requires the employer to grant the bonus if the worker does a good job? And why did the worker accept the job in

---

[14] See Section 7.6.

the absence of such a clause if he did not trust the employer? As to the first question, the standard view is that the judgment of whether an employee has done a good job can rarely be reduced to a set of rules against which behavior can be reliably measured. An assembly line worker who meets his quota but also reduces worker morale because of irritating habits should not receive a bonus, one might think. But although a quota is easy enough to enforce, how do we describe in advance behavior that reduces morale? Any such description would surely be vague enough to be manipulated by an opportunistic employer, and so is no solution to the problem. Indeed, one way that unions put pressure on employers short of a strike is to "work to rule," which means following the employment rules to the letter, rather than engage in activities that maximize profit. A safe generalization is that optimal work cannot be reduced to a set of rules in advance, though it may be identifiable by a knowledgeable insider. An insider, not a court.

Employment contracts are thus quite vague, and the employee is disciplined or encouraged by bonuses, promotions, demotion, firing, and so forth, rather than clearly defined contractual rights. This leads to the second question, and the answer must be that workers enter vague contracts because they expect employers to act "fairly" — that is, roughly in conformity with the requirements of value-maximizing behavior. Employees who do good work will be rewarded, and those who do bad work will not be rewarded; moreover, employees will be treated consistently, given a clear sense of expectations, forgiven for minor infractions, and so forth. Many students have an unshakable conviction that employers cannot be trusted to act in this way, and on their side one must concede the unrepresentative sample of employment disputes that appear in the cases and the felt need in some industries for workers to unionize. This does not mean that employers never act unfairly. But except in extreme cases, courts cannot distinguish good and bad practice, and so should not intervene in the absence of contractual instructions to the contrary.

As another angle on this question, you might compare two terms of a contract: the wage term of, say, $20 per hour and the termination-at-will term. Courts virtually never rewrite the wage or price term of a contract. Why not? Because they have no idea what the proper price would be, and trust the market to get it right enough of the time. But if you agree that courts have no basis for modifying the price term, what grounds do they have for modifying the termination-at-will term? If they do not have enough information to choose the optimal price, it is hard to see why they would have enough information to choose the optimal termination rule. If they have enough information to choose the optimal termination rule, then why not enough to choose the optimal price term as well?

§2.9   Timing

Another aspect of contract design concerns the timing of the obligations of the two parties. In a buyer-seller contract, the buyer can (1) pay in advance of the seller's performance,(2) pay simultaneously with the performance, (3) pay after the performance, or (4) pay in installments.

The timing of payments matters because the buyer or seller may be judgment-proof. Judgment-proofness means that a party can avoid paying damages for breach of contract. This can arise from numerous conditions: the party declares bankruptcy, or the party has assets that cannot be collected because they are hidden or protected by law, or the victim cannot discover information necessary to prove the breach, or the victim does not bother to sue because the litigation costs exceed the expected recovery.[15]

If the seller believes that the buyer might be judgment-proof, she might insist that the buyer prepay: the seller gets cash in hand before turning over valuable goods. If the buyer believes that the seller might be judgment-proof, he might insist that the seller deliver before the buyer pays — the buyer "postpays." If neither trusts the other, they might agree on a simultaneous exchange — where the seller hands over the goods and at the same time the buyer hands over the money. There are other variations. The buyer could pay half or some other portion of the price in advance (often called a "deposit") and the remainder after delivery.

As we will see, the design of the contract can have implications for remedies if breach occurs. To anticipate, the standard measure of damages — expectation damages — puts the victim in the position he would have been in if the contract had been performed. If the buyer has agreed to postpay, then fails to do so after having received the goods, he must pay the full price as damages — this ensures that the seller obtains her profit (the contract price minus the cost of the goods). If the buyer has agreed to prepay, then fails to do, the seller will normally not have to deliver the goods. Now the full price would overcompensate her because she has not given away

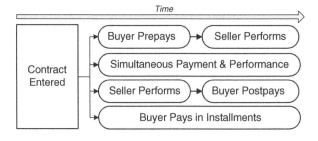

---

[15] See Chapter 7.

the goods; she should receive as damages just her lost profit — the contract price minus the (avoided) cost of the goods.

§2.10 Form Contracts

Contract doctrine arose at a time when most contracts were bargained individually. Seller owns a pig, Buyer wants a pig, the two haggle over the details of the transaction, and then the deal is consummated. When a dispute arises, the court will try to figure out what exactly the two parties agreed to, an exercise that will usually involve taking evidence on what each party intended to accomplish, and how their words and actions should be reasonably understood.

Today, most contracts do not work this way. True, many transactions are haggled out, and the details vary from transaction to transaction. Sales of businesses have this character. Employment contracts sometimes do as well, especially for unique or otherwise important types of employees. Informal sales of goods between non-specialists and prenuptial and other agreements that touch on highly personal relations also fall in this category.

Much more important, especially in the case of sales of goods, many services (like car rentals), and financial instruments, are form contracts. Form contracts are written contracts that contain terms that do not vary, or vary minimally, across transactions. When you rent a car from Avis, the contract will be almost identical to the contracts between Avis and thousands of other customers. You also use form contracts when you ship goods with Federal Express or UPS; purchase automobiles, televisions, furniture, cell phones, and fishing rods; enter service agreements with phone companies, electric companies, and gas utilities; sell or buy a house; hire a real estate agent; become employed in a large factory; or lease space from a landlord.

Some contracts fall between these two extremes. The sale of a house will involve some haggling, and the buyer and seller might agree on some special obligations aside from price. The seller might agree to fix up the back porch, for example, or to release the buyer from the deal if the buyer cannot get financing. The buyer might agree to allow the seller to stay in the house a few days after the closing. Such parties will typically use a form, one often supplied by the local real estate agents association, and write in the special agreements that deviate from the default terms on the form. But, in the end, the form will govern most of the possible disputes that might arise.

Forms contracts can be long or short, but whatever the case, they contain many terms that the parties do not negotiate. These terms cover a range of contingencies: what law applies if there is a dispute, and what forum will be used; whether liability is limited or not, and in what way; whether the buyer may rely on representations of seller's agents; what happens if goods are damaged in transit; and so on. We will see these terms and others later on. For now, it is important to see that these terms do not necessarily reflect the mutual agreement of the parties in the way that the haggled-out details of the pig transaction do. How and whether this matters is the topic of Section 3.5.

§2.11   Ex Ante / Ex Post

One of the peculiarities of the common law system is that courts invent new rules in order to do justice ex post, and yet the chief effect of these rules will be with respect to future behavior. That is, the ex ante effect of rules is usually more important than their ex post effect. Courts understand this tension, but they rarely talk about it in explicit fashion.

Let us begin with an example. Imagine that Creditor has a business of lending money to relatively poor people, at a high rate of interest. Creditor lends $1000 to Debtor, Debtor defaults, and Creditor brings suit for breach of contract. Debtor defaulted because he lost his job, his kids are sick, and he argues that Creditor should have given him some breathing room. The interest rate — say, 50 percent — seems extremely high, and the court is tempted to refuse to enforce the contract.

Ex post thinking focuses on the two parties and the events that gave rise to their dispute. A court might think that Creditor was too harsh and the interest rate was too high, and rule in favor of Debtor. Or the court might think that a deal is a deal, and rule in favor of Creditor. Whatever the case, the thinking here is purely ex post.

Ex ante thinking focuses on people in general, and how they will act in the future. If the court rules in favor of Debtor, then creditors in general will think that if they lend money to people, and those people default in sympathetic circumstances, courts will refuse to let them collect on their loan. As a result, creditors will refuse to lend to poor people, or perhaps they will raise interest rates or make other demands. The ex ante effect of the ruling, then, is to reduce the amount of credit available to poor people, or, more particularly, the type of person who might find himself in circumstances similar to those of Debtor.

All rules of contract law can be analyzed in ex ante fashion, and that is indeed how we will think of them. Courts are clearly influenced by ex post considerations at times, but my impression is that when they think carefully about what the rule ought to be, they are mainly concerned with ex ante effects.

§2.12 Default Rules and Bargaining Around

Contracts often fail to mention contingencies that give rise to disputes. These omissions are sometimes called "gaps" in contracts, and courts may or may not feel compelled to "fill" the gaps with terms. This simple description masks some complexities, however.

Consider our example above, of a sales contract that does not say what happens if the goods are destroyed in transit. Is there a gap? Buyer might well deny that such a gap exists. If the contract simply says that Seller must deliver the widgets, Buyer will say that Seller has an absolute obligation, and if she cannot deliver the widgets because they have been destroyed in transit, she has violated that obligation and must pay damages. Only Seller will argue that a gap exists. Seller will argue that because the contract lacks a term that assigns the risk of destruction in transit, the court needs to fill the gap, and ideally, from Seller's perspective, with a term that assigns the risk to Buyer.

If courts in such cases routinely assign the risk to Buyer in the absence of a term to the contrary, we might say that a "default rule" exists. This is academic terminology; courts rarely use this term. A default rule is a rule providing that a particular term will govern if the parties do not say otherwise. "Saying otherwise" is often put in terms of "bargaining around." If Seller and Buyer agree that Seller should bear the risk, they can bargain around the default rule that assigns the risk to Buyer, by providing explicitly in the contract that Seller bears the risk of destruction of goods in transit.

Much of contract law consists of default rules, as we will see. The traditional view is that default rules reflect the terms that most similarly situated parties would prefer — that is, the efficient terms or the profit-maximizing terms. Some scholars argue that some default rules provide for inefficient terms, as a means for encouraging parties to reveal information to each other. This is not a plausible view.[16] Efficient default terms will result in bargaining around, and hence information revelation, and so the case for inefficient default terms turns out to be narrow. We will return to this argument when we discuss specific default rules.

---

[16] For the traditional view, see Ian Ayres & Robert Gertner, Filling Gaps in Incomplete Contracts: An Economic Theory of Default Rules, 99 Yale L.J. 87 (1989). For my criticisms, see Eric A. Posner, There Are No Penalty Default Rules in Contract Law, 33 Fla. St. U. L. Rev. 563 (2006).

§2.13 Third-Party Effects (Externalities)

The conventional, utilitarian or welfarist explanation for why courts should normally enforce contracts is that if the parties are rational and fully informed, the contract will make both parties better off (ex ante) without making third parties worse off. However, some contracts do make third parties worse off. This third-party effect is, in economic terms, called an "externality."

Consider, for example, a contract in which Seller sells an apple to Buyer in return for $1. Buyer prefers the apple to $1 and Seller prefers $1 to the apple; no third party is affected by this transaction. Therefore, the contract is presumptively efficient.

By contrast, a contract between Murder, Inc., and Buyer, where Buyer pays Murder, Inc., to murder his business rival, does create a negative externality — the business rival is made worse off by this contract. Laws against criminal conspiracy address this problem. Buyer and the managers and employees of Murder, Inc., will go to jail.

But this rule is "outside" contract law; it is a rule of criminal law. Contract law itself presumes that contracts do not produce negative externalities, or, if they do, that they will be governed by other laws. Environmental law restricts transactions between sellers and buyers that create pollution that harms third parties. Antitrust law restricts transactions between sellers and buyers that concentrate market power and result in higher prices.

This basic economic distinction is vulnerable to some objections. From within economics, Ronald Coase pointed out that, depending on how property rights are allocated, third parties can pay to protect themselves or be paid to give up their rights to be free from external sources of harm.[17] The idea of externality collapses into a more basic notion — that of transaction cost. When parties can transact with each other cheaply, third parties will not be harmed except when the benefits are greater than the harms for others — so a kind of efficiency is achieved, regardless of whether externalities exist. Legal regulation is needed only when transaction costs are sufficiently high that bargaining is not possible.

One of Coase's famous examples is a railroad whose trains produce sparks as they travel along the tracks. From time to time, these sparks ignite and destroy a crop. The railroad's activity creates a classic externality — it harms a third party. One might think of the railroad acting "on its own"; or one can see it as the product of a series of contractual relationships (involving investors, managers, employees, consumers). In either case, it creates externalities because it does not enter contractual relationships with the farmers who own the land that abuts the tracks.

---

[17] Ronald Coase, The Problem of Social Cost, 3 J.L. & Econ. 1 (1960).

The railroad poses a classic problem for economic analysis. Because the owners of the railroad do not bear the cost of the fires, they will engage in a level of economic activity greater than what is socially optimal. The socially optimum level of railroad activity will take into account the harm to farmers. The classic solution is to impose what is known as a Pigouvian tax (after the economist Pigou) on the railroad, where the tax equals (roughly) the cost imposed on the farmer. An equivalent solution is to give the farmers a tort remedy for damages equal to their costs.[18]

Coase pointed out that the socially optimal level of railroad activity would (in theory) be achieved even without a tax or tort remedy. The starting point for understanding his argument is that a high level of railroad activity (frequent trains at high speeds creating a lot of sparks) and a high level of farming activity (crops planted all the way to the edge of the tracks) are economically incompatible. One or the other activity should be reduced, or both should be reduced, so that fires become less common. From a social perspective, we want the less valuable activity to be reduced (it is also possible that the cheapest outcome is for both activities to be reduced a little). If the less valuable activity is farming, then the farmers will voluntarily cut back their crops from the tracks. If the less valuable activity is railroad travel, then (and this point is the heart of the argument) the farmers will pay the railroad to reduce the speed or quantity of trains. The socially optimal activity will be achieved through contracting, and this is true regardless of whether the initial right (to emit or to be free from sparks) is assigned to the railroad or the farmers.

Coase's insight is justly famous but, in fact, it has few if any implications for understanding contract law. The reason is that Coase *assumes* that parties can enter (at low cost) contracts to reassign property rights; if they can, then we can (in theory) do without much of tort and environmental law. But Coase does not tell us how contract law should be designed so that parties can cheaply enter contracts. If contract law is badly designed, people can't "contract around" it because their contracting around will be subject to the badly designed law. (Imagine, for example, a law that says that no contracts will be enforced.) They might be able to fall back on nonlegal forms of cooperation, but nonlegal forms of cooperation are typically weak outside of small, closely knit groups.

From outside economics, commentators point out that virtually every transaction causes externalities. If a homeowner pays someone to paint his house bright orange, neighbors will be harmed. The sale of every energy-using device affects the climate and depletes the reserves of fossil

---

[18] The tort standard would need to be strict liability, not negligence.

fuels at the expense of future generations. Even the sale of the lowly tomato may deplete resources that would otherwise be available to others. The traditional (pre-Coasean) economic prescription that directs government to enforce voluntary transactions while regulating activities that cause externalities is empty if all or virtually all voluntary transactions cause externalities.

The economic and philosophical questions are hard. But contract law is straightforward. As noted above, the common law of contract evolved to address the problems of the contracting parties. It did not do so because judges assumed that contracts necessarily lack external effects. It did so because judges classified the laws that addressed these external effects as belonging to other areas of the common law, or they left these problems for legislatures to deal with.

§2.14   Agency Relationships

Many cases involve corporations and other non-human entities such as governments, organizations, and associations. These entities are not persons, which means that they cannot have intentions, enter agreements, and so forth, except in a metaphorical sense. Instead, they act through agents, human beings. The law cheerfully attributes all of the human characteristics that are presupposed by contract doctrine to non-human entities, which are assumed to do whatever their authorized agents have done.

Most of the time this process is straightforward. If a purchasing agent of Microsoft enters into a contract to purchase office supplies, and then Microsoft's treasurer refuses to sign the check, then Seller can sue "Microsoft" for breach of contract, rather than the purchasing agent or the treasurer. The two agents are not parties to the contract, nor are they parties to the dispute. If it is legally relevant that Microsoft intended to breach or not, the question will be whether the treasurer (or her supervisors) intended to breach or not; if so, then the treasurer's intention to breach will be attributed to Microsoft.

Tricky problems can arise when agents act outside the scope of their duties. Suppose the CEO of Microsoft purports to sell Microsoft to Google, but without obtaining the approval of Microsoft's board of directors or shareholders. Is there a contract? Or suppose that the purchasing agent purports to sell Microsoft's office furniture to a company that buys and sells used office furniture. Is there a contract? The answers to these question lie within the domain of agency law, corporate law, and related fields of law, and thus are outside the scope of this book.

§2.15   Subjective / Objective

We will see references to "subjective" and "objective" approaches or theories to contract law, and so a few words on this distinction are appropriate here. Courts and commentators use the word "subjective" to refer to the mental states — usually intentions — of people; they use "objective" to refer to how a "reasonable" observer would interpret a statement or action.

Consider, for example, a contract involving the sale of "chickens."[19] We can distinguish the "subjective" intentions or understandings of the parties. If Buyer intended to buy broilers — if he understood the word "chicken" to mean "broiler" at the time of contracting — and Seller had the same understanding, then we can say that, using the subjective approach, the contract was for broilers, not for any old chickens. In other words, a court that enforced contracts according to their subjective meaning would interpret this contract to refer to broilers.

We can also distinguish the "objective" meaning of the contract. The reasonable person might interpret chicken, in the context of the contract, as referring only to "broilers" or in some other sense. The reasonable person could be just someone who is experienced in using the English language, or it could mean a relatively sophisticated commercial trader with experience with this type of transaction — courts are not always consistent about this issue. Whatever the case, it is possible for the objective meaning and the subjective meaning to be the same or different.

Note also that the subjective meaning is vulnerable to misunderstanding, in a way that objective meaning is not. If Buyer believes that "chicken" means "broiler," and Seller believes that "chicken" means "any old chicken," then the contract has no subjective meaning. The objective meaning, by contrast, is just whatever the average or representative person believes the meaning to be. A further difference between the two is that subjective meaning is especially vulnerable to false evidence, bad memory, wishful thinking, and the like. However, these evidentiary problems can be overcome if there is a paper trail.

§2.16   Contract Modification

Suppose that Buyer and Seller agree that Seller will deliver widgets on July 1, and in return Buyer agrees to pay $100. A few days later, Seller realizes that the widgets will not be ready until July 3. Seller contacts Buyer and they agree that Seller will deliver the widgets on July 3, and in return

---

[19] Frigaliment Imp. Co. v. B.N.S. Int'l Sales Corp., 190 F. Supp. 116 (S.D.N.Y. 1960).

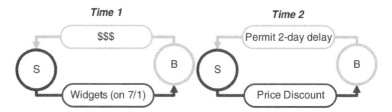

Buyer will receive a $10 price discount. So, in effect, they end up having a contractual relationship in which Seller agrees to delivery on July 3, and Buyer agrees to pay $90.

The second contract is a modification of the first contract. This is important because if a court were to decide, for whatever reason, that the second contract is void, then the first contract would come back into force. One-sided contract modifications — where only one side's obligation changes — are vulnerable to challenges on various grounds, including lack of consideration, duress, and unconscionability.

§2.17   Risk Aversion and Insurance

Two concepts that appear in many cases are risk aversion and insurance. Risk aversion refers to the widely recognized propensity of human beings to prefer certainty over risk. Consider a choice between (1) $100 with certainty and (2) $200 with a probability of 50 percent or $0 will a probability of 50 percent. A person who is risk neutral is indifferent between choices (1) and (2). A person who is risk averse prefers choice (1). A person who is risk preferring will take choice (2).

Economists derive risk aversion from the idea of declining marginal utility of wealth. Consider a person who has no money at all and another person who has $100,000. The person who is broke will get more benefit from a single dollar than the person with the $100,000. The first person can buy some food (though not very much) and satisfy his hunger for a little while. The second person is unlikely to find such an important purpose for an extra dollar.

Now imagine that a person earns $50,000 per year. She believes that with a probability of 1 percent she will become ill and lose her job. More formally, she can imagine two "states of the world" for the following year. In the first, which occurs with probability 99 percent, she continues to have her job and income. In the second, which occurs with probability of 1 percent, she is ill and has no job, and hence has no money (assuming no savings).

If this person experiences diminishing marginal utility of money, then she will want to equalize the amount of money that she has in each state of the world. If she does not have an equal amount in each state of the world, she can improve her well-being (in an expected sense) by "moving" one dollar from the state of the world in which she has more money (and so values the marginal dollar relatively less) to the state of the world in which she has less money (and so values the marginal dollar relatively more). Because the bad state of the world is so unlikely, she can pay an insurance company a small amount in return for a large payout in that world.

For example, the insurance company could pay this person $49,000 in the bad state of the world if she paid it $490 in the good state of the world. ($490 is 1 percent of $49,000.) So rather than facing a 1 percent chance of 0 and a 99 percent chance of $50,000, our insurance client faces a 1 percent chance of $49,000 and a 99 percent chance of $49,510.[20]

The insurance company is willing to enter this deal as long as it can find numerous people who face uncorrelated risks and want to buy insurance. "Uncorrelated" means that the fact that one person becomes ill does not increase the probability that another person will become ill. The cause of illness is particular to the individual (such as a heart problem) rather than common to all (such as an epidemic). Suppose 1000 people want to buy the same insurance. The insurance company receives $490,000 each year (1000 times the premium of $490) and pays out, on average, $490,000 (1 percent of 1000 times the payout of $49,000), so it breaks even. The insurance company will need to add a few dollars to the premium to cover its administrative expenses and protect itself in years where the number of illnesses is greater than average, but it can still offer an attractive deal to people seeking insurance.

Not all people are risk averse, and people who are normally risk averse will sometimes act differently — for example, they will gamble. People can also self-insure (save) and tend to do this when potential losses are small (no one buys insurance against the common cold). Analysts usually assume that businesses are risk neutral. The reason is that the shareholders who own businesses can insure themselves against bad outcomes by diversifying their holdings — buying shares in diverse firms. However, this assumption is probably not always accurate. Firms frequently buy insurance; it may be that they do this so that they are not driven out of business by a large negative shock, which would dissipate the corporate experience and organizational capital that have accumulated over many years.

---

[20] Technically, she would want to exactly equalize the amount in each state of the world because of the declining marginal utility of dollars. The insurance company would also charge extra to cover administrative costs and allow it a profit.

§2.18   Recurring Cases

Cases in a typical casebook will at first look bewilderingly diverse, but beneath the diversity are some patterns, and students who recognize these patterns will develop a better understanding of the law.

It turns out that most cases can be classified along the following lines.

Start by distinguishing sales of goods and personal services transactions. Sales of goods are generally simpler than personal services; and possibly because of this, the common law of contract, as it pertains to sales of goods, has been codified (and modified) in the Uniform Commercial Code. Personal services contracts usually involve more obligations and more complicated obligations, usually on both sides, which makes them harder to resolve.

In the classic *sales of goods* case, Buyer and Seller agree that Buyer will pay a price, P, for the widget. On Buyer's side, breach typically involves either nonpayment or late payment. Determining whether Buyer complied with his obligation is thus relatively straightforward: did he pay, and on time, or not?

On Seller's side, breach can be more complex. Failure to deliver, or to deliver on time, arises frequently, but sellers do not always have an obligation to deliver; maybe Buyer is supposed to pick up the widget. Most commonly, Seller fails to deliver a good of adequate quality. The question becomes whether Seller had any obligation with respect to quality and, if so, whether she breached it. This question can be tricky.

Then there are a host of relatively collateral obligations that can give rise to disputes. Seller might have an obligation to deliver or not, as noted above; a question might arise whether one party or the other bears the risk of damage, loss, or destruction of the widget during delivery. In some cases, Buyer might have an obligation to supply models or plans or other information to Seller, and Seller might have an obligation to allow Buyer's agents to inspect the manufacturing process. And so on.

Sales of real estate are not that different from sales of goods, but they are typically more complicated. For one thing, the sale of real estate involves the transfer of title, which requires the conveyance of a deed and the involvement of third parties such as title insurance companies. In addition, the buyer may need time to obtain financing, to hire an inspector to examine the property, and so forth. So typically the signing of the contract occurs a few weeks from the closing.

Personal services contracts comprehend a range of transactions, where at least one side, and sometimes both, must engage in a series of actions over time, actions that often involve highly discretionary elements. Consider the following examples.

An *employment contract*, where the employee does the work, and the employer pays the employee, with both obligations extending over time.

The contract might provide all kinds of restrictions on what the employee can and cannot do (for example, arrive late, bring family members onto the worksite) and all kinds of obligations (the employee must work so many hours a week, provide training to subordinates, and so forth). But often the contract will say nothing, and it is understood that the employee's main obligation is simply to follow the instructions of the employer. The employer might similarly have many obligations — to pay the employee a certain amount, to maintain a certain quality of work environment, to provide regular evaluations, to give the employee process before discipline — or virtually none.

Employment disputes arise over all these sorts of obligations, but many of the most prominent cases involve workers who believe that employers have violated explicit or implied terms to fire them only for good reason. Workers also sue because they believe that employers have not paid them according to the right formula or supplied promised pensions or shares of profits. Employers do not sue workers very often because workers are usually judgment-proof; the most common case seems to be the attempt to enforce covenants not to compete, where the worker sets up a competing business or goes to work for a competitor in violation of her promise not to.

"Seller"	"Buyer"
Seller	Buyer
Worker	Employer
Contractor	Owner
Subcontractor	Contractor
Borrower	Lender
Lawyer/Doctor	Client
Insurer	Client/Insured
Licensor	Licensee
Landlord	Tenant
Business	Business (merger)

A *construction contract* involves the building or repair of a house or other edifice. Construction contracts produce frequent disputes because of the complexity of the transaction. The contractor sells services; these include obtaining material, installing it, and so forth. The buyer makes payments, typically by installment, for reasons that we will discuss in due course.

In the case of a *loan*, it might be tempting to classify the lender, who supplies cash, as the seller. In fact, the borrower is the seller, which is indeed recognized in common parlance: when a corporation borrows money on the market, it sells bonds. A bond is a promise to repay plus interest. The corporation sells bonds to lenders in return for cash. The reason we think of the lender as the buyer is that the lender transfers cash, like any buyer, and gets in return a less liquid asset: a promise to repay in the future. Although this will eventually take the form of cash, a promise to pay is less liquid than actual cash because an extra step is involved to convert it into cash (as when a bondholder sells the bond to another person).

Leases are contracts between the owner of real estate (the landlord or lessor) and a person who occupied the property for a period of time (the tenant or lessee). (One can, of course, lease other items, such as automobiles.) The landlord is the "seller," who offers, in effect, a service — allowing the tenant to occupy a space — in return for money (rent). Other obligations exist on both sides. The landlord usually promises to maintain the premises, fix leaky faucets, and so forth; the tenant may promise to keep the hallway clean, install a rug so as not to disturb neighbors in the floor below, alert the landlord of problems, and in other ways minimize disruption for other tenants and limit depreciation of the landlord's property.

The difference between a lease and a sale is that in a lease the owner retains a residual interest in the property. The tenant departs; the owner gets the property back and can use it or lease it again. Leases are attractive when the person who takes out the lease expects to use the property for less than its useful life, and doesn't want to go through the bother of reselling it. The tenant also avoids the risk that property will depreciate (but also does not enjoy the benefit if the property appreciates). The structure of the lease therefore creates a conflict of interest between the lessor and the lessee. The lessor wants the lessee to use the property carefully; the lessee prefers to avoid the expense or trouble of doing so. Drivers take less care of cars they rent while on vacation compared with the cars they own because they do not enjoy the residual value of the rental. Lessors try to limit this behavior (which is called "moral hazard") through contractual provisions that require the lessee to take care.

Licenses are typically contracts in which the owner of property gives someone else permission to use the property in certain ways. In this way, licenses are similar to leases, but typically the term is used in connection with intellectual property. Microsoft invents an operating system, then licenses people to use the operating system in return for a fee. Microsoft doesn't sell them the operating system because then it would no longer own the software code and wouldn't be able to modify it, improve it, and license it to other people. Microsoft might also license code to other software companies, giving them the right (for example) to consult the code and even use pieces of it to develop software that can be used with the operating system.

Disputes over licenses often raise complex issues at the boundary of contract law and property law. Microsoft licenses its operating system software to Game Company so that Game Company can develop a computer game that works on a PC. The license includes a term prohibiting Game Company from using the code for any other purpose. Violating this term, Game Company copies some of the code into an operating system that it develops and hopes to sell on the market. Breach of contract? Yes — Game Company violated a term. But Microsoft can also argue that Game Company stole its intellectual property — a more serious act that gives rise to more generous remedies.

To understand why this could happen, imagine that in an ordinary lease the tenant promises never to enter the landlord's garage. If the tenant does so, she violates the lease, giving rise to a breach of contract claim. But she also trespasses on the landlord's property, giving rise to a tort claim. However, in the intellectual property context, it can be difficult to determine whether a term is merely a contractual term or also establishes that licensor retains a property interest in certain resources.

Businesses often enter complex contracts with suppliers, purchasers, and other entities. Two distinctive contracts that pose special problems are *requirement* and *output* contracts. In a requirement contract, a seller promises to provide all of the goods a buyer orders (what the buyer requires); in an output contract, a buyer promises to buy all of the goods the seller produces (the seller's output). As we will see, courts are sometimes troubled by these contracts because they are vague and present opportunities for abuse.

Another common type of business contract is the *franchise* agreement. The franchisor (the seller) is typically a large company with a valuable brand. It contracts with numerous franchisees (the buyers), who set up stores that exploit that brand identity. McDonald's, for example, licenses entrepreneurs to set up a McDonald's restaurant. McDonald's overriding goal is to protect its brand, so it requires the franchisee to undergo training, to maintain standards of hygiene and décor, and to offer the food items for which McDonald's is so justly famous. McDonald's, in turn, will supply advertising, market research, and other services and products that benefit all franchisees. The franchisee pays royalties to McDonald's, while McDonald's permits the franchisee to use its name, trademark, and so forth. Franchise agreements vary a great deal, and often involve various other types of transactions (for example, the franchisee might purchase supplies or rent buildings from the franchisor). But the essential element of the contract is the licensing of intellectual property in return for royalties and a promise to engage in behavior that maintains the value of the brand.

In a *sale of business*, a business sells itself. What this means is that the owner or shareholders of the business sell their ownership interest or their shares to a buyer. The business itself consists of real property, inventory, intellectual property, and other assets; the new owner may also inherit employment and other contracts that the seller assigns to it. *Merger* agreements take place when two businesses combine; the identities of the buyer and seller may be obscure. Two firms, X and Y, might merge into a new firm, XY. The new firm could just as easily be called X, Y, or something else. However, typically one firm actually buys the other: the buyer hands over cash or shares in itself or other things of value to the shareholders of the seller.

The important thing to remember is that although contractual relationships are often complex and vary greatly, some simple patterns recur. It helps when trying to understand an unfamiliar contract to figure out first which party belongs in the buyer position and which party belongs in the seller position; then you can compare the contract under consideration with other contracts that are simpler and more familiar.

§2.19   Breach of Contract or Void Contract?

Many breach of contract cases are not about whether a breach occurred at all; they are about whether a valid contract exists. One party sues the other for breach, and the defendant defends by claiming that a valid contract does not exist, in which case he could not have breached.

Buyer announces that he will not take delivery of, or pay for, Seller's widget. Seller sues for breach. Buyer defends by arguing that the contract is void because it is not in writing under the Statute of Frauds, because consideration was absent, because there was not a valid offer and acceptance, or because he agreed under duress. If Buyer prevails, Seller has no claim for breach of contract. If Buyer's argument fails, Seller does have such a claim.

Sometimes, a party must make a strategic decision whether to argue that a contract should be rescinded or enforced on his terms. In response to Seller's claim, Buyer might argue that the contract is enforceable but that an interpretation more favorable to him should be enforced. In some cases, Buyer may have the right to void the contract or enforce it (for example, if Seller committed fraud); in some cases, Buyer has no such right (for example, if the contract is illusory), but nonetheless he can choose to press one claim or the other with the court, not being sure which one the court will accept.

§2.20   If Breach, When Does Breach Occur?

Most contracts are bilateral contracts — a promise for a promise — and cases can be categorized according to when the breach occurs, an issue that can matter for determination of liability and of damages.

Consider a promise by Buyer to pay and for Seller to deliver. We can distinguish the following possible moments in time.

Before any performance. Buyer announces that he will not pay, or Seller announces that she will not deliver. In either case, an "anticipatory breach" occurs — anticipatory, because the time for performance has not yet occurred. The victim of breach, the promisee, sues the promisor for breach of contract. Because the promisee has not performed, he will need damages that cover only the "profit" of the contract — the difference between the value of the promisor's performance for the promisee, and the cost of performance for the promisee.

After the performance of one party. Buyer pays in advance, and then Seller announces that she will not perform. Or Seller delivers, and then Buyer refuses to pay. In either case, a breach occurs. The victim of the breach, the promisee, will seek damages not only for the "profit" but also for the cost already incurred.

After partial performance of one or both parties. The contract provides that Buyer pays in two installments. Buyer pays the first installment but not the second. Or the contract provides that Seller deliver a high-quality widget. Seller provides a widget but it is low-quality. In either case, one party has partially performed, while the other has either not performed or fully performed. And there are cases where both parties partially perform: Buyer pays only the first installment and Seller delivers the low-quality widget. These cases arise for obvious reasons. Buyer believes that the second installment is due only after the widget survives inspection, which it did not; Seller believes that her obligation to replace the widget is contingent on full payment by Buyer. So each sues the other.

§2.21   What Is a "Promisor"?

Students sometimes get confused by the terms courts use to describe the parties. Consider a bilateral contract, say, with a seller and a buyer. In an opinion, the court refers to the "promisor" and the "promisee." But aren't both parties "promisors"? Both make promises. And so both parties are "promisees" — the parties to whom a promise is made. What's going on?

The answer is that the court uses "promisor" to refer to the party that is being accused of breach, usually (but not always) the defendant. Suppose that Buyer sues the Seller for late delivery — that is, breaching her promise to deliver on time. The court will refer to Seller as the promisor and Buyer as the promisee. Now suppose that Seller sues Buyer for failing to pay. The court will refer to Buyer as the promisor and Seller as promisee. I said that the promisor is usually the defendant because in most cases the victim of breach brings suit. But there are also cases where the promisor brings suit — for example, where a promisor admits to breach but also seeks restitution.

Courts sometimes use the term "obligor" as a synonym for promisor, and "obligee" as a synonym for promisee.

Chapter *3*

Contract Formation

§3.1   Mutual Assent

"Mutual assent" is a guiding concept in contract law, but it is not a doctrinal requirement. By guiding concept, I mean that it can be said, very roughly, that many doctrines of contract law ensure that an enforceable contract exists only when parties mutually consented to it, and not when parties did not mutually consent to it.[1] But courts use these doctrines, not the notion of mutual consent, when deciding whether a valid contract exists. For example, if a contract is invalid, it will be because a valid offer was never made, or it was withdrawn before acceptance, or the acceptance was defective. One needs to understand the doctrines of offer and acceptance; "mutual assent," as a concept, falls by the wayside.

One should also understand that the concept of "mutual assent" hides a number of complexities. Despite the common statement that a contact is enforceable only if there is mutual asset, mutual assent in fact is not always required. We will discuss these complexities in due course, but for now

---

[1] See Restatement (Second) of Contracts §17(1) (1981) ("the formation of a contract requires a bargain in which there is a manifestation of mutual assent to the exchange and a consideration").

consider a case where a buyer manifests assent to a contract (says "I accept your offer") but does not in fact assent to the contract (he believes that the offer is a joke, for example). In such cases, as we will see below, courts may find an enforceable contract. We will revisit the idea of mutual assent in Section 6.2 after we have seen the relevant doctrine.

§3.2 Offers

Black-letter doctrine says that a contract can exist only if there is an offer and an acceptance.[2] An offer is "the manifestation of willingness to enter into a bargain, so made as to justify another person in understanding that his assent to that bargain is invited and will conclude it."[3] What does this mean? Whether an offer exists is a question of interpretation. The factfinder must decide whether a reasonable person would understand the statement in question to be an offer. At a minimum, there must be words or gestures or other behavior (for example, the placing of an item with a price tag on a shelf in a store) indicating that one party seeks to enter a legally enforceable contract.

In Moulton v. Kershaw,[4] Sellers sent a letter to Buyer as follows:

> Dear Sir: In consequence of a rupture in the salt trade, we are authorized to offer Michigan fine salt, in full car-load lots of 80 to 95 bbls., delivered at your city, at 85c. per bbl., to be shipped per C. & N.W. R.R. Co. only. At this price it is a bargain, as the price in general remains unchanged. Shall be pleased to receive your order.

Buyer replied, "Your letter of yesterday received and noted. You may ship me two thousand (2,000) barrels Michigan fine salt, as offered in your letter. Answer." Sellers changed their minds and informed Buyer that they would not enter into a contract for the sale of salt. Buyer sued for breach of contract.

The issue is whether a contract was formed. A contract requires an offer and an acceptance. Buyer's reply is an acceptance, as we will see later, if Sellers' letter counts as an offer. Was it? Sellers argue that the letter was merely an advertisement or invitation to negotiate.

---

[2] Restatement (Second) of Contracts §22(1) (1981) ("[t]he manifestation of mutual assent to an exchange ordinarily takes the form of an offer or proposal by one party followed by an acceptance by the other party or parties").

[3] Restatement (Second) of Contacts §24 (1981).

[4] 18 N.W. 172 (Wis. 1884). For a similar case, see Nebraska Seed Co. v. Harsh, 152 N.W. 310 (Neb. 1915) (concluding that a telegram with an estimated quantity available and approximate price did not use sufficiently definitive language to be considered an offer).

To resolve the dispute, one must interpret the letter. Was it a manifestation of an intention to be legally bound, or not? The court noted that the letter did not use the word "sell" or the phrase "we offer to sell you." If the letter had said, "we offer to sell you salt . . . ," then the letter would probably have been an offer. The court also noted that the letter did not fix a maximum. This had dual significance. If a seller seeks to be legally bound, he does not want to expose himself to possibly unlimited liability, as he would if the offeree demanded an enormous quantity of goods, far beyond what the seller can supply. And if offers nominally to sell an unlimited quantity of goods were permitted, courts would have to determine what parties really mean, which is more likely that only a reasonable amount of goods may be demanded. This difficult inquiry is best avoided.

But one shouldn't think that an offer must contain the word "sell" or must be limited in quantity. People speak in many different ways, and courts understand this. An offer can exist even without the word "sell" or any other magic word. In addition, courts will permit people to make unlimited offers as long as they have made it clear that this is what they want to do. In *Moulton* the court believed that the lack of a maximum, along with the wording and the business setting, suggested that the seller sought to enter negotiations, not to be legally bound to deliver whatever quantity a buyer might demand.

Courts struggle with a basic tension in the way people speak to each other. Communication is costly — it takes time and thought and sometimes money — and so people don't want to go into elaborate detail when they offer goods or services for sale. At the same time, people want to communicate accurately, and that requires the expenditure of effort to describe future contingencies and obligations. A great level of detail probably does signal that people seek to make firm obligations, but the level of appropriate detail varies from case to case. In markets where people constantly interact with each other, they often develop highly economical procedures for entering deals — which are unintelligible to outsiders but perfectly clear to insiders. Courts need to be aware that a brief, vague-seeming statement signals an intention to be legally bound in one market but not in another market.

It is useful, but not entirely accurate, to say that the offer and acceptance doctrines are used to distinguish cases of agreement from cases of preliminary negotiation, in which information is sought and exchanged but no agreement is reached. This proposition is not accurate because of the ambiguity of the concept of agreement. The parties do not need to agree on every last detail; it is sufficient that they agree on the major elements of the contract. On the other side, if the parties do manifest an intention to be legally bound, but do not agree in sufficient detail, a court will refuse to find an offer and acceptance. The question then becomes, How much detail is the right amount?

One cannot answer a question like this in the abstract. If you read a lot of cases, you will get a sense of what courts find acceptable. Here we will note that the ultimate standard of what counts as offer and acceptance has less to do with the parties' intentions than with the amount of information that the parties make available to the courts. Courts usually but not always demand a price term; where one is lacking, sometimes they can assume that the parties intended to use the market price. Courts almost always demand a quantity term; there is no "market quantity" that they can rely on, though sometimes custom or past practice will do the trick. When one shifts the focus from the question, How much detail shows that the parties reached an agreement? to the question, How much information does the court need to enforce the contract?, the inquiry becomes more straightforward. Courts find an offer and acceptance when the terms that are discussed or written down, together with custom and past practice, provide them with enough detail that they can determine whether a breach has occurred, and supply a remedy. Of course, there can't be merely detail; there must also be a signal from each party that he intends to be legally bound. But that can usually be inferred when the parties are saying the same thing, and not contradicting each other, and shake hands, lay down a signature, or do any of the other things that conventionally establish an intention to be bound.

A final consideration involves the strategic difficulties with negotiating a contract. Imagine that Seller owns a widget and would like to sell it, but for no less than $100. When Seller approaches a potential buyer, Seller might offer to sell the widget, but in doing so, she is likely to reveal information that could be to her disadvantage. If Seller offers the widget for a price of $100 or $110, she might end up selling for a low price to a buyer who would be willing to pay $200 or more. Alternatively, Seller could ask the potential buyer to suggest a price; if the buyer complies, then Seller obtains the advantage. But the buyer might not comply.

The vulnerability of Seller, and also the credibility of her offer, depends on the law. If the offer is not legally enforceable, then Seller could change her mind after Buyer accepts, and demand a higher price. But if that is the case, Buyer would not trust Seller's offer in the first place, and would refuse to accept. If the offer is legally enforceable after acceptance, Seller cannot change her mind, and she might find herself stuck with a bad deal, but at least she can commit herself. If not legally enforceable after acceptance, an offer would be worthless; there would be no way to make a contract.

Seller can revoke her offer before Buyer accepts. Since Buyer can convey information about his valuation only by accepting, Seller cannot — in ordinary cases — take advantage of Buyer by revoking an offer. But this conclusion changes when Seller invites Buyer to rely on the offer's being kept open for a period of time. Often Buyer needs time to invest in information about competing offers, and Seller can attract a buyer at a good price only by keeping the offer open.

It follows that Seller should not be permitted to revoke what is called a "firm offer," an offer plus a promise to keep the offer open for a period of time. When Seller makes a firm offer, she balances two considerations: the higher price she can demand from a buyer who has time to inquire about the value of the widget, and the risk that someone else will come along with an offer to pay a price higher than that stipulated in the offer.[5]

§3.3 Acceptance and the Mirror Image Rule

The mirror image rule says that a statement (or action) counts as an acceptance and hence results in a valid contract if that statement "mirrors" the offer.[6] If someone says, "I offer to sell you this widget for $100," one can accept by saying, "I hereby accept your offer for that widget for $100," but a simple "yes" will do. The mirror, then, is just a loose metaphor; the key point is that a statement, even an agreeable, affirmative statement, cannot count as an acceptance if it introduces new or different terms from those that are contained in the offer. A "yes" does not introduce new or different terms, so a "yes" suffices. So does a handshake. So does delivery or acceptance of delivery. One can accept a contract simply by taking the goods in question or delivering them, in response to an offer.

Let us consider a simple example:

1. X: "I offer to sell you my car for $3000."
2. Y: "I accept, however, only if you pay for a tune-up."
3. X: "Okay."

Even though Y uses the word "accept," he does not really accept the contract; he is making a counter-offer, albeit one that proposes only a minor adjustment to X's offer. At point 3, X accepts.[7]

It is often the case that X and Y negotiate for quite a while — hours, days, years — before reaching a deal. Courts do not bother to review all the statements going back and forth, and classify them as offers and counter-offers. The courts need to identify only the last statement (or

---

[5] See Section 3.11.

[6] See Restatement (Second) of Contracts §50(1) (1981) ("Acceptance of an offer is a manifestation of assent to the terms thereof made by the offer in a manner invited or required by the offer."). See also Ardente v. Horan, 366 A.2d 162 (R.I. 1976) (concluding that an offer for sale of real estate was not accepted because the purchaser's signed sale agreement and down payment were accompanied by a letter requesting that several fixtures remain with the property).

[7] Compare Livingstone v. Evans, 4 D.L.R. 769 (Alta. S.C., 1925).

Acceptance of Offers

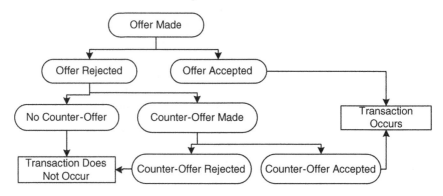

action) that shows an intent to make a deal — to be legally bound, as the courts say — while not varying whatever came before. The final statement or action might be a "yes" or "you've got a deal!" or an "okay" or a handshake or delivery or acceptance of delivery. Then look at whatever came before it. That statement will be considered the offer (or counter-offer; it doesn't matter).

This simple process is of great importance as it establishes the terms of the deal, namely, the terms that are contained in the offer. The offer, then, will essentially be the contract. Consider the following sequence of events.

1. Seller: "I hereby offer you this widget, for $100, and on these terms." Seller hands over a form that contains dozens of clauses governing issues of warranty, choice of forum, and so on.
2. Buyer: "I hereby accept your offer to sell the widget, for $100, on these terms." Buyer hands over a form that contains dozens of clauses governing issues of warranty, choice of forum, and so on — some, many, or all of them different from the terms of Seller's form.
3. Seller delivers the widget, which arrives at Buyer's place of business with Seller's form tucked in the box.
4. Buyer sends a check for $100 to Seller's place of business, along with Buyer's form.

So whose form prevails? The mirror image rules provides a simple guideline: whoever's form is sent last — Buyer's, at time 4. If Seller cashes the check, that will be considered acceptance of Buyer's offer at time 4. If Buyer hadn't sent the form at time 4, then his acceptance of delivery would be considered acceptance of Seller's offer at time 3. If Seller hadn't included the form in the box at time 3, her delivery would be considered acceptance of Buyer's offer at time 2. Buyer's statement at time 2 can't be an acceptance because the form he supplies is different from Seller's offer: Buyer's statement at time 2 can only be a counter-offer. As the sequence of events was originally described, the contract is made at time 4; before then, there is no contract, so either party could have backed out without risking legal liability.

The mirror image rule, however, does not govern this transaction. Because it involves the sale of goods, the transaction would be governed by the U.C.C., which involves a different rule, as we will see in Section 3.6. But the mirror image rule remains the common law rule and governs all transactions aside from sales of goods.[8]

§3.4 Offers Stipulating Silence as Acceptance

The old chestnut is that the "offeror is master of the offer." This slogan restates the mirror image rule. The offeree cannot accept an offer that the offeror did not make but that the offeree wishes that the offeror had made. If, for example, the offeror says, "I'll sell you some widgets for $100 as is," the offeree can't accept by saying, "It's a deal, with the understanding that you'll take them back if they are defective." As we saw, the offeree's statement would be construed as a counter-offer, leaving the offeror the option to accept or reject it or propose yet another counter-offer.

The idea that the offeror is master of the offer has led to some confusion about how far the offeror can go toward designing his offer. Suppose, for example, the offeror says, "I offer you widgets for $100 a bushel, and if you don't say anything, that will count as acceptance." Offerors can stipulate that certain types of behavior count as acceptance, but the problem here is that by stipulating silence to be acceptance, the offeror is trying to force the offeree to take action. The offeree can always say "no," but what if he has better things to do with his larynx? Or suppose that the offeror sends the offer by mail to the offeree and states that failure to respond will be construed as acceptance? Now the offeree must devote time to fending off offers, and offerors have an incentive to mail their offers in the hope that some offerees will overlook them or fail to respond for some other reason.

The law addresses this problem with a simple doctrine: silence cannot be acceptance unless the circumstances of the parties' relationship suggest that they understand silence in that way.[9] Requiring an affirmative act or statement from the offeree eliminates the offeror's incentive to use manipulation to obtain an acceptance from an unwilling offeree. The exception contemplates repetitive business relationships, where, for example, a seller periodically sends goods to buyer, who routinely accepts

---

[8] However, the Restatement, under the influence of the U.C.C., suggests that parties may be able to form a contract without complying with the mirror image rule. See §22(2).

[9] See Restatement (Second) of Contracts §69(1) (1981).

them without any communication.[10] After a while, it is reasonable for the seller to expect the buyer to reject offers only by making an explicit statement to that effect.

§3.5 Offers with Hidden Terms

A more complex problem arises when the offeror "hides" terms in a contract. Consider a literal form of the term *hiding*. A buyer takes a box off the shelf of a store. The label on the outside of the box identifies the item and its price, and says that "additional terms are inside the box." The buyer buys the item, takes it home, opens the box, and reads the enclosed contract, which includes the following term: "Surprise! You owe us $10,000!" Now, to be sure, such terms are exceedingly rare, but other surprise terms are not so rare. For example, the contract might say that "you agree to arbitration in case of dispute," or "you must pay a $2000 arbitration fee if there is a dispute," or "you have no warranty." I will call these "Surprise Clauses" and stipulate that they make the buyer unhappy.

Now, in the real world, one does not come across cases where terms are literally hidden. More frequently, they are just hard to find or hard to respond to. In ProCD v. Zeidenberg,[11] the Surprise Clause stated that the telephone number database, which came on a CD in the package, could be used only for personal (not commercial) purposes. In Hill v. Gateway,[12] the buyer ordered a computer over the phone. The Surprise Clause was an arbitration clause that effectively made arbitration or dispute resolution of any sort impossible (the fee was high and the procedures onerous). The arbitration clause was not read over the phone for the obvious reason that no one has the time or patience to listen to the recitation of a lengthy contract. Buyers did, however, have the right to return the computer within 30 days if they did not like the terms of the contract. The plaintiffs did not take advantage of this right because they did not read the contract.

Terms can hide in plain sight in the midst of lengthy contracts, so even if consumers have the opportunity to read the contracts in advance — as they usually do if they buy items at stores — they rarely take that opportunity. Nowadays, a lot of products can be bought online. Certain online services give you the opportunity to read the terms and may even insist

---

[10] See Section 3.12.

[11] 86 F.3d 1447 (7th Cir. 1996).

[12] 105 F.3d 1147 (7th Cir. 1997). For a similar case, see Specht v. Netscape Communications, 150 F. Supp. 2d 585 (S.D. N.Y. 2001) (determining that an arbitration clause in a contract agreed to with the click of an web page button would not be enforced because the website did not provide sufficient notice).

that you click "I accept" before paying for the product; does anyone read the terms in such agreements, which go on for pages and pages in dense legalese? Probably not.

Here, we just want to focus on the following question. If a person buys a good without understanding all the terms of the contract, is the contract invalid?

The traditional answer is no. You might think that a person who does not read the contract cannot be bound to it; after all, there has been no mutual assent to the terms. But if the person has the opportunity to read the contract and forgoes it, his or her assent is presumed. This is the common law duty to read; if one violates that duty, one has no remedy.[13] The rule makes a great deal of sense. If a contract is written down, the parties can reasonably assume that it will be read. If there is no duty to read, then one party can always pretend to read it and not read it, and then he can escape the contract if it is profitable to do so. Indeed, applying this reasoning, neither party will read the contract and no contract will be enforceable!

Yet the rule has problems. Contracts are hard to read and harder to understand. Lawyers draft them with an eye to cases and doctrines that the non-lawyers who sign the contracts rarely know about; they are written with care so that courts will enforce them correctly, but not with the literary flourishes that make for a good read. It seems doubtful that consumers ever read the consumer product contracts they enter.[14] I certainly don't. Who has the time?

As a result, sellers can easily sneak in terms that buyers do not want. There are limits to what they can do, however. When famous companies like Apple, Facebook, and Microsoft bury contract terms that a great many people do not like, these terms are ferreted out by watchdogs and broadcast over the Internet. Truly offensive terms may garner bad publicity. For example, sellers often try to limit their exposure to litigation by including arbitration clauses, choice of forum clauses, and other terms that make it difficult or expensive for buyers to bring claims for breach of contract and to win damages. In recent years, Internet companies have reset default privacy settings, which can result in the disclosure of information that users assumed would remain private. When the firms are exposed, they may be forced to backtrack.

But this is not always the case, or so it is thought. The conventional wisdom is that firms frequently hide terms in lengthy form contracts that buyers do not read; these terms unreasonably favor sellers in ways that

---

[13] See Allied Van Lines, Inc. v. Bratton, 351 So. 2d 344 (Fla. 1977); see also Restatement (Second) of Contracts §23 cmt. b, Reporter's Note to cmt. e.

[14] See Omri Ben-Shahar, The Myth of the "Opportunity to Read" in Contract Law, 5 Eur. Rev. Cont. L. 1 (2009). On the general problem of boilerplate, see Boilerplate: Foundations of Market Contracts (Omri Ben-Shahar ed., 2007).

we will consider when we address substantive unconscionability.[15] Courts have responded by demanding that sellers highlight such terms, or otherwise draw buyers' attention to them. For example, rental car companies ask customers to initial waivers of insurance. Thus, a number of cases involve fact-intensive evaluation of the contract. In Henningson v. Bloomfield Motors, for example, the court objected because a clause that excluded liability in case of accidents appeared as the phrase "[the car manufacturer's] obligation under this warranty being limited to making good at its factory any part or parts thereof."[16] The phrase seems designed to mislead consumers who might otherwise assume that if they are injured as a result of a design defect, the company would have to pay them money. Rather than saying, "you get nothing if you are hurt," the form mentions what *is* covered. Of course, the buyer admitted that he never read the form, so he could hardly have been misled by the clause.

Rules that penalize sellers for misleading their customers seem sensible. Why not demand the seller to be as clear as possible? But putting the rules into practice has turned out to be a challenge. Buyers have limited cognitive capacity, time, and patience. Modern products and services are often very complicated; explaining how they work and what can go wrong can take a long time. Making these explanations in a way that produces clear legal rights and obligations is even harder. And then throw in all the trivial but necessary terms governing dispute resolution, delivery, insurance, warranties, and the like. No buyer wants to read the contract and hear all the terms. Thus, the rules force sellers to guess at which three or four terms are most important to buyers, and then draw their attention to them. But how does one know what matters to buyers? Maybe in some cases it is obvious, but probably not often.

Legislative efforts to mandate disclosure have been disappointing. The Truth in Lending Act, for example, is a federal statute that governs the disclosure of information for certain types of loans, such as mortgages. Lenders must provide buyers with all relevant information — the length of the loan, monthly payments, how interest is calculated, the fees (for example, for getting the loan in the first place, for missing a payment, for terminating it early), whether the loan can be sold to someone else, and so on. Additional documents explain the borrower's rights under the Truth in Lending Act, and still more documents describe rights under state law. The result is a massive pile of documents that no one can get through, many of which present the same information in confusingly different ways. Academic research suggests that only a few salient pieces of information penetrate the buyer's skull, not enough to make the informed comparisons that the law is aimed at.

---

[15] This issue arises under the offer and acceptance doctrines as well, most famously in the *ProCD* case. See Section 4.10.

[16] Henningsen v. Bloomfield Motors, 161 A.2d 69, 93 (N.J. 1960).

Let us turn back to the common law. Seller offers a product along with a lengthy written contract that contains all sorts of complicated terms. What should be the legal consequences?

The district court in the ProCD case supplied one possible answer: no contract.[17] The court held that because buyer did not learn the terms of the offer until after he brought the box home, there was never any mutual assent. A contract could not have been formed. In so holding, the district court implicitly assumed that a contract could have been formed only at the point of sale — when Buyer handed over money to Seller and took the box. The circuit court reversed, holding that a contract could have been formed and was formed when Buyer retained the item after having opened the package, read the terms (or enjoyed the opportunity to read them), and declined to return the package.[18] The offer was, in essence, "you may buy this database, and acceptance takes place when you fail to return it after opening the box and reading the terms."

The circuit court cleverly resolved the tension between two factors — our reluctance to demand that Buyer learn all the terms of a contract before handing over his money, and the classic idea that Buyer must understand the terms of the contract before consenting to it. The court did this by extending the offer temporally — Buyer would have the leisure to read the terms at home. But the court's decision did not resolve the underlying problem, which is that buyers buy things without taking the trouble to understand the contracts, meaning that unscrupulous sellers can "hide" unfavorable terms in plain sight. Most buyers will not take the opportunity to read the contract at home; it's just too much trouble.

The uneasy compromise, for now, is that contracts will be enforced, including terms that seem unfavorable to Buyer, as long as Buyer has an opportunity to read the terms and Seller takes the trouble to point out especially unfavorable or surprising terms. The contract also must satisfy other legal doctrines that protect the consumer, notably the unconscionability doctrine, which we discuss in Section 4.10.

§3.6   U.C.C. §2-207

The mirror image rule is simple and easy to understand, but it is no longer the law for sales of goods, which is governed by the Uniform Commercial Code. U.C.C. §2-207 marks a departure from the mirror-image rule.

---

[17] ProCD, Inc. v. Zeidenberg, 908 F. Supp. 640 (W.D. Wis. 1996).
[18] ProCD, Inc. v. Zeidenberg, 86 F.3d 1447 (7th Cir. 1996).

U.C.C. §2-207 provides:

(1) A definite and seasonable expression of acceptance or a written confirmation which is sent within a reasonable time operates as an acceptance even though it states terms additional to or different from those offered or agreed upon, unless acceptance is expressly made conditional on assent to the additional or different terms.

(2) The additional terms are to be construed as proposals for addition to the contract. Between merchants such terms become part of the contract unless:

(a) the offer expressly limits acceptance to the terms of the offer;
(b) they materially alter it; or
(c) notification of objection to them has already been given or is given within a reasonable time after notice of them is received.

(3) Conduct by both parties which recognizes the existence of a contract is sufficient to establish a contract for sale although the writings of the parties do not otherwise establish a contract. In such case the terms of the particular contract consist of those terms on which the writings of the parties agree, together with any supplementary terms incorporated under any other provisions of this Act.

Against the background of the mirror image rule, §2-207 has two major effects. First, it provides that a contract will exist in situations where the mirror image rule prevents contract formation. Suppose, for example, that Seller provides a form and Buyer responds with a mismatching form. Under the mirror image rule, no contract exists. Under §2-207, a contract *may* exist. We will discuss shortly whether one does or not. For now, just note that if the mismatch is not excessive, a contract will be deemed to exist.

This difference disappears for contracts that are partially performed. If Seller responds to Buyer's mismatching form by delivering, the delivery will be deemed an acceptance, and so a contract will exist even under the mirror image rule. But prior to performance on either side, §2-207 provides for the existence of an enforceable contract in cases where the mirror image rule does not.

Second, when partial performance does occur, the mirror image rule will produce a contract with terms that are different from those that follow from §2-207. The mirror image rule is sometimes called the "last shot rule" because the terms of the last form that was issued will be the terms of the contract. The reason is that earlier forms were met with mismatching forms and thus could not be accepted. The last form is the offer; delivery or acceptance of delivery is the "acceptance." The terms of the offer control. Section 2-207 provides for a different result. Speaking very loosely, §2-207 provides that the terms will be those of the first form, plus minor adjustments in the second form. But that is speaking very loosely; §2-207 poses a number of interpretive challenges.

Consider the following example.[19]

1. Seller issues an offer to sell a widget accompanied by Form X, which says that Seller is *not* liable if an injury occurs as a result of a defect in the widget.
2. Buyer says, "I accept" the offer to sell a widget and sends Form Y, which says that Seller *is* liable if an injury occurs.
3. Seller delivers.
4. Buyer takes delivery.

Under the mirror image rule, the contract will be Form Y (Seller is liable). Buyer rejects Form X by replying with an inconsistent form. Buyer's Form Y is the counter-offer. Seller's delivery counts as acceptance. Note that the contract does not come into existence until delivery at time 3.

Under §2-207(1), one must first ask whether Form Y is a "definite and seasonable expression of acceptance." This seems likely.[20] Form X is the offer; Form Y, despite the inconsistency, seems like an acceptance or part of the acceptance. Note that Buyer does not say that his acceptance is conditional on Seller's "assent to the additional or different terms." If he did, then Buyer's form would be regarded as a counter-offer. Seller's delivery then might be deemed acceptance, or alternatively one might jump to subsection (3), which we will discuss shortly.

But if we conclude that Buyer's Form Y is an acceptance, we go to subsection (2). This subsection starts off with the phrase, "The additional terms are to be construed as proposals for addition to the contract." This phrase has caused some confusion. Recall that subsection (1) refers to the offeror's possible assent to *additional or different* terms (not just "additional terms"). Is this difference in language of significance? Some commentators argue that if the terms in Form Y are different, then we go directly to subsection (3); if they are additional, we can go to subsection (2). Others argue that in either case we go to subsection (2); subsection (3) is reserved for cases where Buyer's response at time 2 does not express even "partial" acceptance, and yet the parties end up acting as though they have entered a contract. In our example, the terms are different: in one form Seller pays; in the other she does not. But imagine that Buyer's form did not say that Seller pays but said nothing at all, while incorporating an

---

[19] These facts are based on Idaho Power Co. v. Westinghouse Elec. Corp., 596 F.2d 924 (9th Cir. 1979).
[20] For an example of when assent is not sufficiently apparent, see Step-Saver Data Sys., Inc. v. Wyse Technologies, 939 F.2d 91 (3d Cir. 1991) (holding that a boxtop license was not binding on a buyer because there was not sufficient evidence to demonstrate assent from the purchaser).

integration clause. Do we now say that the terms are different or additional? The question is hard to answer.

Let us continue through subsection (2). We immediately see that subsection (2) comes into play only if both parties are merchants. What if they aren't? Presumably, the terms of the first form control (Seller doesn't pay). If both parties are merchants, we must consult the first form to see whether it says that the offer expressly limits acceptance to the terms of the offer (§2.207(2)(a)). If yes, then the first form controls. This clause creates additional interpretive difficulties: don't all offers expressly limit acceptance to the terms of the offer? If not, the offeror can solve this problem by adding boilerplate to that effect, which many offerors have done. Let's move onto (b), which is probably the most important clause in subsection (2). If Buyer's form "materially alters" Seller's form, then Seller's form controls (Buyer pays if there is an injury); otherwise, Buyer's form controls (Seller pays). How does one tell whether an inconsistent term is "material"? Courts have tended to distinguish more peripheral clauses (e.g., choice of forum), but there is no obvious answer to this question. Finally, Seller can avoid Buyer's terms by objecting to them in advance or within a reasonable time (c).

In practice, subsection (2) boils down to an inquiry into whether the offeree's inconsistent term is a material alteration or not. But we still haven't addressed subsection (3), which says that inconsistent terms are knocked out and replaced by the default rule in the Code. In the current case, if the Code has a default rule making Seller liable, then that is the result. Some courts pretty much ignore subsection (2) and apply this rule — the so-called knockout rule — to every case.

Consider, for example, Richardson v. Union Carbide.[21] Seller (Rage) sold a piece of equipment (a "powder transporter system") to Buyer (Hoeganaes). Each side submitted forms. Seller's form contained an indemnity clause that required Buyer to protect Seller from any claims arising from the use of the equipment. Buyer's form did the opposite: it required Seller to protect Buyer from any claims. When an employee of Buyer was injured by an explosion and sued both Buyer and Seller, Buyer and Seller tried to force each other to bear the entire liability. If Buyer's form controlled, then Seller must pay; if Seller's form controlled, Buyer must pay. Whose form controls?

The court applied the knockout rule on the ground that the major alternative approach would give an advantage to the offeror (Seller, in this case), which seems arbitrary. Under that alternative approach, Seller's

---

[21] 790 A.2d 962 (N.J. 2002).

form would prevail because Buyer's pro-buyer indemnity clause would (probably) be construed as either a "different" (rather than additional) term, so that subsection (2) does not apply; or as an "additional" term under subsection (2), which materially alters the contract and thus does not become part of the contract. The court does not take seriously the traditional idea, reflected in the mirror image rule, that the first offeror does not really enjoy an advantage because the offeree can always reject and make a counter-offer. In the U.C.C. world, that is harder to do. The knockout rule avoids these difficulties.

Section 2-207 is a masterpiece of ambiguity, and a proposed revision simplifies it by adopting the "knockout" interpretation:

> Subject to Section 2-202, if (i) conduct by both parties recognizes the existence of a contract although their records do not otherwise establish a contract, (ii) a contract is formed by an offer and acceptance, or (iii) a contract formed in any manner is confirmed by a record that contains terms additional to or different from those in the contract being confirmed, the terms of the contract, are:
>   (a) terms that appear in the records of both parties;
>   (b) terms, whether in a record or not, to which both parties agree; and
>   (c) terms supplied or incorporated under any provision of this Act.

However, current law remains a morass.

Nonetheless, the goal of the drafters of the U.C.C. is relatively clear. They believed that the mirror image rule did not reflect the reality of business. Commercial buyers and sellers knew very well that their forms did not match in every detail but nonetheless would have been surprised to learn that a contract did not exist prior to delivery. Thus, it seems reasonable to hold that a contract can exist despite disagreements over certain terms. Section 2-207 tries to recognize this fact by distinguishing between cases where the differences matter (are "material") and cases where they don't. At the same time, the drafters acknowledge that the offeror herself might sometimes want to avoid being bound to a contract that even nonmaterially differs from what she offered (hence the escape hatches in subsections (1) and (2)(c)).

Which rule is superior? The mirror image rule is certainly simple, and its application is predictable. However, it can result in courts refusing to recognize contracts when the parties intended to create them, and its implication that the last form supplies the terms seems arbitrary. Section 2-207, if applied sensibly, can ensure that a contract exists when the parties so intend, and yet its penultimate-shot implication hardly seems less arbitrary than the mirror image rule's. The more serious problem is that §2-207's provisions are ambiguous and hard to apply.

§3.7   The Mailbox Rule

The mailbox rule provides:

Unless the offer provides otherwise,

> an acceptance made in a manner and by a medium invited by an offer
> is operative and completes the manifestation of mutual assent as soon
> as put out of the offeree's possession, without regard to whether it
> ever reaches the offeror.[22]

To understand what is at stake, imagine that Seller owns some property, which she would like to sell. She hears that Buyer might be interested. Seller mails an offer in the form of a writing for Buyer's signature.
Buyer receives the writing, signs it, and places it in a mailbox, but before
the post office delivers the writing to Seller, Buyer has a change of heart
and phones Seller and informs her that he rejects the offer. The writing
arrives a few days later. Seller argues that a contract has been formed;
Buyer disagrees.[23]

1.   Seller/Offeror mails offer to Buyer/Offeree.
2.   Buyer signs writing and places it in the mailbox.
3.   Buyer calls Seller and revokes the offer.
4.   Seller receives signed writing.

An offer was made; that is clear. The question is whether Offeree (Buyer)
accepted the offer and thereby formed a contract. Offeror (Seller) argues
that Offeree manifested his assent by signing the writing and placing it in
the mailbox — at that point, mutual assent existed. When Offeree tried to
revoke, he merely engaged in an anticipatory repudiation of the contract.
Offeree argues that mutual assent never existed because Buyer changed
his mind before communicating to Seller — just as if Buyer had initially
signed the writing and then torn it up rather than mailed it. Under the mailbox rule, Offeror wins — a contract is formed — because the acceptance
(the signed writing) was put out of Offeree's possession when Offeree
mailed it.

The idea of mutual assent does not get one very far toward understanding what is at stake. Instead, consider the risks that the parties face. When
Offeree mails the acceptance, he loses the ability to accept another, possibly better offer instead. Thus, Offeree faces the risk that he will want to
change his mind while the letter is in transit. Under the mailbox rule, he
must take that risk. Under an alternative rule — say, where the acceptance

---

[22] Restatement (Second) of Contracts §63(a) (1981).
[23] See Morrison v. Thoelke, 155 So. 2d 889 (Fla. App. Ct. 2d Dist. 1963); the rule comes
from Adams v. Lindsell, 1 Barn. & Ald. 681 (K.B. 1818).

becomes valid only when Offeror receives it — Offeree does not take that risk. Instead, Offeror takes the risk that Offeree will find a better opportunity and change his mind — in the sense that Offeror cannot insist on a contract until she receives the letter.

Which rule is superior? It is hard to know. In other countries, the mailbox rule is not used. It probably does not matter—there are very few cases where this problem arises because delivery rarely takes very long—as long as the rule is clear. The mailbox rule is no less clear than the alternative; given that it has been the rule for many years, there is no good reason to change it.

§3.8 Offer and Acceptance and Unilateral Contracts

Offerors can seek an acceptance in the form of a promise or an action. The offer "I will pay you $100 if you promise to mow my lawn every week this month" seeks an acceptance in the form of a return promise. The offeree can accept by saying, "I promise to mow your law every week this month" or just by saying "yes" or "okay," but in the latter case the response is interpreted in the same way—as a return promise to mow every week this month. The offer "I will pay you $100 if you mow my lawn right now" seeks acceptance in the form of an action: mowing the lawn. The offer "I will pay you $100 if you mow my lawn today" is ambiguous regarding the proper form of acceptance. A person might accept the offer by mowing the lawn immediately or later that day, or by promising to mow the lawn later today.

If an offer can be accepted only through an action, then it is interpreted as an offer to enter a unilateral contract. A unilateral contract is the exchange of a promise for an action; by contrast, a bilateral contract is the exchange of a promise for another promise.[24] Unilateral contracts often appear as offers of rewards. "If you catch the thief John Doe, then I will pay you $10,000." "If you catch the fish Diamond Jim, then I will pay you $100." "If you return my cat, I'll pay you $100." But they show up in other ways as well. "If you pay me $50, then I promise to deliver you a toaster." "If you pay me $1000, I promise to paint your portrait." The last two offers can be accepted just through payment, rather than through a promise.

A number of cases deal with the problem of the unknowing or unmotivated performer. Suppose that a person catches the thief, or catches the fish, or returns the cat, without knowing about the offered reward, or

---

[24] See Section 2.4.

knowing about the reward but not being motivated by it.[25] Should the person have the right to the reward?

It is hard to see why he should. The purpose of announcing the reward is to influence people's behavior. If some fraction of the population will engage in the desired act even in the absence of the stimulus of the reward, then nothing is gained by allowing these people to claim the reward. Allowing them to claim the reward simply increases the offeror's expected liability without increasing the chance of the desired outcome. If the offeror were free from this extra liability, then he could offer an even higher reward, thus creating a greater incentive for those who would not act in the absence of compensation. Nonetheless, courts tend to grant the award in these cases where there is knowledge even if there is no proof of motivation — perhaps under the belief that figuring out who is motivated and who isn't is more trouble than it's worth.

Another set of cases address offers that are unclear as to whether they seek acceptance in the form of a return promise (creating a bilateral contract) or in the form of an act (creating a unilateral contract). An ambiguous offer creates problems for offerees because if they interpret the offer wrongly, they can end up with terms they do not like. In Allied Steel & Conveyors v. Ford,[26] Ford and Allied had a contract under which Allied supplied and installed machinery in Ford's factory. Partway through Allied's performance, Ford sent Allied a new offer to buy additional machinery. The offer included a statement reading, "This purchase order agreement is not binding until accepted. Acceptance should be executed on acknowledgment copy which should be returned to buyer."[27] The offer also included an indemnity provision that required Allied to pay for any harm arising out of the contract. The order of events was as follows: (1) Allied began installation of the new equipment; (2) an Allied employee was injured; (3) Allied signed the acknowledgment and sent it to Ford. Allied argued that it was not liable under the indemnity provision of the second contract because it had not yet "accepted" the second offer. Ford argued that Allied accepted the offer by beginning installation and therefore the indemnity provision bound Allied. The court agreed with Ford.

The decision might seem puzzling at first sight. The language seems clear that Allied must accept by signing and returning a piece of paper. Until Allied has done that, there can be no contract. But the court believed that Ford supplied the acknowledgment copy just as a convenience and that a reasonable offeree should not interpret that as ruling out acceptance by action. Otherwise, Allied could evade the indemnity clause by waiting to return the acknowledgment copy until it had completed installation.

---

[25] Glover v. Jewish War Veterans of the United States, Post No. 58, 68 A.2d 233 (D.C. Mun. Ct. App. 1949).

[26] 277 F.2d 907 (6th Cir. 1960).

[27] Id. at 909.

Ford had no reason to insist on a return promise rather than an act. The principle that the offeree can accept an ambiguous offer in any reasonable way can be found in section 32 of the Restatement.

Davis v. Jacoby[28] provides another illustration of this idea. This soap opera case contains colorful facts, but stripped down involves a promise from Uncle to Niece and her husband. Uncle, who had suffered some business difficulties and health problems, wrote to the two relatives, saying, "Now if Frank [Niece's husband] could come out here and be with me and look after my affairs, we could easily save the balance I mentioned, provided I dont [sic] get into another panic and do some foolish things. . . . So if you can come, Caro [Niece] will inherit everything. . . ."[29] Frank and Caro, who lived in faraway Canada, wrote back that they would come to California to help out, and began to wind down their affairs. But Uncle killed himself before they arrived; after their arrival, Caro provided care to her aunt, who died soon thereafter. It turned out that Uncle's will left the estate to other relatives.

The issue was whether a contract had been formed. If so, the estate goes to Frank and Caro; if not, the estate goes to the heirs. The answer depends on whether the offer was to enter a unilateral or bilateral contract. If the offer was to enter a unilateral contract, then Frank could accept it only by helping Uncle; but because Uncle died before Frank had a chance to do so, the offer was revoked prior to acceptance (death of the offeror terminates an offer). By contrast, if the offer was to enter a bilateral contract, then Frank could accept by mail, in which case Uncle's death would be legally irrelevant. Like most people, Uncle did not write in legalese. He certainly could have chosen to be clear about which type of offer he was making, but he did not.

The court held that Uncle had implicitly made an offer to enter a bilateral contract, and therefore Frank and Caro win. The court gave three reasons. First, it believed that courts should presumptively treat offers as offers to enter bilateral rather than unilateral contracts. It did not provide a justification for such a presumption, and sometimes one hears that such a presumption protects the offeree. This is not necessarily true, but in any event today the rule is that, when the offer is ambiguous, the offeree gets to choose how to accept it, as noted above.

Second, the court held that Uncle wanted a return promise because he sought assurance that things would turn out all right. That assurance could be given only by a return promise delivered by mail or telegraph. Once Frank and Caro make a return promise, they are bound, and Uncle has nothing to worry about. By contrast, if Uncle had made an offer to enter a unilateral contract, Frank and Caro would have had the right to change

---

[28] 34 P.2d 1026 (Cal. 1934).
[29] Id. at 1027-1028.

their decision up until they arrived in California and actually completed the task of taking care of Uncle and his wife.

Third, the court observed that Uncle must have known that he might die before his wife (even if he didn't plan to commit suicide), while he asked Frank and Caro to commit themselves to giving care to her until her death. Such a commitment cannot be made through a unilateral contract; it can be made only in a bilateral contract. As noted above, if the contract were deemed unilateral, then Uncle's death would terminate it, thus releasing Frank and Caro from their obligation to care for Uncle's wife (as well as depriving them of their right to payment except for what they could obtain through restitution).

The argument on the other side is that Uncle could best motivate Frank and Caro by providing that their payment would be due only upon performance. This would make Frank and Caro vulnerable to a change of mind by Uncle, and therefore cause them to work harder. The court rejected this argument because their relationship was not arms' length and Uncle didn't seem so hard-nosed, at least in his dealings with his niece and her husband.

It is hard to generalize about cases like these, other than to note that one needs to be sensitive to context. Rather than follow hard-and-fast rules, courts interpret the language and actions of the parties, and this requires sensitivity to the setting in which their actions take place.

§3.9   Offers and Reliance: Unilateral Contracts

In the famous (and absurd) Brooklyn Bridge example, the offeror offers $100 to an offeree if he crosses the Brooklyn Bridge. The Brooklyn Bridge is more than a mile long. When the unfortunate offeree has trudged halfway across, the offeror shouts, "I've changed my mind and I revoke the offer." Has the offeree wasted time and effort; does he have a remedy?

Traditional doctrine said the offeree has no remedy. An offer is revocable; that is what an offer means. It is a kind of conditional promise — "I will pay you if you accept" — but without consideration.[30] Walking halfway across the bridge is a legal detriment but it does not count as consideration because the offer stipulated that performance, and hence acceptance, would require traversal of the entire bridge. The traditional idea is that the offeror is master of the offer, as we saw above. If the offer says that acceptance requires that the offeree cross the entire bridge, then that is what acceptance requires. If the offeree does not like the offer, he can choose not to accept it.

---

[30] See Section 5.1, on the consideration doctrine.

This doctrine was deemed too harsh for the tender conscience of twentieth-century contract scholarship. The image of a forlorn figure standing at the midpoint of that great expanse of bridge was too much to bear. The Restatement solves the problem in section 45 as follows:

> (1) Where an offer invites an offeree to accept by rending a performance and does not invite a promissory acceptance, an option contract is created when the offeree tenders or begin the invited performance or tenders a beginning of it.
> (2) The offeror's duty of performance under any option contract so created is conditional on completion or tender of the invited performance in accordance with the terms of the offer.

An option is an important concept to which we will return.[31] A person with an option has a right, but not a duty, to do something. Someone else — the person against whom the option is held — has the duty to do that something if the option holder demands that it be done. Here, once the offeree steps onto the bridge, an option is given to the offeree, meaning that the offeree can decide either to cross the bridge (in which case the offeror must pay him) or to not cross the bridge (in which case the offeror has no duty to pay him). That is to say, the offeree exercises his option by crossing the bridge, but retains the option not to cross the bridge until he actually crosses it.

The upshot is that the offeree's reliance is protected. If he walks half-way across the bridge, he need not worry that the offeror will change her mind and revoke the offer; she has lost the power to do that. At the same time, the offeree *can* change his mind. If he prefers, he can turn around and return, or jump off the bridge, or make it his home — and he incurs no penalty, though he cannot demand compensation, either.

It is important to see that the Restatement did not solve the problem of reliance so much as shift the cost of reliance from the offeree to the offeror. Once the offeror makes the offer, she loses the ability to revoke it if she decides she would prefer to use her money in some other way. This means that if the offeror finds a better use for her money while the offeree is halfway across the bridge, the offeror cannot change her mind and pursue this other project.

In both settings, the parties face a risk that the performance will turn out to be worth less to the offeror than she had thought, or to be more costly to the offeree than he had thought. In the first case, the offeror wants to revoke; in the second case, the offeree wants to discontinue performance, leaving the offeror in the lurch. The original rule put the risk on the offeree; the Restatement puts the risk on the offeror. It is not clear why the Restatement writers thought this risk shift was an improvement.

---

[31] See Section 3.11.

Note that Restatement 45 does not protect all forms of reliance. Suppose that the offeror announces the offer, and the potential bridge crosser decides to buy a pair of comfortable shoes before stepping onto the bridge. After he has done so but the moment before he steps on the bridge, the offeror revokes the offer. Restatement 45 does not give the offeree a remedy because performance — the actual crossing of the bridge — has not yet begun. You might say that the offeree bore the risk and should not have purchased the shoes on the strength of a mere offer — but that was the argument behind the rule that the Restatement replaced, that the offeree should not have begun crossing the bridge if he did not want to take the risk that the offeror would change her mind.

§3.10   Offers and Reliance: Bilateral Contracts

The case of James Baird v. Gimbel Company[32] sets the stage. As always, one should abstract from the facts in order to understand the analytic structure of the doctrine. Contractor wants to bid for a project. To submit a bid, Contractor needs a pretty good idea of the project's costs — that is, the sum of the costs of the inputs, including labor and materials. Otherwise, Contractor doesn't know how much to bid. So Contractor announces that it is looking for suppliers and other subcontractors, or these people independently learn about the project and send (sub-)bids to all potential contractors. In any event, Contractor receives a bid from Supplier stating, "We offer to supply materials (or perform a part of the job) for the price of X." Contractor receives several such bids for a particular component of the job, and chooses the lowest bid, or perhaps a relatively low bid submitted by a reputable firm. Contractor turns around and calculates its bid on the project using this bid as well as the low bids it received for the other parts of the project. Contractor wins the project using Supplier's bid. The next day, Supplier says, "Sorry, we made a mistake" and withdraws its bid. Contractor must find another supplier, and if the new price is higher Contractor may lose money on the project. If Contractor tries to pull out of the project, it loses an opportunity to make a profit and may forfeit a bond.

The sequence of events is as follows:

1. Supplier offers bid.
2. Contractor uses bid to calculate its own bid.
3. Contractor submits bid and wins.
4. Supplier withdraws bid before Contractor can accept.

---

[32] 64 F.2d 344 (2d Cir. 1933).

Under the old doctrine, Contractor has no remedy against Supplier. Supplier's bid is most plausibly interpreted as an offer to enter a bilateral contract — under which Supplier supplies the materials in return for money. Contractor can accept the offer only by saying, "I accept." Contractor never did that. It did not want to say, "I accept" before bidding on the project, because if Contractor's bid was not accepted, Contractor would not want to be bound to pay Supplier for materials it would not need. So Contractor must wait and see whether it wins the bid before accepting the offer. However, this means that Supplier can change its mind after Contractor has made its bid — just as long as Supplier says, "I revoke" before Contractor says, "I accept." Supplier can revoke because it made a mistake, but it can also revoke simply because it finds a better deal somewhere else. One is not bound before an offer is accepted.

Note that Contractor could not do any better by arguing that Supplier made an offer to enter a unilateral contract. The offer stipulated that Contractor's performance was payment of the money. So if the offer was for a unilateral contract, Contractor could not accept it without paying money to Supplier. If the offer had indicated that Contractor could accept it by using it in a bid that was awarded, Contractor would be fully protected. But suppliers and other subcontractors do not make such offers — no doubt because they value the flexibility of a revocable offer.

The Restatement changes the rule so as to extend protection to the offeree. Restatement 87(2) provides:

> An offer which the offeror should reasonably expect to induce action or forbearance of a substantial character on the part of the offeree before acceptance and which does induce such action or forbearance is binding as an option contract to the extent necessary to avoid injustice.

Now Supplier cannot revoke the offer (it is "binding") once Contractor relies on it (by submitting a bid) as long as Supplier should reasonably have expected the reliance, as surely it should have. The "extent necessary to avoid injustice" part is thrown in so that judges can rely on their sense of justice if they want, which in fact they would do in any event.

The rule shifts the risk from the offeree to the offeror. The offeree does not have to worry about the offeror changing her mind, but the rule solves this problem by creating another: now the offeror must worry about being bound to an offer that she may come to regret.

The rule was invented by Justice Traynor in Drennan v. Star Paving Co.[33] and subsequently codified in the Restatement. Traynor justified the rule on the basis of promissory estoppel.[34] Offers provoke reliance, and people who rely on promises to their detriment should be protected with a legal

---

[33] 333 P.2d 757 (Cal. 1958).
[34] See Section 5.3.

remedy. A contractor who calculates a bid on the basis of proposals from subcontractors and suppliers, wins the bid, and then discovers that his costs are higher because subcontractors and suppliers have revoked their offers — well, the plight of such a person tugs at the heartstrings, doesn't it? Maybe, but Traynor's reasoning is circular. If offers are revocable, then they should not provoke reliance. The offeree knows that the offeror can revoke the offer, so the offeree should protect himself — for example, factoring in a large margin above the sum of the proposals he receives. Traynor argued that when a person makes an offer, he makes an implicit promise to hold the offer for a reasonable time — and it is on this promise that the offeree may rely. But a person who makes an offer does not necessarily promise to keep it open; she may want the right to revoke it at any time. There are no grounds — at least, none identified by Traynor — for holding that such a person always implicitly promises to keep the offer open, or should be treated as having done so.

So what should the rule be? It is hard to answer that question without knowing more about how people conduct business, but at least the question can be posed precisely.[35] If offers are irrevocable (after reliance), then offerees can rely more (which saves costs) but the offeror cannot change her mind (which adds costs). If offers are revocable, the opposite is true. We want to minimize the sum of these costs. We just don't know which type of costs is higher.

Note the parallel between section 87(2) and section 45. Section 45 addresses the case where a person offers to enter a *unilateral* contract, the offeree embarks on performance, and the offeror revokes before the offeree has completed performance. Under the old rule, the offeree has no remedy and must swallow the cost of partial performance. Under section 45, the offeror may not revoke the offer once the offeree begins. Section 87(2) addresses the case where a person offers to enter a *bilateral* contract, the offeree relies on the offer (for example, by using it to calculate a bid), and the offeror revokes before the offeree has a chance to accept by making a return promise. Under the old rule, the offeree has no remedy; under section 87(2), the offeror may not revoke once the offeree relies. Both rules solve old problems and create new problems. The new problem is that if the offeree dawdles rather than accepts or rejects, the offeror is stuck until the offeree finally acts. The offeree can also shop

---

[35] On precontractual liability, as it is called, see, e.g., Alan Schwartz & Robert E. Scott, Precontractual Liability and Preliminary Agreements, 120 Harv. L. Rev. 661 (2007); Richard Craswell, Offer, Acceptance, and Efficient Reliance, 48 Stan. L. Rev. 481 (1996); Avery Katz, When Should an Offer Stick?: The Economics of Promissory Estoppel in Preliminary Negotiations, 105 Yale L.J. 1249 (1996); Lucian Arye Bebchuk & Omri Ben-Shahar, Pre-Contractual Reliance, 30 J. Legal Stud. 423 (2001).

around for better bids,[36] which he can then use as leverage to force the offeror to lower her price. The law addresses this problem by putting a limit on how long the offeree can take to reply: he must reply within a "reasonable" time, which is whatever a court thinks appropriate under the circumstances.

§3.11 Firm Offers and Option Contracts

In the previous sections, we saw how courts and the U.C.C. drafters developed ways to protect the reliance (or investment) of offerees on offers. It is striking that for some time before these developments offerees could not rely on offers — in the sense of having legal protection if offerors tried to revoke them — even when offerors intended to keep the offer open, to make a "firm offer," to use the term of art.

Imagine that a person wants to sell her house. The asking price is $400,000. The offeror cannot attract interest at first, but finally a prospective buyer shows up and likes the look of the house. However, Buyer tells Seller that he needs time to think about such a substantial purchase. Buyer wants to get to know the neighborhood better, do some more research, and perhaps talk to some neighbors. To do this, Buyer needs time — maybe just a week. But Buyer does not want to take this trouble unless he can be sure that the offer will remain open. So Seller says that she will keep the offer open for a week.

A week later, Buyer has finished his research and comes back to accept the offer. However, Seller informs him that in the meantime she sold the house. Someone came along and offered $410,000, and Seller couldn't resist. The sale was a sure thing (whereas it was possible that Buyer would decide not to buy the house), and the new buyer offered an additional $10,000. Does Buyer have a remedy?

Under old doctrine, the answer was no. A firm offer has two elements: (1) an offer (to sell the house for $400,000) and (2) a promise to keep the offer open (for a week, in this case). The promise (2) was not supported by consideration and so was unenforceable. As we will see in Section 5.1, a promise that is not made in return for something else ("consideration") is not enforceable in most cases. If you delete element (2), you are left with a naked offer, which, as we have learned, is revocable. So Seller had the right to revoke the offer even though she had promised not to.

The analysis has a kind of logic to it but makes no sense from the standpoint of policy. Why prevent Seller from making a firm offer? As we saw, a firm offer served both parties' interests. Its effect is to transfer the risk

---

[36] It is not clear whether this practice is socially undesirable; it seems unfair to the supplier but may lead to lower costs.

that a third party will come along, from the buyer (who would lose the purchase if the offer is revocable) to the seller (who cannot take advantage of the materialization of the third party if the offer is irrevocable). There are many business situations where such a transfer of risk makes sense.

Indeed, firm offers are also known as options. Options are familiar from the financial world. You can buy stock in Microsoft, or you can buy an option to purchase shares of Microsoft at a certain price within a certain time. (These are known as calls; you can also buy options to sell assets, which are called puts.) When you buy an option to purchase Microsoft stock, you pay the seller to make an offer to you (Microsoft stock at price of X) and to promise to hold that offer open for a certain period of time. However, as we saw before, it can also make sense to give options away, that is, agree to hold open an offer in return for nothing at all.

The logic of the consideration doctrine had to yield to business realities — as logic always does. Courts carved out exceptions to the consideration doctrine for firm offers or options. The Restatement provides in section 87:

> (1) An offer is binding as an option contract if it
>
> (a) Is in writing and signed by the offeror, recites a purported consideration for the making of the offer, and proposes an exchange on fair terms within a reasonable time; or
> (b) Is made irrevocable by statute.

The U.C.C. imposes even more limited requirements in section 2-205:

> An offer by a merchant to buy or sell goods in a signed writing which by its terms gives assurance that it will be held open is not revocable, for lack of consideration, during the time stated or if no time is stated for a reasonable time, but in no event may such a period of irrevocability exceed three months; but any such term of assurance on a form supplied by the offeree must be separately signed by the offeror.

Both provisions make options enforceable as long as certain formalities are satisfied. "Purported" consideration in the Restatement means that no consideration has to pass, and it is doubtful that parties even have to "purport" to provide consideration. All that is really necessary is that the offer be put in writing.

The procedural formalities and the substantive limitations no doubt reflect concerns about abuse. As we will see, one of the functions of the consideration doctrine is to prevent fraudsters from inventing gratuitous promises out of whole cloth and persuading a jury of their existence. Perhaps it is easy for Jones to go before jurors and persuade them that Smith promised to give Jones $1 million, when Smith had done no such thing.

The consideration doctrine reduces the incentive to commit fraud on the court in this way. If gratuitous promises are unenforceable, then Jones can at best persuade the jury that Smith promised him $1 million in return for some object or service. So if Smith loses $1 million, he will at least get that object or service in return, which costs Jones. In addition, juries are not likely to believe Jones if the object or service is worth a great deal less than $1 million. But now it turns out that Jones can just tell the jury that Smith gave him the option to buy Microsoft at some price — and hey!, the price of Microsoft has since appreciated. Jones gets something for nothing. The Restatement and the U.C.C. try to head off this type of fraud by requiring a writing, and they try to minimize the adverse effects of this type of fraud by putting a time limit on the option.

§3.12 Implied Contracts

People don't always say, "I offer . . . " and "I accept . . . " or use near synonyms, even when they mean to offer and accept. Courts may infer that contracts exist from behavior or words that do not include contractual language. That is why §2-203 of the U.C.C. can refer to "conduct by both parties which recognizers the existence of a contract."[37] But what does such conduct consist of?

One scenario involves a commercial seller and commercial buyer with a long relationship. Seller has been making monthly deliveries to Buyer, and Buyer has sent back checks. No one says anything in particular about offering or accepting or contracting. One day Buyer refuses to send a check, and Seller sues for breach of contract. A court may well find that a contract exists. In Hobbs v. Massasoit Whip Co.,[38] Buyer not only retained the goods for quite some time but also disposed of them. The court held that Seller had a cause of action for breach of contract.

This case could be interpreted differently. An offeror cannot normally stipulate that silence is acceptance; that would make it easy for offerors to trick people into entering contracts or otherwise forcing them to incur the burden of response. But if a course of dealing builds up in which both parties do accept silence as acceptance, then the normal rule is relaxed.[39] But this is just to say that an implied contract can be formed, that is, a contract where it is clear that both parties consented to perform albeit without saying anything. If a course of dealing does not exist, some kind of more general custom or pattern of commercial activity must. People

---

[37] See also §2-204(1).
[38] 33 N.E. 495 (Mass. 1893).
[39] See Restatement (Second) of Contracts §69(1) (1981); for a discussion of this rule, see Section 3.4.

sometimes impose themselves on others and argue that the others "implicitly" agreed to a deal. Courts are skeptical of these arguments.[40]

Implied contracts, however, do not always involve consent. In Collins v. Lewis,[41] a deputy sheriff took possession of cows from someone who did not own them and tried to return them to the owner. The owner did not take them and after some time passed, arranged for the cows to be sold. In the meantime, the deputy sheriff paid for their care. The deputy sheriff sued for damages and won. Now, it is clear that the owner never consented to pay the deputy sheriff for the care of the cows, so there is not a real contract. The implication of the contract in this case occurred by operation of law, that is, as a matter of policy: the court believed that the owner should pay the sheriff because the sheriff conferred a benefit to the owner, and did so pursuant to his duty rather than as a gift. The underlying theory was that of restitution, not of contract. That could have been the theory in *Hobbs* as well: the seller conferred a benefit on the buyer with the expectation of being paid (though the buyer later destroyed the goods).[42]

Courts do not distinguish very carefully between these two cases: the "real" implied contract, where both parties consented to mutual obligations but without using clear language to that effect, and the phony implied contract, where the party being sued consented to nothing but nonetheless is required to pay under a theory of restitution. Numerous confusing synonyms muddy the waters. An "implied-in-fact" contract usually is one where the parties consent; an "implied-in-law" contract usually is one where consent is lacking. "Implied contract" and "quasi-contract" are used in both ways, sometimes to refer to cases of consent, sometimes to refer to cases where consent is lacking.[43]

§3.13 Summary

Mutual assent seems like a simple idea but the concept masks numerous complications. The central idea is that people know what their interests are and will bind themselves to contracts only when they believe those contracts advance their interests. Welfare-maximizing courts should respect those interests and hence enforce contracts when they reflect mutual assent.

---

[40] See, e.g., Martin v. Little, Brown & Co., 450 A.2d 984 (Pa. Super. Ct. 1993).

[41] Collins v. Lewis, 283 S.W.2d 258 (Tex. Ct. Civ. App. 1955).

[42] For another example, see Seaview Ass'n of Fire Island, N.Y., Inc. v. Williams, 510 N.E.2d 793 (N.Y. 1987).

[43] We discuss restitution in Section 9.2.

However, when people assent to a contract, they rarely if ever understand the full consequences of entering the contract. The future is unpredictable: can one really consent to consequences that one does not foresee? Contracts themselves are often highly complicated and people rarely take the trouble of understanding them. Even sophisticated businesses do not: they exchange forms without thinking about which one will prevail when the forms are inconsistent. Thus, consent is a matter of degree. A contracting party can know more or less about the consequences of a contract; the degree of consent tracks the extent of knowledge.

One approach to this problem is simply to insist that people clearly announce their intention to enter a contract and refuse to find contracts when those clear signals are absent. The mirror image rule exemplifies this approach. But a mirror image in contract is not a necessary or sufficient condition of consent. Not necessary, because people do agree to enter legally enforceable deals without bothering to iron out every detail. Not sufficient, because the person who says, "I accept" does not necessarily understand the offer, in which case he does not fully consent to the terms.

Courts respond to these problems in several ways — some of which we will see in the next two chapters, but which we will anticipate here. First, they give parties incentives to inform themselves — for example, by constructing a contract so as to reflect the understanding of the better-informed party. The duty to read penalizes the party that failed to inform itself about the content of a writing. However, courts do not press these incentives very hard. It is not always rational to read a contract or in other ways fully inform oneself of its content: this takes time and sometimes money (if one hires a lawyer), and the gains from contracting are not always high enough to justify this cost.

Second, courts penalize a party that deliberately misleads the other party or (more controversially) fails to take steps to inform the other party of terms or consequences that are not in that party's interests. Here again we see limits on what courts are willing to do. Strong duties to disclose may discourage parties from gathering information in the first place, and can penalize parties for failing to predict what other parties care about.

Third, courts will sometimes refuse to enforce contracts because of a lack of information or a misunderstanding on both sides. Because the parties did not understand what they were getting into, there is no reason to believe that the contract makes anyone better off. But courts also understand that people rarely have the time to fully inform themselves, and are often willing to gamble that the contract serves their interest.

Fourth, courts do not insist on an acceptance that mirrors the offer, and look for any adequate sign that the parties intended to enter, or would have benefited from, a legally enforceable relationship. They find contracts in long-term relationships even though terms are left out. They find implied contracts when agreement can be inferred from behavior. They find contracts under U.C.C. §2-207 as long as the major terms in the forms agree. However, the modern inclination to find contractual relationships even in highly indefinite agreements and relationships has led to some confusion about how the "implicit" terms should be determined. The doctrine seems unstable; formalism has not been fully vanquished.

Casebooks often split up the "policing the bargain" doctrines (like duress and unconscionability) and the "contract formation" doctrines (such as the mirror image rule). The division seems natural because contract formation doctrines require parties to comply with formalities, while policing doctrines attempt to determine whether or not the contract is socially desirable — free from force and fraud. But it is important to recognize the overlapping subject matter of these doctrines. Both sets of doctrines attempt to determine that the parties "really" consented to the contract, in the sense of giving (voluntary) assent to terms that they understood. Formalities such as the mirror image rule attempt to screen out agreements that the parties do not want legally enforced or semi-agreements that are not really agreements, in the sense of not being fully concluded or adequately spelled out. Formalities work best when both parties are sophisticated and informed, but they can trip up less sophisticated parties and parties in a hurry, and can be exploited by unscrupulous parties. When the formalities are complied with, the policing-the-bargain doctrines can then be invoked by the party seeking to persuade a court that even though she complied with the formalities, she did not intend to be legally bound to the terms now being pressed against her.

Chapter 4

Policing the Bargain

§4.1   Misunderstanding

There are two issues that often arise in the same case: assent and interpretation. Suppose that Buyer and Seller agree on the sale of cotton to be delivered by the ship *Peerless*. It turns out that there are two (or more) ships named *Peerless*; Buyer insists that he meant one ship (the ship that left in October, or the "October *Peerless*"), and Seller says that he meant either of the two ships (the other of which left in December, or the "December *Peerless*"). The market price of cotton is lower than the contract price when the October *Peerless* arrives (favoring Buyer), and higher than the contract price when the December *Peerless* arrives (favoring Seller).[1]

Buyer wants to avoid a decision that there was a valid contract and that under the contract the identity of the ship did not matter. If the court comes to this decision, then Buyer will have to pay expectation damages to Seller equal to the difference between the contract price and the market price upon arrival of the December *Peerless*. First, he might argue that there was a valid contract, but the proper interpretation of the contract was that the October *Peerless* was the correct ship. On this theory, Seller breached

---

[1] Or so I infer; these facts are omitted from the case.

the contract by refusing to deliver upon the arrival of the October *Peerless*, and owes Buyer expectation damages equal to the difference between the contract price and the market price at that time. Second, he might argue that there was no valid contract in the first place; thus, he has no obligation to pay damages to Seller, though of course he cannot claim damages from Seller either.

We will discuss the interpretation issue elsewhere; for now, observe only that Buyer's argument is not necessarily as much of a loser as it sounds. It sounds like a loser because the contract does not specify the October *Peerless*. But if a court decides that the contract is ambiguous and allows in parol evidence,[2] and the parol evidence shows that both Buyer and Seller had the October *Peerless* in mind, then Buyer could win on the interpretation issue. Alternatively, it may turn out that trade usage is concrete: when parties talk in this way, they always mean the next ship to arrive — or something like that.

Seller wants to argue, and did argue in Raffles v. Wichelhaus,[3] that the contract entitled him to deliver from either of the two *Peerless* vessels in question. Notice that on this view the contract is not ambiguous: it says exactly what it means, that any *Peerless* is okay. The court disagreed and held that no contract existed because there was no "consensus ad idem," now usually translated as no "meeting of the minds." This is a good outcome for Buyer; it means that he does not have to buy the cotton at a price higher than the current market price, and he can buy the cotton at the lower market price if he still wants it.

It is tempting to agree with the court that there cannot be a contract because the parties never agreed on which ship would carry the cotton. However, parties rarely agree on all elements of the contract: they just do not have enough time to remove every source of ambiguity (which is surely impossible). Apparently clear terms contain latent ambiguities that become visible when unanticipated events come to fruition. The better reading of *Raffles* is that the contract provides the court with no basis for preferring one interpretation (Buyer's or Seller's) to the other. Non-enforcement, then, gives future parties an incentive to anticipate latent ambiguities and write clearer contracts. That explains why the Restatement decrees non-enforcement when neither party knows that the other party attaches a different meaning to a term, or both parties know but do nothing about it. When one party knows the other party's meaning, or should know, the Restatement directs courts to interpret ambiguous terms consistently with the second (ignorant) party's meaning.[4] This ensures that

---

[2] For more on the parol evidence rule, see Section 6.8.

[3] 1864 WL 6161 (K.B. 1864).

[4] See Restatement (Second) of Contracts §20(2) (1981):

   The manifestations of the parties are operative in accordance with the meaning attached to them by one of the parties if

parties who suspect a misunderstanding on the other side's part will clear it up before entering the contract.

§4.2 Misrepresentation, Fraud, and the Duty to Disclose

Mistake cases are usefully divided into cases involving a mistake by Buyer, cases involving a mistake by Seller, and cases of mutual mistake. Let us start with the first category. In the typical fact pattern Seller has some vital piece of information — a "fact" — that Buyer does not have. The information indicates that the product is not as valuable as Buyer thinks it is. This fact might be that Seller's house is infested with termites or located in a floodplain, that Seller's car has a history of engine problems, or that Seller's legal claim is unsupported by strong evidence.

The law prohibits Seller from deliberately lying about the fact. If Seller says that her house is not infested with termites, and it is, Buyer will have a fraud claim against Seller. Buyer must also show that he relied on the misrepresentation, and in some cases that can be hard to do. In the termite case, however, the court would infer that Buyer would not have bought the house, or would have insisted on a lower price, if he had been informed of the termites. Buyer has a fraud (or deceit) claim. Fraud is a tort claim, but it is used here to avoid a contract. In fact, the contract is "voidable" (rather than necessarily void): Buyer has the option to affirm or disaffirm the contract.

The logic behind the fraud claim is straightforward. Contracts should make both parties better off. Buyer has less information about a product than Seller does, and the main source of information for Buyer about the product will often be Seller. If Seller can tell lies without fearing a penalty, then Buyer has no reason to believe Seller, in which case Seller has no credible method for disclosing (favorable) information about a product that will induce Buyer to purchase it. Thus, if sellers can commit fraud, they will have trouble selling things. Meanwhile, if Buyer does believe Seller, and Seller tells a lie, then Buyer will usually end up with something that he values less than the money he paid.

The same logic might be used to argue that Seller should be liable if she fails to disclose the fact. Seller offers to sell her house and does not tell Buyer about the termites. Seller doesn't lie; she just doesn't disclose relevant information. To be sure, if Buyer asks specifically about termites,

---

(a) that party does not know of any different meaning attached by the other, and the other knows the meaning attached by the first party; or

(b) that party has no reason to know of any different meaning attached by the other, and the other has reason to know the meaning attached by the first party.

the game is up for Seller. Either Seller must tell the truth or say nothing at all, in which case Buyer will infer that Seller has something to hide and be unlikely to consummate the deal. But if Buyer does not think to ask Seller about termites or other unappealing features of the house, then Seller can avoid informing Buyer of those features, and Buyer will end up with a house that he does not want. To prevent this from happening, there should be a duty to disclose.

The argument is appealing, but faces some limits. First, frequently Seller will not know what "fact" is relevant to Buyer. Seller's old house has many things wrong with it: a clogged chimney, some termite infestation, lead paint, noisy traffic in the morning, unfriendly neighbors, occasional air pollution drifting through when the wind blows from the south, the possibility (but only that) that construction will soon take place across the street, and so on. Buyer might not care about some or all of these things. Buyer might be old and deaf and indifferent to these problems; he could be a developer who plans to tear the house down anyway. Thus, if the transaction can be nullified on the basis of any negative feature of the house, Buyer could easily escape his obligation for opportunistic reasons.

Second, Buyer might find it easier to do a thorough inspection, or even just to ask Seller about particular things that concern him, than for Seller to anticipate everything that Buyer wants to know about. Indeed, standard practice is for Buyer to hire an inspector, who may discover things that Seller did not know. No duty to disclose, or a limited duty to disclose, encourages buyers to continue this sensible practice.[5]

Third, there may be some concern that Seller might not make proper inspections of her own product if she expects to be held liable if she discovers something and neglects to tell Buyer about it. Seller might not have a termite inspection done, for example. She reasons that if she has it done and termites are discovered, she will have to inform Buyer. But if she fails to have it done, she might find a buyer who does not insist on a termite inspection. To prevent this type of opportunism, the duty to disclose would need to be extended to cover facts that Seller could reasonably have discovered, not just facts that Seller knew. Such a rule might not be workable.

For these reasons, the rule is (roughly) that sellers must disclose facts that they know or should reasonably know about the thing they are selling that buyers cannot discover by reasonable inspection. The opposite is not true, however. Buyers do not usually have to disclose facts about the

---

[5] There is a separate problem: Seller discloses in forms that buyers do not read. See Omri Ben-Shahar & Carl E. Schneider, The Failure of Mandated Disclosure, 159 U. Pa. L. Rev. 647 (2011).

thing they are buying — facts they happen to know and the sellers do not know.[6]

The classic example involves a geologist who discovers that some valuable minerals exist below the surface of property owned by someone else. The geologist incurred great expense to discover the minerals — for example, he needed to rent expensive detection equipment. The owner does not know about these minerals. The geologist purchases the property without disclosing that those minerals exist. Such a contract is enforceable even if the seller could not have discovered the minerals through reasonable inspection.

Why? The simplest answer is that if the geologist must disclose the hidden information, then he cannot profit off it. If he discloses it, Seller will raise the price, depriving the geologist of the return on his investment in searching for minerals in other people's property. That means that no one will discover the minerals, and they will remain underground, unused, which is a social loss.

The explanation is appealing but it has some problems. First, note that the owner, if she is savvy, can always ask the geologist why he wants to purchase the land. If the geologist lies and tells her that he just wants a vacation home, then the seller has a fraud claim if she ever discovers the truth. If the geologist doesn't answer the question, then the seller is given a clue that something is not right — that the potential buyer knows something about her property. The seller can invest in finding out, again depriving the buyer of the return on his investment in detection. One might argue that buyers in these situations should be permitted to lie — that is where the logic of our explanation leads — but courts do not do that.

Second, there is subtler problem having to do with the economics of information. Consider Laidlaw v. Organ,[7] a famous old case involving the sale of tobacco. The buyer had learned that the War of 1812 had ended and that a blockade on New Orleans would be lifted. This meant that foreign demand for tobacco would shoot upward, leading to a higher price. The buyer approached a seller who had not yet learned of this event, and offered to purchase tobacco at the existing low price. Shortly after the sale, the seller learned that the blockade had been lifted and that he had therefore let the tobacco go at a price much too low. He managed to get the tobacco back from the buyer, whereupon the buyer sued to enforce the contract. The seller defended by alleging fraud.

---

[6] See Restatement (Second) of Contracts §161 cmt. d (1981) ("If the other is indolent, inexperienced or ignorant, or if his judgment is bad or he lacks access to adequate information, his adversary is not generally expected to compensate for these deficiencies. A buyer of property, for example, is not ordinarily expected to disclose circumstances that make the property more valuable than the seller supposes.").

[7] 15 U.S. 178 (1817).

The buyer never made a misrepresentation, so the fraud claim failed. However, it is not clear that this type of hoarding of information is socially valuable. Information has social value only to the extent that it enables people to allocate resources more efficiently. The end of a blockade is useful information, as it enables farmers to adjust their planting — more land for tobacco, for example, and less land for other crops. So it is good to get this information out quickly, and allowing a buyer to profit on his private information is a way to do this. The prospect of profits gives people an incentive to acquire intelligence and act on it, which — in this case — causes the price of tobacco to adjust upward slightly earlier than it would have otherwise, which in turn causes farmers to plant more tobacco. But a day or two does not make much difference in farming. The effect of the buyer's action was to cause tobacco prices to increase a few days before when they would have otherwise. The benefit for farmers was close to zero. But the profits to the buyer were very high. This mismatch between the social value of information and the private benefits can cause people to invest excessively in information acquisition. Think of all the people hovering around the port of New Orleans to see the outcome of the battle, and then racing away to find buyers before the newspapers could reach them. These people could be doing something socially productive.

These and related complexities make it difficult to know whether the rules governing fraud and disclosure are economically efficient.

§4.3 Constructive Fraud

Constructive fraud arises when two parties have a confidential or fiduciary relationship, and the party in the superior position enters into a transaction with the other party that does not serve that other party's interest. A confidential relationship is one in which one party "confides" in the other, that is, depends on the other for advice. Confidential relationships arise naturally, not through a formal transaction; if a friend or relative relies on you for financial advice, which you freely give, creating a relationship of dependence, then a confidential relationship exists, and you have certain duties toward your friend. Fiduciary relationships arise between lawyers and clients, investment managers and clients, trustees and beneficiaries, and so on.

Once a confidential or fiduciary relationship is formed, the party in the superior position can no longer enter arm's-length relationships with the party in the inferior position. The party in the superior position must act with care and ensure that that the transaction is in the other party's interest.

Consider the case of Jackson v. Seymour.[8] Widow owns a tract of land and has depended on her brother for advice on how to manage it. One day she decides to sell a part of the land to Brother for $275. It turns out that this piece of land has valuable timber on it, worth $3200 to $5000. Brother did not know about the timber. Widow sues for rescission and prevails.[9]

The first thing to understand is that the contract would have been enforced if the parties had not had a confidential relationship. No fraud was committed. Brother did not have a duty to disclose information he did not have; even if he knew about the timber, it is doubtful that he would have been required to disclose this information (see the geologist example). No other problems mar the bargaining process.

Because of the confidential relationship, Brother has a duty to take care that the transaction serves Widow's interest — a duty that he could have discharged by doing a thorough survey of the land before buying it. He would also have had the duty to disclose the existence of the timber if he had already known about it.

No fraud took place because there was no misrepresentation. That is why the court had to draw on the doctrine of constructive fraud — "constructive" meaning not real. Why is such a duty created? One might fear that people in Brother's position would be reluctant to form confidential relationships in the first place — to Widow's detriment — if they know that they will have extra legal duties.

But, by the same token, one might fear that in the absence of this doctrine, ill-motivated people will encourage vulnerable people to rely on them. Once vulnerable people put their trust in others, they can be easily taken advantage of. The con artist knows the trick. Start by doing a favor for someone, obtain that person's trust, then move in for the kill. The doctrine of constructive fraud recognizes that the essence of fraud — the use of deception to transfer wealth from one person to another — can exist in situations where explicit misrepresentations are avoided.

§4.4 Mutual Mistake

Discussion of the mutual mistake doctrine unavoidably begins with Sherwood v. Walker.[10] Buyer purchases a cow named Rose 2d of Aberlone from Seller. Seller believed that Rose was infertile and sold her at a

---

[8] 71 S.E.2d 181 (Va. 1952).

[9] See Restatement (Second) of Contracts §161(d) (1981) ("A person's non-disclosure of a fact known to him is equivalent to an assertion that the fact does not exist in the following cases only . . . where the other person is entitled to know the fact because of a relation of trust and confidence between them.").

[10] 33 N.W. 919 (Mich. 1887).

price reflecting her value as beef. A fertile cow is more valuable than a sterile cow because a fertile cow can produce more cows. Buyer may or may not have believed that Rose was sterile; the facts are unclear. But the majority opinion is premised on the factual assumption that both Buyer and Seller believed that Rose was sterile; in fact, she was fertile and indeed "with calf" (that is, pregnant) at the time of sale. Seller discovered this fact before Buyer had a chance to pick up the cow, and refused to permit Buyer to do so.

Buyer and Seller both wrongly believed that Rose was infertile. What of it? People rarely understand fully the products that they buy and sell. The seller and buyer of a used car might both believe that the car is more fuel-efficient than it really is. The seller and buyer of a washing machine might believe that it makes less noise than it really does. The seller and buyer of a work by an old master might mistakenly believe that it is worth less than its market value. The seller and buyer of a book might believe that it is better written than it is. Because the buyer and seller rarely have full information about the product they exchange, then surely there is always a mutual mistake of some sort, about some aspect of the product.

We might think that both parties should bear the risk of adverse facts: for the buyer, that the product is worth less than the buyer thinks; for the seller, that the product is worth more. Each party can take precautions against the adverse event by inspecting the product, bringing it to experts or appraisers, and so on.

Note the difference between this setting and the case of fraud and non-disclosure. In fraud and nondisclosure cases, one party (usually the seller, but sometimes the buyer) is informed about the relevant fact and the other is not. In the mutual mistake case, both parties are uninformed about the relevant fact — that some unknown characteristic of the product renders it more or less valuable than the parties believe.

The law does not let the loss fall where it may. Instead, it distinguishes between what one might roughly call major and minor mistakes. In the case of major mistakes, rescission will be granted at the request of the disappointed party (the seller if the product is worth more than the parties thought, the buyer if the product is worth less than the parties thought). Sherwood v. Walker states the rule as:

> [A] party who has given an apparent consent to a contract of sale may refuse to execute it, or he may avoid it after it has been completed, if the assent was founded, or the contract made, upon the mistake of a material fact, — such as the subject-matter of the sale, the price, or some collateral fact materially inducing the agreement; and this can be done when the mistake is mutual.

But the Restatement subsequently revised it in section 152 to:

(1) Where a mistake of both parties at the time a contract was made as to a basic assumption on which the contract was made has a material effect on the agreed exchange of performances, the contract is voidable by the adversely affected party unless he bears the risk of the mistake under the rule stated in §154.

(2) In determining whether the mistake has a material effect on the agreed exchange of performances, account is taken of any relief by way of reformation, restitution, or otherwise.

Section 154 states:

A party bears the risk of a mistake when:

(a) the risk is allocated to him by agreement of the parties, or

(b) he is aware, at the time the contract is made, that he has only limited knowledge with respect to the facts to which the mistake relates but treats his limited knowledge as sufficient, or

(c) the risk is allocated to him by the court on the ground that it is reasonable in the circumstances to do so.

For an example, let's return to Sherwood v. Walker. The parties believed that Rose was an infertile cow; she turned out to be fertile and with calf. The court styled the question as one about whether the mistake was about the "substance" of the transaction or an "accident" of it. The Restatement uses the language "basic assumption" instead. Was the infertility of Rose a "basic assumption" of the contract? One might say yes — if one believes that the price did not reflect the chance that Rose was fertile. Then we must ask whether the adversely affected party — the seller — bore the risk of the mistake. Section 154 does not provide much guidance. Section (a) is an easy call: if the contract says, "Seller bears the risk that cow is fertile," then Buyer wins. Section (b) is always applicable: any party knows he has limited information. And section (c) also provides no guidance.

Why not enforce these contracts? One possibility is that a contract that reflects mutual mistake should be presumed not to make both parties better off — unlike a contract where there is no such mistake. One party will feel intense regret. But this happens all the time. Think of the sale of Microsoft stock: only one party will make money on it. Indeed, suppose neither party knows that the day before the sale Microsoft discovered some fantastic new technology (the share is now worth more, as in *Sherwood*), or that Microsoft is in fact bankrupt (the share is now worth less, as in counterfeit cases where the mutual mistake doctrine is applied[11]). Surely,

---

[11] See, e.g., Smith v. Zimbalist, 38 P.2d 170 (Cal. Dist. Ct. App. 2d Dist. 1934); Beachcomber Coins, Inc. v. Boskett, 400 A.2d 78 (N.J. Sup. Ct. App. Div. 1979).

we would enforce the sale. When one buys or sells a share of a company, one takes the risk that the company is worth more or less than one believes it to be. But isn't this always the case when goods are sold?

Contracts involving mutual mistake involve an element of surprise that is lacking in other contracts. A recurring idea in contract law is that courts should protect parties from low-probability or unforeseeable risks. When two parties enter a contract, there is a usually low risk that the facts are substantially different from what the parties believe. These facts favor one party and hurt the other. It may well be that people would be willing to give up the chance for a windfall (when the facts favor them) in order to avoid the risk of a significant detriment (when the facts favor the other party). The mutual mistake rule sets up an insurance policy, where each party is protected from the hazard (the contract is rescinded instead) but in return gives up a "premium" consisting of the expected value of the windfall.

But do parties really want these insurance policies? It's not clear. It would be surprising if businesses were risk-averse, at least with respect to run-of-the-mill contractual transactions. Corporations have shareholders who can diversify. Even smaller businesses are sufficiently diversified — in the sense that they enter multiple different types of transactions simultaneously — that they would probably not want to buy insurance against particular contractual disappointments. And if they do, they can always buy insurance from the market or self-insure by retaining some earnings. Parties can also protect themselves using warranties and other contractual terms, though it can be difficult to predict all of the possible aspects about which one might be mistaken. The mutual mistake doctrine might make more sense in the case of major transactions involving individuals, such as the purchase of a house.

§4.5   Unilateral Mistake

A unilateral mistake occurs when only one party has a false belief about the facts of the transaction. One might assume that a unilateral mistake presents a weaker case for rescission than mutual mistake, because error does not so fully pervade the contract, but this is not necessarily the case.

In a mutual mistake case, neither party knows or can suspect that the other party is mistaken. In a unilateral mistake case, the non-mistaken party may know or infer that the other party is mistaken. The law can harness this information in order to reduce the risk that parties enter transactions that are against their interest.

Let's consider a standard construction contract case, where Contractor submits a bid to Owner.[12] Contractor's bid is $100,000, but it reflects a clerical error: Contractor failed to add in one of the proposals that it received from a subcontractor. If Contractor had not made the error, its bid would have been $120,000. Because of the error, Contractor wins the auction — the next highest bid is $115,000. Contractor learns of its error after being informed that it has prevailed, and seeks to rescind the contract.

We focus on two factors: (1) the care with which Contractor performs its calculations, and (2) the obviousness of the error to Owner. We want Contractor to use some care but not excessive care, which would be costly and time-consuming. And we want Owner to correct errors when it is easy to do so, but not otherwise. The way to do this is to hold Contractor to the disadvantageous contract when it fails to take adequate care in performing calculations, or where it did take such care but there was no opportunity for Owner to detect the mistake.

With respect to the last point, Owner has an advantage over Contractor — namely, that Owner (unlike Contractor) has information about the other bids. If Contractor's bid is substantially lower than the second lowest bid, this is a clue that Contractor made an error. In our example, the $15,000 difference may not be enough to create such an inference, but if Contractor had bid, say, $50,000, then Owner would have good reason to believe that Contractor had made a mistake. At this point, Owner would have a duty to alert Contractor of the possible mistake, and give it a chance to withdraw its bid.

The doctrinal solution is not perfect. One might fear that Contractor would deliberately make a mistake — that is, not make a true mistake at all, but underbid and then claim to have made a mistake — as a way to get an advantage over its competitors. If Contractor learns that its bid is far lower than the next highest bid, it can claim mistake and then raise the bid substantially and still win. However, in other settings, this isn't possible.

The Restatement presents the rule in section 153 as follows:

> Where a mistake of one party at the time a contract was made as to a basic assumption on which he made the contract has a material effect on the agreed exchange of performances that is adverse to him, the contract is voidable by him if he does not bear the risk of the mistake under the rule stated in §154, and
> (a) the effect of the mistake is such that enforcement of the contract would be unconscionable, or
> (b) the other party had reason to know of the mistake or his fault caused the mistake.

---

[12] These facts are loosely derived from Elsinore Union Elementary Sch. Dist. v. Kastorff, 353 P.2d 713 (Cal. 1960).

The rule seems too broad, but in practice courts tend to apply the unilateral mistake doctrine to mistaken bids and other cases where the error reflects mathematical miscalculations — "clerical errors" — rather than what are called "judgment errors."[13] If a buyer believes that a product is underpriced and offers to pay a great deal more, he is exercising judgment, and courts will not interfere with the bargain if the buyer turns out to be wrong. In these routine cases, the seller has no reason to infer that the buyer has made a mistake; it's just as likely that the buyer has a strong preference for a good or service and is willing to pay a great deal to get what he wants.

Another question that arises is whether Contractor (or any other mistaken party) should be released from the contract if Owner has not yet been hurt. In construction bidding cases, this often seems to be the case. Contractor discovers its error a few hours or days after winning the bid; Owner can easily take the next highest bidder. Contrast this situation to one where Contractor discover its error months later and the other bidders have gone on to other projects, so Owner cannot easily find a substitute. Here, the contract should be enforced. However, even in the first case, harm can arise from permitting Contractor to escape the contract. As noted above, if this is the rule, Contractor can fabricate an error, make a low bid, and then try to renegotiate after winning the contract. Owner can avoid this strategic behavior by refusing to deal with Contractor, but if there are not many bidders this might be difficult. Contractor in this case is undermining the auction system, a device for eliciting information about bidders' valuations, which will not function properly if bidders are not bound to their bids.

§4.6 Implied Warranty

The unilateral and mutual mistake doctrines resemble the implied warranty doctrine. The implied warranty doctrine says that when a seller of goods does not provide otherwise (through a warranty disclaimer), the seller is deemed to promise that the goods will be free of defects ("merchantable") and fit for the buyer's purpose ("fitness"). If the goods are not merchantable or fit, then the buyer can sue the seller for breach of contract and obtain damages.

One difference between the doctrines is that the implied warranty doctrine protects only the buyer while imposing a duty on the seller. The mistake doctrines protect both parties (from their mistakes) and impose a duty on each party to correct the mistake of the other. In the construction

---

[13] See, e.g., S.T.S. Transp. Svc., Inc. v. Volvo White Truck Corp., 766 F.2d 1089 (7th Cir. 1985).

bid cases, the "seller" — the party making the bid — is rescued by the unilateral mistake doctrine.

Another difference is that a seller can always disclaim an implied warranty by clearly stating that the good is being sold without warranties, or "as is." A seller cannot so easily avoid the mistake doctrine by making stipulations in the contract. In principle, the seller could try to do so by providing in the contract that buyer bears the risk (and the words "as is" might work), but a court may disregard such terms if it believes that the mistake is fundamental.

A final difference is the remedy. As noted above, breach of implied warranty gives the buyer the right to sue for damages — seller has breached the (implied) promise. Buyer will also usually have the right to rescind the contract. The mistake doctrines give the mistaken party *only* the right to rescind the contract, sending both parties back to the status quo.

Let's see how the two doctrines apply differently to a contract for the sale of land. In Hinson v. Jefferson,[14] Buyer purchased a tract of land for the purpose of building a house, but the land turned out to be unusable because of a high water table. Neither Buyer nor Seller knew about the problem. Buyer sued to rescind the contract on grounds of mistake, but the court held that Buyer was protected by an implied warranty that the land could be used for a house. As a result, Buyer could obtain damages (or possibly rescind the contract on the ground of breach).

Both doctrines penalize Seller; the difference is that the penalty will be greater under the implied warranty doctrine. Buyer has the option to rescind or demand damages, and will threaten whichever is worse for Seller in order to extract the most generous settlement. This greater threat may encourage sellers to investigate their land before trying to sell it. By contrast, the rescission remedy just sends Seller back to the status quo. She will have to try to sell it again, presumably at a lower price to someone who does not mind the problems with it.

The implied warranty doctrine has an additional effect. It recognizes that even when a product is defective in some way, frequently the sale will go through. To understand this point, suppose that Seller sells a car to Buyer for $10,000. The car turns out to have a leaky carburetor that neither party knew about (or only Seller knew about). Under the implied warranty doctrine, Buyer would sue and obtain the cost of repairing the carburetor — say $100. Under a mistake doctrine, Buyer would obtain rescission. But Buyer may well prefer the car with a leaky carburetor for an effective price of $9,900 to no car at all. If so, the rescission remedy would require the parties to renegotiate. By contrast, the implied warranty remedy produces the modified deal to which they would renegotiate under the mistake remedy. A step is skipped and some costs are saved.

---

[14] 215 S.E.2d 102 (N.C. 1975).

The "information doctrines" reconsidered. The duty to disclose, misrepresentation, unilateral and mutual mistake, and implied warranty doctrines overlap in often subtle ways. Some basic distinctions, displayed (very roughly) in the following table, may be helpful. Two parties enter a transaction for the sale of a widget. The value of the widget is different from what one or both parties believe: it is higher (disappointing Seller) or lower (disappointing Buyer). Information about the actual value of the widget may be known to one party or to neither party. If both parties have the information, they will not consummate the sale. If neither party possesses the information, it may nonetheless be the case that one party is in the better position to obtain it.

Representation

Mental State	Doctrine
Intentional	Fraud
Negligent	Negligent misrepresentation
Innocent	Breach of contract / warranty if representation is a promise

No Representation

Mental State	Doctrine
Both parties ignorant	Mutual mistake
One party ignorant	
Informed party should have known of first party's ignorance	Unilateral mistake / breach of implied warranty / violation of duty to disclose
Ignorant party could have discovered information through reasonable inspection	No liability

Consider first the case where one party makes a representation that turns out to be false. The party may make that representation knowing that it is false (intentional misrepresentation), believing it to be true when she could easily have discovered that it is false (negligent misrepresentation), or innocently. If the other party relies on the misrepresentation, she may have a claim. In the case of intentional misrepresentation, the victim can claim fraud and obtain rescission. The law throws the book at the fraudster because fraud leads to the misallocation of resources, and the fraudster can avoid engaging in fraud simply by not doing it. In the case of negligent misrepresentation, the victim usually can obtain a remedy. Here, the law punishes the person who makes the misrepresentation to encourage her to do research before entering the transaction. In the case of innocent misrepresentation, the victim is out of luck unless she can show that the representation was a promise, that is, that the other party promised that the represented conditions existed or would come to pass.

Now consider the case when no representation takes place. The law offers remedies but less enthusiastically than in the other case because the promisor does not always know that the information is important to the victim, and the victim should be encouraged to raise any concerns with the promisor. Further, the party with the superior information may have that information because she invested resources in obtaining it; if she were not permitted to exploit her informational advantage, she would not invest those resources and the information might never be obtained, resulting in a misallocation of resources. So the law treads cautiously. When both parties lack the relevant information (the cow is fertile, for example), and neither party could reasonably have been expected to obtain it through investigation (as the *Sherwood* majority assumed), there is little reason to enforce the contract. The contract just transfers resources from one party to another, not necessarily from the party who values them less to the party who values them more. But courts must be careful. In most transactions, neither party knows everything there is to know about the product or service being sold; thus, the mutual mistake doctrine is reserved for extreme cases.

In other cases, one party has the information and the other party does not, or one party can make reasonable inferences on the basis of information that the other party lacks (the contractor cases). These cases are like accidents. If the uninformed party had taken more care (by acquiring more information) or the informed party had taken more care (by disclosing information), the dispute would never have arisen. But the uninformed party cannot always acquire additional information at reasonable cost; and the informed party may not know that the other party is uninformed, may have obtained the information through the investment of valuable resources, or may be unable to inform the other party without incurring large costs. Courts take into account all of these factors in unilateral mistake and implied warranty cases, engaging in something like a comparative fault analysis, but with a presumption in favor of enforcement.

§4.7   Infancy

Infants (the legal term for children) may enter contracts, but they retain the right to void these contracts.[15] Some states mitigate the harshness of this rule by giving the other party the ability to obtain restitution, including the return of the goods sold if they exist; if contracts involve "necessaries" — goods or services that the infant needs to live — then the infant *must* pay restitution if he disaffirms the contract.

One might think that the infancy doctrine is supposed to protect children, but the truth is more complex. The doctrine deters people from entering contracts with children, and that helps children only if children usually enter bad contracts. And yet if that were the case, the exception for necessaries would make no sense. If children have bad judgment, they will pay too much for, or buy the wrong, necessaries, and there is no reason to permit them to do this. If the purpose of the infancy doctrine were to protect children against their bad judgment, a more straightforward rule would authorize courts to evaluate the transaction, and reverse it or otherwise change the terms if they think that the infant made a bad deal. Sellers and other contracting parties would give infants a good deal on all goods they wanted — rather than a bad deal on necessaries and no deal on "luxuries" — because they would fear that otherwise a court would release the infant from the contract ex post.

An alternative explanation for the infancy doctrine treats it as a tax on children who leave home. Under the infancy doctrine, the child who leaves home will encounter sellers who will not sell him things he wants unless the things are necessaries. The doctrine serves as a funny kind of tax on the child's income. This will make the world outside the home seem less attractive to the child, and encourage him to stay home until he reaches majority. Now some children have good reason to leave home. They might seek to escape brutal parents. These children will prefer being out of the home even if they are not permitted to purchase non-necessaries. Thus, the infancy doctrine permits children to leave home if they have a compelling reason, but otherwise discourages children from leaving home.[16]

By contrast, an infancy doctrine that gave courts the power to enforce all good deals and reform bad deals would give children an incentive to leave home. They could enter the world and not worry too much about being taken advantage of.

It hardly needs to be said that the infancy doctrine is a throwback to a time when teenagers left home and obtained work in great numbers. It has little relevance today.

---

[15] See Restatement (Second) of Contracts §14 (1981) ("Unless a statute provides otherwise, a natural person has the capacity to incur only voidable contractual duties until the beginning of the day before the person's eighteenth birthday.").

[16] See Webster St. P'ship v. Sheridan, 368 N.W.2d 439 (Neb. 1985).

§4.8 Incompetence

As the infancy doctrine illustrates, the ever-present paradox in contract law is that the privilege to disaffirm a contract is a privilege you do not want. If you have the right to void your contract, then people will not contract with you. But this paradox can be resolved. If children have bad enough judgment, then their contractual choices will be poor, so they are better off not being permitted to enter contracts in the first place. Better to encourage them to stay at home or, in the worst case, a public institution than to allow them to go out on their own and enter contracts without parental guidance.

Not all children have poor judgment, and so, as is always the case in the law, the rule is overbroad. It is also the case that some adults have poor judgment. These adults do not benefit from the infancy doctrine, but they can invoke a related rule: the incompetency doctrine. An incompetent person can avoid a contract if — roughly speaking — the counterparty had reason to know of the first party's incompetence, the terms were unfair, and the counterparty can be compensated for his reliance.[17] The rule is somewhat less protective than the infancy doctrine is, at least in standard formulations. The counterparty cannot defend herself by proving that she did not have reason to know that the other party was a child, whereas one can defend oneself by providing that one did not have reason to know that the other (adult) party was incompetent. The distinction is easily explained. One can usually tell whether a person is an adult or child just by looking at him, and in cases of doubt one can demand identification. One cannot usually tell if an adult is incompetent, except in extreme cases.

Consider the well-known case of Faber v. Sweet Style Mfg. Corp.[18] A businessman diagnosed with what would now be called bipolar disorder bought some commercial property during a manic phase and then later sought rescission of the deal. The evidence of his disorder was that after seeing a psychiatrist for a while, he canceled his appointments, began to

---

[17] See Restatement (Second) of Contracts §15 (1981), which provides:

(1) A person incurs only voidable contractual duties by entering into a transaction if by reason of mental illness or defect

(a) he is unable to understand in a reasonable manner the nature and consequences of the transaction, or
(b) he is unable to act in a reasonable manner in relation to the transaction and the other party has reason to know of his condition.

(2) Where the contract is made on fair terms and the other party is without knowledge of the mental illness or defect, the power of avoidance under Subsection (1) terminates to the extent that the contract has been so performed in whole or in part or the circumstances have so changed that avoidance would be unjust. In such a case a court may grant relief as justice requires.

[18] 242 N.Y.S.2d 763 (N.Y. Sup. Ct., Nassau Cty. 1963)

drive around at high speeds, took his wife out to dinner (!), became more sexually active, purchased expensive cars, and zoomed around making expensive real estate deals. Eventually, he was hospitalized. From the seller's perspective, the buyer probably seemed like an ordinary hard-charging businessman. Indeed, the court did not find that he was cognitively impaired. He was not delusional. But the court did believe that his judgment was impaired, and for that reason granted rescission.

A person with a psychological disorder, unlike a child, can enter and exit his impaired state. Courts do not want to disable him when he is mentally healthy. This comes up frequently with elderly people who lapse in and out of senility. One temptation is to evaluate the terms of the contract directly. If the contract is crazy, then the person who entered it is probably crazy as well. However, except in extreme cases, it is hard to tell whether or not a contract is crazy. The contract in *Faber* was well within the bounds of commercial reasonableness. In Ortelere v. Teachers' Retirement Bd.,[19] a retired teacher suffering from "involutional melancholia" (presumably, clinical depression) switched her retirement benefits option from $370/month plus death benefits for her husband, to $450/month with no death benefits, and then died soon thereafter. The court reasoned that the teacher would not have agreed to such a bad deal unless she had been mentally impaired. She enjoyed the extra money for only a few months and then her husband, who had taken off work to care for her, got nothing. But the deal was a bad one only with the benefit of hindsight. The teacher could have reasoned that she and her husband needed the extra income because the husband had stopped working, and that the husband could support himself after she died. This is a perfectly rational course of reasoning even if the choice turned out to be the wrong one because the teacher died so promptly. This case indicates the hazard of permitting courts to reason backward from unfairness to incompetency.

What does it mean to be incompetent? Something more than having poor judgment. Usually a psychiatrist diagnoses a mental disease and the factfinder decides whether the person in question understood the transaction itself or the consequences of the transaction — for example, that it subjected the person to great financial risk. As noted, the court's judgment of the fairness of the transaction may play a role in this determination, for better or worse; but the cases focus on all the small details that accumulate around incompetency. Crazy people do crazy things. They neglect their children and friends, forget to do daily chores, dress strangely, and make bizarre claims about themselves and others.

Like the infancy doctrine, the incompetence doctrine addresses a risk of contracting: that one of the parties does not understand what he is doing, and thus may enter a contract that is not jointly beneficial. This risk must

---

[19] 250 N.E.2d 460 (N.Y. 1969).

be allocated to one party or the other. It make sense to put the burden on the adult (or the competent party) to the extent that this party can protect himself by making inquiries and not entering a contract with someone with observably impaired judgment. The hard case occurs when the impairment is not detectable to a non-specialist. Here, the court splits the difference by (in most cases) voiding the contract and giving the competent party a right to restitution, as long as the contract seems to have been fair in the first place.

§4.9 Undue Influence

The undue influence doctrine is a rule that protects people from being pressured into entering an unfavorable contract. The Restatement, section 177, provides:

> (1) Undue influence is unfair persuasion of a party who is under the domination of the person exercising the persuasion or who by virtue of the relation between them is justified in assuming that that person will not act in a manner inconsistent with his welfare.
>
> (2) If a party's manifestation of assent is induced by undue influence by the other party, the contract is voidable by the victim.
>
> (3) If a party's manifestation of assent is induced by one who is not a party to the transaction, the contract is voidable by the victim unless the other party to the transaction in good faith and without reason to know of the undue influence either gives value or relies materially on the transaction.

"Unfair persuasion" is a nebulous idea, however. It is best to start with an example.

Odorizzi v. Bloomfield School District[20] involved an agreement between a schoolteacher, Odorizzi, and the school district, under which the teacher agreed to resign and the school district agreed not to subject him to a termination procedure. The case arose after Odorizzi had been arrested by the police on suspicion of engaging in homosexual activity — which was, at that time and place, illegal. The police had booked and held the teacher overnight. When he was back home, the principal and district superintendant asked to see him. They came over and on the spot told him that if he did not resign, they would initiate termination procedures that would be public. Odorizzi, exhausted after being awake for 40 hours, and no doubt in fear of being exposed (or taken) as a homosexual, agreed. Later, the

---

[20] 246 Cal. App. 2d 123 (1966).

police dropped the charges, presumably because of insufficient evidence of illegal behavior. Odorizzi sued for reinstatement, and won in court.

Agreements to resign like this one are common. When employees enjoy job security—as must have been the case with Odorizzi—they have the right to a procedure before being fired, which can be expensive and time-consuming for the employer and can have an uncertain outcome. Employers want to avoid these costs. The employee wants to avoid the stigma of termination; he will have less trouble finding a new job if he can tell potential employers that he resigned rather than that he was fired. Each side gains from a deal in which the employee resigns and the employer keeps quiet about the reason for resignation.

What, then, was objectionable about the contract between Odorizzi and the school district? It is easy to say that Odorizzi acted while in emotional distress, but that is often the case when employees are asked to resign. Imagine that Odorizzi had been caught beating one of his students or faking test scores, and the same deal was offered. Odorizzi benefits from the deal; if we were to say that he could not enter a contract while in emotional distress, then it would be impossible for him to enter it even though it is in his interest. One might also argue that Odorizzi should be let off the hook because the charges were dropped—the school district never had a right to fire him. (We must assume that the school district would have been justified in firing a teacher who violated the law.) But, again, if we were to come to this conclusion, then courts would never enforce contracts to resign because it is always possible that the person in question might have prevailed if the termination procedures had been used.

The best explanation for the result rests on the unusual circumstances of the deal: it took place at Odorizzi's home, and before he had a chance to get some sleep. The school district never provided a justification for why this was necessary, leading to the inference that the principal and the district superintendant hoped to intimidate Odorizzi and take advantage of his exhaustion—so that he would enter into a contract that was not in fact in his interest. Assume that, with a little more sleep and the advice of a lawyer, Odorizzi would have realized that it was unlikely that the police would charge him with a crime, in which case the school district would not be able to fire him. There is no reason to allow parties to take advantage of the temporary cognitive impairments of others. That can only lead to the enforcement of contracts that are not mutually beneficial.

The undue influence doctrine resembles the infancy and the incompetence doctrines. First, the victim is impaired, like a child—albeit temporarily—and like an incompetent person. Second, the other party has a chance to avoid the problem in the first place simply by refraining from exerting unreasonable pressure. In this respect, the undue influence doctrine has an even stronger basis in policy than the incompetence doctrine, where it is often difficult for the competent party to realize that the other party is incompetent and refrain from entering the transaction. However, it is often difficult to distinguish undue influence from the regular hurly-burly of commercial behavior ("Buy now, or you will lose your chance to make a killing!").

The undue influence doctrine differs from fraud, constructive fraud, the duty to disclose, and mistake. Fraud requires an affirmative misrepresentation and reliance. Mistake requires an incorrect belief. Constructive fraud requires a confidential or fiduciary relationship. The school district did not lie to Odorizzi, nor did Odorizzi make a mistake about the factual basis of the deal, as far as we are told. Nor did Odorizzi and the school district have a confidential or fiduciary relationship. But the doctrines have some similarities. A person who enters a bad deal may be able to escape it if the party on the other side took advantage of him—either by misstating the facts, failing to correct mistakes or provide certain information, or putting unnecessary pressure on him. Telling the truth, disclosing information, and refraining from using pressure are all actions that are relatively cheap for one party (albeit with exceptions we have discussed) and that confer substantial benefits on the other. Courts encourage these actions by refusing to enforce contracts that benefit people who did not engage in them.

§4.10 Unconscionability

The various doctrines we have discussed—mistake, duty to disclose, fraud, and so on—focus on the bargaining process, which can be contrasted with the "substance" of the contract, that is, the actual terms of trade. The bargaining process refers to the back-and-forth between the two parties leading up to the contract. Traditional thinking about contract law holds that courts should police the bargaining process, but not the substantive terms of exchange. This thinking largely remains current, but, as we will see, it has been eroded in some aspects. The trends are encapsulated in the unconscionability doctrine.

The unconscionability doctrine provides for the rescission of contracts that are "unconscionable."[21] The term is nowhere defined, but in practice

---

[21] See Restatement (Second) of Contracts §153 (1981), which provides:

Where a mistake of one party at the time a contract was made as to a basic assumption on which he made the contract has a material effect on the agreed exchange of performances that is adverse to him, the contract is voidable by him if he does not bear the risk of the mistake under the rule stated in §154, and
    (a) the effect of the mistake is such that enforcement of the contract would be unconscionable, or
    (b) the other party had reason to know of the mistake or his fault caused the mistake.

courts distinguish between "procedural" and "substantive" unconscionability. Procedural unconscionability refers to bargaining defects; substantive unconscionability refers to the substantive fairness of the contract. Courts sometimes say both forms of unconscionability must be present in order for rescission to take place; but there are cases in which only one or the other exists. We will consider these two ideas in turn.

Procedural Unconscionability

What types of bargaining defects justify a finding of procedural unconscionability? Many cases feature a recurring pattern. On one side, the seller is an established merchant such as a department store. On the other side, the buyer is (often, but not always) poor, poorly educated, unsophisticated, inexperienced, and vulnerable. Sometimes the buyer does not speak English. Sometimes the buyer is approached at home by a door-to-door salesman. The contract may be written on a lengthy form that is hard to read and contains obscure or complex terms that favor the seller, and that the buyer does not understand or know about. In these cases, the other procedural doctrines do not come into play. The seller does not commit fraud because it does not make a misrepresentation — the unfavorable terms are explicit in the contract. There is no confidential relationship that could give rise to an action for constructive fraud. The buyer does not make a unilateral mistake in the sense of a miscalculation; he just does not fully understand the contract.

The classic case is Williams v. Walker-Thomas Furniture.[22] Mrs. Williams was a welfare recipient with several children. She purchased a stereo from Walker-Thomas Furniture on credit. When she missed a payment, she forfeited not only the stereo, but also a number of items she had bought from Walker-Thomas previously — because of the operation of a clause of the contract that I will describe below, and that she did not know about or understand. Recall our duty to read cases — courts often require sellers to draw buyer's attention to obscure terms in contracts. But when the buyer is poor and uneducated, the problem seems more pressing. Courts often cite two ideas in connection with procedural unconscionability — lack of sophistication and unequal bargaining power.

Is the argument for rescission or nonenforcement stronger if the buyer is poor and uneducated? It seems reasonable to expect a seller to take a little more time and effort to explain the contract to an uneducated person if the seller actually knows that the person is uneducated — which will not often be the case. Sellers may sometimes recognize that buyers are poor, but sometimes not; and even when they do, poverty is not the

___

[22] 350 F.2d 445 (D.C. Cir. 1965).

same thing as lack of sophistication. Mrs. Williams was poor but she had repeatedly bought goods on credit from Walker-Thomas Furniture. She may well have been a sophisticated buyer of consumer goods, for all we know. The court did not address this issue, perhaps because it relied on stereotypes about the competence of poor people.

The rationale for procedural unconscionability is the same as for the other bargain defect doctrines. The seller writes the contract and accordingly understands it. If she has slipped in some obscure and complex terms that are unfavorable to the buyer, she knows it. Most buyers are not in the position to spot these terms, so either they waste a lot of time reading and trying to understand the contract or they end up with a deal that does not make them better off. A doctrine that discourages sellers from relying on such terms — or forces them to draw the buyer's attention to those terms when they are in fact value-maximizing on average but not in the interest of all buyers — minimizes inefficient contracts and reduces transaction costs.

But the doctrine must be carefully applied. Most form contracts contain dozens of terms that are reasonable but may disappoint the buyer if a dispute arises — arbitration clauses, choice of law clauses, limitations on liability, and so forth. It is not realistic to expect the seller to explain all these terms to buyers; it would take a great deal of time and no buyer would have enough patience to listen to them all. As a result, courts find themselves distinguishing terms that seem to matter a great deal from terms that seem to matter less (for example, choice of forum clauses[23]). But how does one make such a distinction? We return to this question shortly — when we turn to substantive unconscionability.

Unequal bargaining power is another term that is often used but not precisely defined. Sometimes it is just another term for inequality of sophistication — Seller knows more than Buyer. But bargaining power has a more precise meaning. It refers to the capacity of a contracting party to obtain a large share of the surplus of a transaction by threatening not to enter the transaction unless the other party agrees. The party with bargaining power is, in effect, a monopolist. If the buyer does not pay a high price, the seller will refuse to sell, and the buyer cannot go elsewhere for the good. But most markets for consumer goods are not monopolized; there is a great deal of competition, and buyers can go to another store if one store charges a high price. Competition drives down prices; consumers have bargaining power, not sellers. That is why you can buy all kinds of things for prices vastly below how much you value them. Even when markets are monopolized, the unconscionability doctrine is not the tool for addressing the problem. For this problem the antitrust laws are used, as I will discuss in the next section.

---

[23] See Carnival Cruise Lines, Inc. v. Shute, 499 U.S. 585 (1991).

Critics make another argument against a broad understanding of procedural unconscionability. Imagine that sellers cannot distinguish between their ordinary buyers and sophisticated buyers who read forms and understand them. If sellers were to include terms that are excessively favorable to the sellers and unfavorable to the buyers, then the sophisticated buyers will withdraw their business. Competing sellers will try to draw buyers' attention to the unfair terms in order to siphon them away from the original sellers. Indeed, the competing sellers will try to make the unfair terms known to the unsophisticated buyers as well as to the sophisticated buyers. To avoid losing customers to competitors, the original seller will remove the unfair terms. Independent outfits like Consumers Union also reveal information about shoddy marketing practices. In this scenario, legal regulation is unnecessary.

The argument turns on a number of empirical premises that are hard to verify. It may turn out that the market is segregated. Sophisticated buyers read form contracts, *Consumer Reports*, Internet sites that discuss marketing practices, and so forth, while unsophisticated buyers do not, and end up paying more and receiving worse terms than sophisticated buyers. Competitors might have insufficient incentive to reveal what the sellers are up to because by revealing information each competitor may end up benefiting other competitors. For example, if Dell uses hidden terms that customers oppose but do not know about, and Gateway launches an expensive advertising campaign to inform consumers, it will end up helping Hewlett-Packard as well as itself. And firms have no incentive to disclose information that is bad for the whole industry.

Substantive Unconscionability

Let us turn to substantive unconscionability. What does this term mean? No one is entirely sure. Substantive unconscionability could be inequality — one side gets more than the other from the contract. Or it could mean unfairness in some more general sense. Both of these ideas are more complex than they first appear.

Consider inequality, or what is sometimes called price disparity. One interpretation of this idea is that the seller gains more from the contract than the buyer does. The seller receives $p - c$ (called producer's surplus); the buyer receives $v - p$ (called consumer's surplus), where p is the price of the good, c is the seller's cost, and v is the buyer's valuation. Inequality exists when the producer's surplus and the consumer's surplus are not equal. However, producer's surplus and consumer's surplus are rarely equal. In a well-functioning market, producer's surplus should be competed away to zero, while consumer's surplus could be very large. Most people who buy ordinary household items — television sets, chairs, food — are willing to pay more for those items than they do. By contrast, when sellers make large profits, other sellers will enter the market and offer a lower price, reducing profits for all. Thus, if inequality of producer's and consumer's surpluses were a concern, we should normally provide a remedy for the seller, not the buyer.

Another possible concern is not inequality, but that the buyer pays too much for a product — that is, more than necessary to cover the seller's cost. This can happen when the seller has bargaining power. As noted above, bargaining power refers simply to the power to charge a price higher than the market price. This problem arises when the seller is a monopolist or when there are a small number of sellers in the market (oligopoly).

It is conceivable that the unconscionability doctrine can be used to challenge market power. If courts strike down contracts with above-market prices, then monopolists will have to offer lower prices. However, there is a problem with such an approach: determining whether a price is "above market" is extremely difficult. It would be wrong to think that the price of a good should be just its cost of production. Production costs include fixed costs (for example, building a factory) and variable costs (the labor and material used for each good that is produced). Because fixed costs must be allocated to each good, the cost of a single good is a function of how many other goods are produced and sold. If many goods are sold, then the fixed costs are spread across many goods, and so each good will be cheaper. The pricing decision is immensely complex, and must account for possible future sales.

Nor can one determine whether a price of a particular good is fair by comparing it to other goods being sold on the market; subtle differences (such as branding, convenience, and so forth) can make a difference. The price of a good might seem high because a competitor offers a much lower price — but only because the competitor hopes to use that low price to bring customers to its store, where they will buy other products ("loss leaders"), in which case the low price does not reflect a lower cost of production. Except in extreme cases — to which we will return — a court cannot tell whether the price of a good is too high.

This is why government addresses the problem of overpricing through antitrust law rather than contract law. Antitrust law requires courts to evaluate market structure and efforts by firms to change it. When firms drive up prices by agreeing to hold down production, they engage in an antitrust violation. Note that the court evaluates antitrust claims by looking at behavior — meetings between executives where agreements are hammered out — rather than at pricing alone. Finally, note also that antitrust policy permits certain types of monopolies — including those granted by patent to developers of intellectual property and innovators in general — suggesting that as a matter of public policy "high" prices will be tolerated because they sometimes lead to social gains. Indeed, if a firm gains a monopoly through innovation or other ways that benefit consumers, antitrust law permits it to charge a monopoly price. That is how the market works. The firm's excess profits should attract competitors and lead to further innovation, and eventually to lower prices. Court-imposed price caps would halt this process. For these reasons, it is rare to find a case where courts strike down a contract simply because the price is too high. Unconscionability cases almost always focus on nonprice terms. In Williams v. Walker-Thomas,[24] the court struck down a cross-collateral clause. In Henningsen v. Bloomfield Motors,[25] the court struck down a limitation on liability. In Broemmer v. Abortion Services,[26] the court struck down an arbitration clause.

A starting point for understanding these cases is that the objectionable clauses all involved the parties' obligations when the contract goes awry — the buyer has failed to comply with his obligations, or the seller has delivered a defective product or service, and a dispute arises. Because buyers usually enter contracts without much thought as to what will happen if things go wrong, courts may believe that buyers pay little attention to the clauses that govern in those situations. If so, sellers can dictate terms that are unfair to buyers.

But unfair in what way? Many contracts put a limit on the disappointed party's remedy if a dispute arises. There is nothing wrong in principle with limitations on liability. They protect the seller from high upside risk, and the seller should pass the cost savings on to the buyer in the form of a lower price. The principle remains valid even if liability is limited to zero. The buyer should either trust the seller's incentives to maintain a brand or its reputation, or go elsewhere. To be sure, there are troubling cases that involve misleading or confusing language and one-sided terms. In Brower v. Gateway 2000, Inc.,[27] buyers knew at the time of purchase that they would have to arbitrate, but they could not know that arbitration would cost so much as to never be worthwhile. Rather than refuse to buy, buyers either did not think about this problem or (wrongly) assumed that arbitration would not be too expensive. If this assumption is reasonable, one can criticize the seller for misleading buyers but not necessarily for failing to make available a remedy.

Consider again the clause at issue in *Williams*. When a debtor like Mrs. Williams defaults, creditors can bring a lawsuit and demand repayment. The court will award a judgment against the debtor, and the creditor can take this judgment to a local official such as the sheriff and demand that the sheriff collect from the debtor. In theory, the sheriff can go to the debtor's house or place of business, and seize the debtor's property. The

---

[24] 350 F.2d 445 (D.C. Cir. 1965).
[25] 161 A.2d 69 (N.J. 1960).
[26] 840 P.2d 1013 (Ariz. 1992).
[27] 246 A.D.2d 246 (N.Y. App. Div. 1998).

property is auctioned off, and the proceeds are given to the creditor up to the size of the debt. The balance, if any, is returned to the debtor.

So much for theory. In practice, there are significant constraints on what the creditor can obtain. All states have exemption laws, which provide that certain types and amounts of property cannot be liquidated to satisfy debts. Exemption laws vary across states, but they tend to protect clothes, furniture, home equity, and other assets up to a certain amount, such as $10,000 or more. For many people, and certainly for all poor people, the exemption laws will protect all of their assets.

Creditors therefore have no recourse, but there are ways around these laws. One way is to demand a purchase money security interest. When a buyer purchases a toaster on credit, the contract provides that title to the toaster will revert to the seller if default occurs. Exemption laws typically do not apply to assets that the buyer purchased with funds secured by those assets. By contrast, credit card debt is not secured.

Walker-Thomas sold several items to Mrs. Williams. All of these items were subject to a purchase money security interest. The effect of the cross-collateral clause was to provide that Mrs. Williams was not paid up on the debt for any one of these purchases until she had paid off the debt for all the purchases in aggregate. Suppose, for example, that she purchases a toaster worth $100 on credit, makes payments worth $90, then purchases a stereo for $200, and then makes payments worth $50. One might think that she has fully paid off the toaster and owes $160 on the stereo. But because of the cross-collateral clause, less than $10 of the $50 payment is allocated to the toaster, so a balance remains on the toaster as well as on the stereo. This means that if Williams defaults, Walker-Thomas can repossess both the toaster and the stereo, rather than just the stereo. (But remember that if the assets are worth more than the debt, Walker-Thomas must return the excess to Williams.)

It may be the case that Williams did not understand the cross-collateral clause (as she testified), and that Walker-Thomas misled her. But imagine that she did understand. The cross-collateral clause enabled Williams to make purchases that would otherwise have been too risky for Walker-Thomas (because the store would not be able to repossess assets of adequate value if she defaulted), although Williams would now have to take the risk that she would lose all the property she purchased if she defaulted. It is hard to see why this clause, which has a marginal impact beyond the default legal regime, is outrageous or shocking. Perhaps we don't want people like Williams borrowing in the first place because of the risk that they will default and lose property that they purchased. If that is the case, then laws restricting lending (usury laws as well as the unconscionability doctrine) may be justified. But it must be kept in mind that if people like Williams are to be protected from the downside of the risks they take, then they won't be able to enjoy the upside either — the ability to purchase and enjoy items today rather than save up for them — because creditors will not supply credit unless they have sufficient protection from default.

It is also common to say that the problem with the contract in *Williams* is that it was "coercive," possibly because the items that Walker-Thomas repossessed were worth less to it than they were to her. This view also betrays a misunderstanding of contract law. Contract law itself is coercive; that is the point. By entering a contract, you agree to be coerced by the law if you breach. As noted above, even in the absence of the cross-collateral clause, Williams must pay her debt. Walker-Thomas would simply demand that the sheriff seize and liquidate her possessions if she does not pay, regardless of how much those possessions are worth to her. Given the high baseline level of coercion in contract law, which is uncontroversial, the additional degree of coercion introduced by the cross-collateral clause is trivial.

A similar point can be made about Henningsen v. Bloomfield Motors.[28] The contract for the sale of the automobile limited the warranty to the replacement of defective parts, so coverage for personal injuries suffered by the plaintiff's wife after an automobile accident were excluded. The court criticized the contract for being written in a misleading way, but the buyer did not read the contract, so he could not have been misled by it. The court also criticized Chrysler, one of the defendants, for refusing to offer a warranty that covers personal injuries. But it does not explain why Chrysler should offer such a warranty.

A warranty is just another feature of a car, like heated seats. If you want a warranty, you have to pay for it, just as you must pay for heated seats. The automobile manufacturer will calculate the cost of the warranty by multiplying the probability of an accident by the average loss that will result from an accident. For example, if 1 out of 1000 cars will have a defect that leads to an accident, and the average accident causes damages of $200,000, then the cost per car is $200.

The car company might offer a warranty as a kind of option, like the heated seats. The base price of the car is $20,000; if you want a warranty, you can have it, but you must pay another $200 for it. Some people will take the deal; others (for example, those with insurance or those who do not mind taking risks) will not. If the market offers this menu, and people understand it, there is no good reason for courts to mandate that car companies provide warranties.

At the time *Henningsen* was decided, however, car companies did not offer warranties covering personal injuries. Buyers who sought warranties and were willing to pay for them could not obtain them. The court

---

[28] 161 A.2d 69 (N.J. 1960).

attached significance to this fact, but there is an innocent explanation. The car manufacturers might have calculated that no one would have been willing to pay for the warranties (perhaps because people had insurance), and therefore there was no point in offering them. Until air bags became cheap and reliable, car companies did not offer them — because no one would want to pay a lot of money for them. Once they became cheap and reliable, car companies began offering them in high-end cars. The absence of warranties that cover personal injuries could just have reflected lack of consumer demand.

There is a less innocent story, however: The car companies had agreed among themselves not to offer warranties covering personal injuries. Maybe they sought to maintain a cartel with above-market prices on cars by limiting nonprice competition. Car companies might have believed that they could maintain above-market prices simply by observing each other's prices and threatening price competition if prices sank too low, but this type of implicit cooperation would be impossible if car companies competed along other dimensions such as warranty coverage. Maybe. But agreements among competitors are not always anti-competitive, and to properly evaluate such agreements, courts must draw on antitrust law,[29] which the *Henningsen* court did not do.

A final point is that some scholars have defended the unconscionability doctrine, or at least its application in cases like *Williams*, on grounds of distributive justice. The picture here is of wealthy firms taking advantage of poor consumers; law that interferes with these transactions can only help the poor at the expense of the rich. However, this type of thinking is at best simplistic. As we have seen, the unconscionability doctrine and similar doctrines may cause sellers to withdraw credit from the poor, which will on average hurt them rather than help them. This is not inevitable, but it is very likely, and in general contract law is a crude instrument to use for redistributing wealth.[30]

* * *

There are tensions in both the procedural and the substantive sides of unconscionability. On the procedural side, the contract is ambiguous, even misleading, yet we often suspect that even if it has been crystal clear, the buyer would have agreed to the offensive term. On the substantive side, the term seems unfair, but one can usually come up with a story about why the term is in the joint interest of the parties. If so, blocking the term

[29] In antitrust disputes, courts make two basic inquiries: they determine whether the defendant(s) had "market power," that is, the ability to set the price above the competitive price; and whether the agreement or practice being challenged has an innocent (that is, pro-competitive, or cost-saving) justification.

[30] See Richard Craswell, Passing on the Costs of Legal Rules: Efficiency and Distribution in Buyer-Seller Relationships, 43 Stan. L. Rev. 361 (1991).

will just increase the price or in other ways harm the consumer. Thus, the unconscionability doctrine remains a controversial doctrine, and courts tend to use it sparingly. The doctrine has also been overtaken by statutory and regulatory developments in consumer protection law, which we discuss in Section 9.3.

§4.11 Coercion and Duress

If a person extracts a promise from another by putting a gun to his head, courts will refuse to enforce the promise on grounds of duress.[31] There is no reason to enforce such a promise: it does not reflect an exercise of autonomy, if that is what you care about; there is certainly no reason for courts to think that the exchange is ex ante jointly welfare enhancing; and people will take self-protective measures if the courts do not protect them from such behavior. These self-protective measures are a social waste; people would be better off if they were not necessary.

There are two harder cases. The first is when a person must deal with a promisee that has all the market power. Suppose I desperately need credit and the only bank in the area charges exorbitant interest rates, or I am starving and the only grocery store charges very high prices for food. People sometimes say that these scenarios resemble the gun-to-the-head case, because the promisor lacks a "meaningful choice." This argument is not entirely wrong, but it is incomplete. In the gun-to-the-head case, voiding the contract (and throwing the promisee in jail) has no negative effects: we are all better off if such people are not allowed to engage in extortion. In the bank and grocery store cases, however, voiding the contract will deprive people of credit they want and food they need.

A better approach is not to void contracts where Seller has monopoly power but to regulate the price. (Note again that such an approach makes no sense in the gun-to-the-head case.) We could ask courts to strike down the credit or food contract if the price is unreasonably high, and to enforce the contract otherwise. But what does it mean for a price to be unreasonably high?

One answer is that a monopoly price is too high; a competitive price is okay. (The technical difference is that a competitive price will just allow the seller to recover marginal costs of production; the monopoly price will be higher, potentially as high as the buyer will pay.) But, as we discussed in Section 4.10, this cannot be a complete answer. Suppose the promisee has market power because he has a patent on an invention — say, a vital drug that I need very much. The policy of giving a monopoly to a patentee

---

[31] See Restatement (Second) of Contracts §175 (1981).

is based on the (debatable) theory that only through such a monopoly can he recover the costs of research. If this is true, voiding the contract would defeat the policy of patent law. More generally, the state does not try to intervene whenever someone obtains a little market power. A little market power might not be such a bad thing: it rewards innovators and it attracts competitors, who will eventually bring down the price. And it is doubtful that courts are capable of detecting a little bit of market power.

Courts do not evaluate prices in breach of contract cases. Instead, they wait for the government or private parties to bring an antitrust action against monopolists and other firms or people with market power. These are complex cases in which the court must evaluate market conditions (does Seller really have market power?) and possible excuses (such as patents), as well as prices and other contract terms. The duress doctrine is reserved for the gun-to-the-head case, and to another type of case, to which we turn now.[32]

The second situation involves a party exploiting a "local monopoly" created by a contract with the promisor. These cases almost always arise under the guise of settlements or contract modifications. Seller (say) performs, then demands payment, and Buyer threatens not to pay unless the Seller agrees to a lower price. Or Buyer pays, and then Seller refuses to perform unless Buyer pays some more. As an example, a crew of fishermen (sellers) strike when the boat is far away from replacement workers;[33] they will not work unless given wages higher than those they agreed to. The supplier (also a seller) refuses to deliver when the buyer is faced with a tight deadline.[34] The supplier will not deliver on time unless the buyer agrees to a higher price or offers other types of consideration. A tenant (a buyer this time) refuses to pay any rent and threatens to vacate the premises unless the landlord agrees to lower the rent for the following year.[35]

In theory, a special doctrine is not needed for cases such as these. The threatened party should refuse to agree to a contract modification and then sue for damages, including any consequential damages. Consider the supply contract. If Buyer refuses to agree to a higher price and Supplier retaliates by delivering late, so that Buyer misses its own deadline and must pay damages to a third party, then Buyer can sue Supplier for these consequential damages. Buyer is made whole; indeed, anticipating this move, Supplier would not threaten Buyer in the first place. However, in practice it may be difficult for Buyer to prove his losses. Suppose that the real problem for Buyer is that if it misses its deadline, its own buyers will stop buying from it. This loss would be difficult to calculate, and a court will not

---

[32] Market power issues arise in unconscionability cases as well; see Section 4.10.

[33] Alaska Packers' Ass'n v. Domenico, 117 F. 99 (9th Cir. 1902).

[34] Austin Instrument, Inc. v. Loral Corp., 272 N.E.2d 533 (N.Y. 1971).

[35] Levine v. Blumenthal, 186 A. 457 (N.J. 1936).

award damages for speculative losses. The duress problem arises because Supplier can exploit this gap in enforcement. If parties were allowed to do this, then contracts such as these would be less attractive ex ante.

The law's solution is to give Buyer (in our example) the right to rescind the contract that was made under duress. If Supplier knows that Buyer will be able to rescind the contract modification, then Supplier will not bother to threaten to deliver late.

However, there is a further problem. Often, parties find it in their joint interest to modify a contract partway through performance. In the simplest case, Seller experiences an unexpected increase in costs and can no longer deliver on time. Seller offers to pay Buyer (in the form of reduced price) to permit Seller to deliver late. The deal could well be attractive to Buyer — if the cost to the Buyer of a late delivery (which could be low) is less than the amount offered by Seller. Such contract modifications are unobjectionable and ubiquitous. But if we had a simple rule — "no contract modifications" — they would not be permitted.

One solution is to distinguish cases where Seller (again, in our example) "threatens" Buyer with non-delivery and cases where Seller offers to pay Buyer to permit her to deliver late. The problem is that these two cases often are the same. Seller says, "I'm sorry but we cannot make the deadline." Is this a threat or an offer to renegotiate the contract? Perhaps the problem is that Seller did not offer to lower the price. Indeed, in the standard duress case, Seller demands a higher price. Courts could strike down any such contract where Seller refuses to perform unless given a higher price, Buyer agrees to a higher price, and then Seller performs. Some courts have applied the consideration doctrine in such cases. Because Buyer does not get anything in addition to the original performance in return for Buyer's extra payment, the promise to pay extra is non-enforceable for lack of consideration.[36]

This approach is vulnerable to a gambit. Seller could always offer something that is new but less valuable to Buyer than the added price. Buyer is really paying for the original performance, but the parties disguise this fact by providing that Seller give Buyer something new. For example, Seller agrees to deliver a little early, or to cover some nominal charge (insurance, transportation) that was originally Buyer's responsibility. To see through the disguise, courts would have to determine whether the additional performance is worth the price — something they are reluctant to do. Doctrine halfheartedly accounts for this problem by permitting the modification when there is a "change in circumstance" — Seller's costs really do go up unexpectedly. But this does not really address this issue, and it is unclear why Buyer would agree to modify the contract and pay more just because Seller's costs increased. Some of the cases suggest that

---

[36] See Restatement (Second) of Contracts §71 (1981) (requiring consideration), *Alaska Packers*, and *Levine*. On the consideration doctrine, see Section 5.1.

if Seller's costs increased in a way that is not anticipated by the contract, Seller would not have an obligation to perform (presumably on grounds of impracticability or impossibility[37]), and therefore Buyer in fact pays for something he is otherwise not entitled to.[38]

The other approach relies on the idea of coercion, similar to the gun-to-the-head case. The Restatement provides that if "a party's manifestation of assent is induced by an improper threat by the other party that leaves the victim no reasonable alternative, the contract is voidable by the victim."[39] Courts reject a duress claim if the victim of the threat has a legal remedy: a legal remedy is a "reasonable alternative."

The duress doctrine has provoked a great deal of controversy, in part because of the sometimes inflated prose of courts. In Austin Instrument v. Loral,[40] Seller refused to perform on an existing contract unless Buyer awarded a second contract to it and agreed to higher prices on the first. Buyer was in a tough spot. It used Seller's inputs to manufacture goods for the Navy during the Vietnam War, and it feared that if it turned down Seller, it would not find substitute sellers in time to meet its obligations to the Navy. In theory, Buyer could say "no" to Seller, breach its contract with the Navy, pay damages to the Navy, and then sue Seller for damages — which would cover the damages Buyer paid to Navy plus the profits it lost as a result of its breach of the Navy contract. The problem for Buyer is that its reputation with the Navy might be irretrievably harmed, so it loses a long stream of future profits from Navy contracts. If (as is likely) a court deemed this loss speculative or unforeseeable under the Hadley rule,[41] Buyer cannot recover from Seller. So it's better to give in to Seller's black-mail then resort to the law.

The court held that Seller's threat to breach "deprived [Buyer] of its free will."[42] But does Buyer really lack free will? Buyer retains the choice to disregard the threat; it possesses free will, the ability to choose. Indeed, its ability to choose is not much different from that of any market actor. You are given a price, and it might seem too high, but you have the choice to accept the deal or not. If it is too high, you reject the deal, but that does not mean you lack free choice.

If we recall what the underlying problem is, however, we can make progress with the doctrine. The problem arises when one contract party demands that an existing contract be modified. There can be two reasons

---

[37] See Section 7.5.

[38] Brian Constr. & Dev. Co. v. Brighenti, 405 A.2d 72 (Conn. 1978); see also Restatement (Second) of Contracts §89(a) (1981) ("A promise modifying a duty under a contract not fully performed on either side is binding ... if the modification is fair and equitable in view of circumstances not anticipated by the parties when the contract was made.").

[39] Restatement (Second) §175(1) (1981).

[40] 272 N.E.2d 533 (N.Y. 1978).

[41] See Section 8.10.

[42] Id. at 536.

for such a demand: (1) an "innocent" change in circumstances (costs go up unexpectedly), which the other party does not want to exploit for self-interested reasons (for example, he wants to maintain a good relationship); or (2) a desire to "hold up" the other party, which has sunk costs. Courts should enforce the first type of contract and refuse to enforce the second. The duress doctrine can be interpreted to advance this agenda. If the victim of the threat has an adequate legal remedy, then it is impossible to hold him up. Therefore, if he agrees to modify the contract, then the first scenario must be in place, and accordingly the court should enforce the contract. If the victim does not have an adequate legal remedy, then the question is whether there has been a change in circumstances. If not, then we have a clear case of hold-up, and the contract should not be enforced.

The problem is that in many cases both conditions will be met. A party who has slightly higher costs might seize on them as a pretext for demanding a much higher price from the other party, who lacks a legal remedy. It is hard to see how a court can resolve a case like this one without doing what courts don't like to do: determine whether the price increase is "fair" in the sense of covering just those additional costs.

Some parties have sought to avoid settlements by claiming duress, arguing that they settled in the first place only because they did not have the money to pursue a lawsuit. In Hackley v. Headley,[43] for example, a logger agreed to accept $4000 for logs that he believed were worth around $6000. The buyer insisted that the $4000 figure was correct (or, in any event, the most that he would pay), and further said that he would not pay any money unless the logger gave up his right to sue for the disputed amount ($2000). The logger agreed, then sued to avoid the settlement so that he could claim the $2000.

The logger had an apparently plausible duress claim. The buyer had "threatened" him by refusing to pay unless the logger agreed to the low amount, and the logger had no adequate legal remedy because he could not afford to litigate. His bills were coming due, and if he did not pay them he would go into bankruptcy. Yet the court rejected his claim.

The court explained that buyers have the right to dispute the bills that are submitted to them, and that if sellers could avoid contracts by claiming duress, then "no one could well know when he would be safe in dealing on the ordinary terms of negotiation with a party who professed to be in great need."[44] The court feared that people will be unwilling to enter contracts with those in financial straits (or who might be in financial straits) because those people will always be able to back out of the contract if they decide they do not like it. But it hardly does such people any good if no one will contract with them. The opposite risk is preferable. Financially distressed people know that they might be taken advantage of

---

[43] 8 N.W. 511 (Mich. 1981).
[44] Id. at 514.

when it comes time for payment, but they can protect themselves in various ways — for example, by demanding installment payments after partial performance.

The real problem is not so much financial distress as the inability to borrow money. Even if the logger is poor, if he has an expected payoff of $6000, a bank should be willing to fund the litigation. Increasingly today, various credit outfits provide just such financing, which further undermines the claim that one cannot sue because of financial difficulties.

Still, we might also ask whether the buyer shouldn't have paid the undisputed amount of $4000. This would have enabled the logger to pay his bills and litigate the disputed amount. Instead, the buyer refused to pay anything unless the logger released him from the disputed claim. If the logger cannot borrow money, then the buyer's behavior seems like opportunism — an attempt to exploit the costs of the legal system in order to avoid being compelled to perform. It might therefore make sense for courts to police such behavior by finding duress (or, say, lack of good faith) if the buyer fails to pay even the undisputed amount. The risk of such a rule is that it might lead buyers simply to exaggerate the dispute; but if this problem can be overcome, the rule would make good sense.

Chapter 5

Which Promises Are Enforceable?

§5.1 Consideration

Courts must decide which promises to enforce. Should they enforce all promises? Or should they enforce just a few — those that are sufficiently "serious" to justify the expenditure of judicial resources, or perhaps those by which the promisor intended to create a legal obligation, as opposed to a moral or personal obligation?

Of course, courts do not want to enforce promises that violate non-contract laws like the antitrust laws, nor do they want to enforce promises that are fraudulent or that are based on poor information or other bargaining defects. But let us put these kinds of promises aside. We are concerned with promises like these:

- Casual promises: "I will meet you for lunch on Thursday."
- Vague promises: "I will hire you when business turns around."
- Gratuitous promises: "I will give you $100 tomorrow so you can buy some groceries for yourself."
- Preliminary negotiations: "Let's merge our companies."

These promises can be contrasted with standard commercial promises — "I agree to buy that car from you for $15,000." This promise does not seem casual (but one must always look at context) or vague. It is not gratuitous — the car, unless it is worth nothing, is being given for the money. And the promise does not seem preliminary, although it may be, if other details need to be hammered out; again, one must check the context.

Courts identify the legally enforceable promises — the promises that should be enforced, as opposed to those that shouldn't be — using the consideration doctrine as well as a host of subsidiary doctrines, including a rule that contracts must not be too vague to enforce, and the offer and acceptance rules, which rule out enforcement of conditional promises (offers) made before agreement is reached. These doctrines overlap with the consideration doctrine to some degree.

Now, why not enforce every promise? The simple answer is that people do not want all of their promises to be enforced. But why not? When one makes a promise, one tries to elicit "reliance," a change of behavior, from the promisee. If the promisee does not know whether the promisor will keep the promise, then he may not rely, which frustrates the promisor's design.

For example, if I invite you to lunch next Thursday at noon, I want you to rely on my promise, and actually show up to meet me. If you don't know whether I will keep my promise, you may not show up. But if my promise were legally enforceable — if you could collect money from me should I break it — then you certainly expect me to show up (or pay you if I do not) and therefore you yourself will show up. So why shouldn't my promise be legally enforceable?

The answer is obvious, but there are some hidden subtleties as well. The answer is that legal enforcement is costly and often inaccurate, so people will not resort to it when cheaper and more accurate alternatives are available. There are such alternatives. Many people keep promises just because it is the honorable thing to do; people also keep promises for reputational reasons. If a promisor keeps breaking her promises, and others get wind of this, they will not trust her when she makes promises to them. Reputation may work as well as the law in many settings. Indeed, in our everyday lives, even our commercial lives, we depend to a much greater degree on reputation than on the law. That is why stores honor warranties even though in most cases a buyer's threat to sue lacks credibility — the cost of the lawsuit would be greater than receiving money back for a toaster, refrigerator, or other item that does not work as advertised. Businesses invest huge amounts of money to develop a "brand" that signals that they will promise to fix or replace products that fail. If they then fail to honor this promise, the brand will lose its value and the investment will be lost.

But then the question is, Why is the law needed at all? If businesses care enough about their reputation, then legal enforceability of promises is unnecessary and might even interfere with commerce (because, again, courts make mistakes). The answer seems to be that sometimes reputation is sufficient, and sometimes it isn't. The challenge for courts is to distinguish these two cases, withholding legal remedies in the first case and supplying them in the second.

The consideration doctrine is one of the legal sentinels that patrol the border between law and reputation. Plausibly, the promisor does not want to legally bind herself in any of the four cases above, and the promisee does not need a legal remedy. Casual promises elicit reliance because the promisee trusts the promisor; if the promise is broken, then the promisee now knows better and the loss is not large enough to justify a lawsuit. Vague promises are similar; in these cases, more may be at stake, but the promisor is not yet prepared to make a commitment. The promisee should avoid relying on a vague promise and instead should wait for specifics. Gratuitous promises present a more complex case: it may well be that people who make gratuitous promises want some of them to be legally enforceable — we will discuss examples below — but most of them probably not, especially in the intra-family setting, where money flows between parents, children, and other relatives. Preliminary negotiations are just that: the two sides want to learn more and are not ready to commit.

One could imagine a law of contract that directed courts to enforce any "serious" promise, or any promise that the court believes the promisor intends to be legally binding. Such an approach relies on a legal standard,[1] a type of legal rule that directs courts to make an all-things-considered judgment that takes into account all relevant evidence about (in this case) the seriousness of the promise.

By contrast, under a formalistic approach, courts lay out in advance certain actions or words that people must use as signals that they want to be legally bound. The formalistic approach in the law of contract essentially identifies two kinds of formalities. The first is the evidentiary ritual: writing down the contract, signing it, attaching a seal to it, and so forth. The second is the requirement of a quid pro quo, a bargained-for consideration.[2] The two kinds of formality merge when courts require a recitation of a quid pro quo but not actual consideration. For example, an option

---

[1] See Section 2.3.

[2] See Restatement (Second) of Contracts §71 (1981):

(1) To constitute consideration, a performance or a return promise must be bargained for.

(2) A performance or return promise is bargained for if it is sought by the promisor in exchange for his promise and is given by the promisee in exchange for that promise.

(3) The performance may consist of

(a) an act other than a promise, or
(b) a forbearance, or
(c) the creation, modification, or destruction of a legal relation.

(4) The performance or return promise may be given to the promisor or to some other person. It may be given by the promisee or by some other person.

contract may be enforceable if the parties recite a consideration, even if it does not pass, or was not intended to pass.[3]

The formalistic approach assumes that the formality sufficiently, not perfectly, distinguishes promises that ought to be enforced and those that ought not be enforced. Suppose for the moment that a promise should be enforced if the promisor wants it to be enforceable at the time that he makes it. Requiring a writing or seal would be justified, then, if most promises are written down or confirmed with a seal only because the promisor wants them to be enforceable. Requiring bargained-for consideration, or its recital, would be justified if most parties intend bilateral exchanges to be legally enforceable, or would not recite that a gratuitous promise is an exchange unless they wanted it to be enforceable.

The substantive approach assumes that there are good promises and bad promises, and courts should enforce only the good promises. What does "good" mean? Reading the cases, one might conclude that courts divide promises into four types: (1) "final" commercial promises, (2) preliminary commercial promises, (3) intra-family gift promises, and (4) charitable gift promises. The consideration doctrine is the main doctrinal approach to distinguishing these types, though it is a poor fit.

Let us begin with final commercial promises. The easiest cases for enforcement are promises that are made as part of an exchange — for a performance or a return promise — at the conclusion of commercial negotiations, or in simple transactions in the absence of preliminary negotiations. The consideration doctrine permits enforcement of a promise when the promisor made the promise in order to obtain the consideration — the return performance or return promise. This is almost always the case in business: the seller promises to deliver the goods in order to obtain the buyer's money; the employer promises to pay the employee in order to obtain the employee's services.

To be sure, not too much stress is placed on the parties' actual intentions, that is, their mental states. The seller's mind could be elsewhere, or the employer might pay the employee in order to please the employee's parents; but if the transaction has the right form, that is enough.[4] If an individual nabs the suspect of a crime, he will usually be entitled to the announced award even if he was not clearly motivated by the reward.[5] Here we see substance merge into form, but in a harmless way: reciprocal intention is surely present in most of the cases; the few deviations do not justify a departure from such a simple principle. By allowing the person

---

[3] See Section 3.11.

[4] See Restatement (Second) of Contracts §81(1) (1981) ("The fact that what is bargained for does not of itself induce the making of a promise does not prevent it from being consideration for the promise.").

[5] See Section 3.8.

to claim the reward, we avoid complex inquiries into mental states in less clear cases.

I distinguish final commercial promises from preliminary commercial promises because there has in fact been some well-known litigation about the latter. Parties often make promises to each other along the way to a deal, and if the deal does not pan out, then the disappointed party might sue to enforce preliminary promises. I will talk more about this issue later,[6] but here I want to point out that if you think that courts should not enforce preliminary promises during negotiations that lead up to failed deals, then you cannot say that promises should be enforced when they are "serious" or "commercial" or "bilateral" — all of this can be true. What distinguishes the preliminary promise from the final promise is that the parties do not intend to create legal obligations in the usual case.

Next, let us consider intra-family gift promises. Courts do not enforce these promises very often, except perhaps when they create significant and reasonable reliance. They do not usually allow parties to obtain enforcement by going through the ritual of a quid pro quo.[7] Thus, the claim that the consideration doctrine is merely a formalism, intended to ensure that the promisor intended to be legally bound, is falsified. Why else would parties go through the ritual unless they had heard about the consideration doctrine, or had some vague sense of it, and the promisor wanted to assure the promisee that she could rely on the promise, even to the point of bringing a legal action if the promise is broken?

On the other hand, courts rarely explain why they object to enforcing intra-family gift promises. Moreover, they are sometimes willing to enforce them when one can make even a superficial case for the existence of an exchange, even when the consequences of doing so are quite odd. I refer to the famous case of Hamer v. Sidway,[8] where Uncle promises to give Nephew $5000 on his twenty-first birthday if he (the nephew) refrains from drinking, smoking, swearing, and gambling. The court enforces the promise because there is a quid pro quo: the uncle makes the promise to induce the nephew to refrain from engaging in certain actions — a legal detriment because the nephew has the legal right to engage in those actions.

Suppose now that Uncle repudiated the contract the day after he made it, before Nephew had dropped his vices, and Nephew sued Uncle for breach of contract. Or suppose Nephew had smoked the next day, and *Uncle* brought suit for expectation damages. Or suppose that, it turns out, Nephew was as innocent of vice as a choirboy — maybe he *was* a choirboy — and so everyone understood that the promise was a bit of a joke: Uncle simply wanted his well-behaved nephew to know that he would be rewarded on his twenty-first birthday for his exemplary behavior. If we

[6] See Section 5.2.
[7] Fischer v. Union Trust Co., 101 N.W. 852 (Mich. 1904).
[8] 27 N.E. 256 (N.Y. 1891).

111

accept the logic of the court, in all these cases there would be a valid contract, and damages would be forthcoming if one side or the other refused to keep his promise. And yet all this seems wrong. We will return to this problem when we discuss gifts and promises.[9]

Because a formality like a writing or recitation of consideration cannot transform an intra-family gift promise into an enforceable promise, one wants to resist the conclusion that formalities make any difference at all.

This view is supported by courts' treatment of charitable gift promises. When the gratuitous promise is made to an institution rather than to an individual, to a stranger rather than a family member, courts are less reluctant to enforce it. In Allegheny College v. Nat'l Chautauqua County Bank,[10] Cardozo tried to treat a charitable gift promise as a kind of contract, with an exchange — memorialization of the donor in various ways. But courts have declined to follow Cardozo. The problem is that as consideration is watered down, and interpreted to mean any benefit, real or imagined, to the promisor, all promises become enforceable, even intra-family gift promises. Courts did not want to go this far. If consideration is to be a serious requirement in contract law, however, one cannot maintain that charitable gifts that are conditioned in some way are not really gifts. Then any gift promise — for example, a promise of money to one's alma mater on the condition that the money be used to renovate the boathouse — would be considered a contract, except in those rare cases in which the money is entirely unrestricted and the donor demands no recognition in exchange.

At the same time, courts do want to enforce charitable gift promises. It is not clear why, but again we defer this question to the chapter on gifts.[11] They have given up treating these promises as contracts, and efforts to bring in promissory reliance were dropped when they realized that it would be difficult to prove that charities rely on gift promises; except in unusual cases, charities will not change their behavior in a measurable way because they expect to receive a little cash in a few years. And so charitable gift promises are enforced just because they are seen as desirable. And to distinguish those that are seriously meant from those that are more casually intended, courts sometimes reintroduce a formality: the requirement that the promise be in writing and sufficiently detailed.[12]

The consideration doctrine does not distinguish intra-family and charitable gift promises, of course, and for that reason one might wonder what it has do with the enforceability of promises. It also does a poor job in commercial contexts. Vague contracts like requirements and output contracts, and one-sided contracts like option contracts and contracts that

---

[9] See Sections 5.4 and 5.6.
[10] 159 N.E. 173 (N.Y. 1927).
[11] See Section 5.6.
[12] Congregation Kadimah Toras-Moshe v. DeLeo, 540 N.E.2d 691 (Mass. 1989).

create a third-party beneficiary, are not objectionable in principle; they have clear commercial purposes, and parties seem to like them. And yet they have from time to time been found to fall afoul of the consideration doctrine, and in the case of the option contract courts have reverted to the formalistic requirement of a recital of consideration, not actual consideration.

Or imagine a case in which an employer awards a pension to an employee upon retirement. The pension is really a promise to make a series of payments over time, and it would be unenforceable under the consideration doctrine because it is not motivated by a benefit or detriment coming from the employee. The real motivation, presumably, is to make the rest of the workforce believe that the employer will reward them if they work hard. Refusal to enforce such a promise deprives the employer of a reasonable tool for providing encouragement to its workforce, and — unless the court relies on subterfuge to justify enforcement[13] — the employer will be forced to use some other tool that might not be as effective.

So what are we to make of the consideration doctrine? As a substantive doctrine, it does not do so well. It implies that charitable gift promises should be struck down, as well as certain commercial promises such as options — yet courts usually enforce these promises when the relevant formalities are satisfied. As a formal doctrine, it implies that an intra-family gift promise would be enforceable if the parties disguised it as a transaction — yet courts do not enforce these promises except when the requirements of promissory estoppel are met.

Underlying the consideration doctrine are two concerns: ensuring that the promisor intended to become legally bound, or perhaps that the promisor was careful about conveying that impression to the promisee; and distinguishing promises that are socially valuable from those that are not. The consideration doctrine will remain ambiguous until courts resolve their thinking about both these issues. The first concern leads to a formalistic conception of the consideration doctrine, the second to a substantive conception, but there is nothing wrong with having both ideas operating as long as it is clear what they are. But it is not.

§5.2   Indefiniteness, Illusory Contracts, and Mutuality of Obligation

The person charging breach of contract must persuade the court that there was a "promise." What is a promise? In ordinary usage a promise is a commitment to do something, usually for the benefit of some other

---

[13] Langer v. Superior Steel Corp., 161 A. 571 (Pa. Super. Ct. 1932).

person. When a person makes a promise, he makes it understood that the person who is addressed, the promisee, can rely on it. The promisor will usually be blamed if he makes a promise and does not keep it.

A promise always refers to action in the future, and in this way it is like a prediction. But a promise, unlike a prediction, creates an obligation. The promise creates the expectation that the promisor will do something in the future; the prediction creates the expectation that something will happen in the future but not that the predictor is obliged to bring it about.

By creating an obligation, the promise invites reliance. Because the promisee expects certain actions to occur, and depends on the promisor's word rather than his predictive abilities, he may act in a certain way that is detrimental to himself if the promise is broken. Promises are different from vows; promises, unlike vows, invite others to rely in a certain way, in anticipation of some action from the promisor.

Promises are also different from threats. A person issues a threat by saying that he will harm someone who fails to do something. But the speaker does not obligate himself, so we do not blame him for failing to carry out the threat. A promisor needs a reason to break a promise without being blamed; a person who threatens does not need a reason in order to avoid being blamed, even if his threat was initially justified.

Promises are usually statements; that is, they usually arise as a part of speech, though they may be inexplicit and they may be couched as predictions, vows, threats, or other statements. Social context will usually resolve the ambiguity unless the speaker wants to confuse. Arguably, a promise can even be implicit in behavior. Two people who have over the years engaged in a great many trades may stop making explicit promises at some point, but it is still understood that each trade creates the same obligations that earlier trades did. One might argue about whether the "implicit promise" — for example, that the goods can be returned if they are below-average quality — should be called a promise or something else, but no one doubts that an obligation is created, and that is all that matters to a court when it must resolve a contractual dispute.

In order to make out a claim for breach of contract one must show that the other party has made a promise in the loose sense described so far. That will not be sufficient, but if there is no behavior giving rise to what in ordinary practice would be considered a promise, or at least obligation-creating behavior, the contract claim will be stillborn. But what counts as a promise in ordinary practice may not be sufficiently "promise-like" to be enforceable by a court.

Courts hold that certain promises do not create obligations because they are indefinite or, in the common doctrinal formulation, "illusory." Because they are illusory, they do not count as consideration, and thus the transaction lacks "mutuality of obligation." All of these words are quasi-synonyms. The easiest case is a statement that is not a promise at all, which a court might call "not a promise" or an "illusory promise." A person invents a recipe and sends it to a food processor, then receives a letter back that says, "We reserve the right to decide whether to use the recipe and to compensate you." The inventor consents.[14] Later, the processor uses the recipe without compensating the inventor, and the inventor sues for breach of contract. The court refuses to find a contract to be breached, because there was no promise. The food processor did not commit itself to do anything.

It is sufficient that the food processor did not make a promise — not an explicit promise and not a promise that can be inferred from its behavior, given that the food processor said explicitly that it did not consider itself bound in any way. One might argue that the court should compensate the inventor on the grounds of quantum meruit, but that is not what we are talking about here.[15] The inventor has no remedy: she should have insisted in advance that the food processor pay her a fee for her recipe. If the food processor does not want to commit itself to pay for a recipe that might not be marketable, the parties could agree in advance that the inventor gets a share of revenues rather than a flat fee.

And yet this approach is not entirely satisfactory, and it should be placed next to another approach, one that puts less weight on the degree of the promise's definiteness and instead focuses on the court's ability to determine the nature of the obligation and the correct remedy.

From this perspective the problem is not that the food processor did not commit itself; perhaps it did in some sense. Ordinary moral intuitions would, I believe, condemn the food processor if it used the recipe, made a profit, and refused to compensate the inventor in some way. Perhaps we could state the implicit promise in this way: "we promise to consider your recipe, and if we decide to use it, to give you some amount of money less than our profit on it, taking account of all costs and perhaps giving us the benefit of the doubt." A court might say that the food processor thereby obligates itself to act in "good faith" or to use "best efforts."

In Wood v. Lucy, Lady Duff-Gordon,[16] a designer of women's fashions, agreed to give Wood the exclusive right to market her fashions as long as he gave her half his profits. When the designer, Lucy, marketed her own goods in violation of the agreement, Wood sued for breach of contract. The relevant question was whether there was a contract at all. For there to be a contract, there must be promises on both sides. Lucy's promise is clear enough, but Wood seems to make an illusory promise like the one in *Davis*, the case involving the recipe. Although Wood would be obligated to pay half the profits if he decided to market Lucy's designs, he did not commit himself to market these designs.

---

[14] Cf. Davis v. Gen. Foods Co., 21 F. Supp. 445 (S.D.N.Y. 1937).

[15] The problem with the quantum meruit claim is that the plaintiff's action was gratuitous; see Section 9.2.

[16] 118 N.E. 214 (N.Y. 1917).

Like many of the promises in the cases that are grouped as illusory contracts cases, this one has a certain structure. The putative promisor says: if I do X, then I will do Y. Y may be definite, but because Y becomes obligatory only if X occurs, and X is within the discretion of the promisor, the obligation as a whole is considered illusory or indefinite. To be sure, if X occurs, *then* the illusory promise is converted into a non-illusory promise. In Obering v. Swain-Roach Lumber Co.,[17] some people (heirs to an estate whose administrator planned to auction off some land) promised to purchase the land from a timber company if that company first purchased it at the auction. The timber company's illusory promise is: if I buy at the auction (X), then I will sell to you (Y). The court held that the contract was valid at the time the dispute arose because the dispute arose after the timber company had purchased the land. X had occurred, so Y is now an obligation on the part of the timber company. But the court said that if the dispute had arisen before the purchase at the auction, there would not have been a contract, and indeed other courts have come to the same conclusion.

Consider Paul v. Rosen,[18] where a liquor store owner promised to sell the store to Buyer "conditioned upon the Buyer obtaining a new lease from" the landlord who owned the premises where the liquor store was located. Before Buyer had a chance to obtain a lease from the landlord, Seller repudiated the deal. The court held that no contract existed because of lack of mutuality. Because Buyer had the discretion to obtain a new lease, Buyer's promise to buy could not be consideration — it was not a "definite" promise. Unlike the facts of *Obering*, the initial step (X) had not been taken; if it had, then presumably Buyer's promise would have matured to the proper degree of definiteness, and Seller would have been bound.

In *Obering*, the Court rested its argument on an offer/acceptance theory. The parties had entered into what they called an "agreement," yet the court interpreted the agreement as an offer by the heirs to buy the land minus the timber if the lumber company purchases the land at auction. Offers are revocable: until the company purchases, the heirs can revoke. The offer here is an offer to enter a unilateral contract; the lumber company accepts the offer by performing an act — buying at auction. Once that act occurs, acceptance takes place, and a contract is formed. The analysis can be applied to Paul v. Rosen as well, except in that case revocation occurred before the act acceptance.

Such an analysis was not used in *Wood*. The court did not say that Lucy's agreement to pay royalties to Wood was an offer that Wood could accept by engaging in marketing (or starting to engage in marketing). If it had, Lucy would have won because Wood had not done anything. If the court had followed *Obering* and Paul v. Rosen, it would have held in favor of

---

[17] 155 N.E. 712 (Ind. Ct. App. 1927).
[18] 122 N.E.2d 603 (Ill. App. Ct. 1st Dist. 1954).

Lucy. There is no contract either because there was no acceptance or because Wood had made an illusory promise and had not yet satisfied the contingency X at the time that he sued Lucy for breach of contract. Judge Cardozo, however, found that a contract existed because Wood had implicitly promised to use best efforts to market the goods. Thus, we have a two-sided deal: Lucy promises not to market her own goods, and Wood promises to use best efforts to market her goods, then give her half the profits. Wood can get his remedy against Lucy.

But if Cardozo's decision is correct, we can transform the *Davis* "agreement," such as it is, and the *Obering* and *Paul* deals into valid contracts at the X stage. The food processor has an obligation to use best efforts to use the recipe; the timber company has an obligation to use best efforts to buy the land at auction; the buyer has an obligation to use best efforts to secure a lease.

Yet this does not seem right, and the reason is that, as Cardozo says, the marketing contract is "instinct with obligation" while the recipe deal is not; it is not even a deal. We are back to the question of how a court decides whether the parties intended to submit to legal adjudication of disputes, or — if you want — to create an obligation, whether legal or not, on the part of one party for the benefit of the other. The food company is constantly pestered by amateur chefs hawking their recipes for grilled marmot and stewed octopus and does not want to devote resources toward tracking their use, negotiating with the senders, and awarding compensation. And even if the parties in *Wood* sought to enter a valid contract, it is possible that they wanted to impose a legally enforceable obligation only on Lucy and not on Wood. To see why, observe that Wood has a strong incentive to market Lucy's goods even if he has no contractual obligation to do so. The reason is that Wood's compensation under the contract depends on successful marketing efforts: the more he markets, the higher his compensation. There is no such incentive for Lucy: she may gain more by breaching the contract and selling her products on her own than by complying with it and giving a share to Wood.

But even if the contract did not have built-in incentives for Wood to act, the court probably would have held the same way — today, at least, that would be standard practice. In Omni Group v. Seattle-First National Bank,[19] for example, Buyer's obligation to purchase property was made conditional on Buyer obtaining a satisfactory feasibility report (regarding whether the property could be developed as planned). Seller, who wished to escape the contract, argued that Buyer's promise was illusory because Buyer could simply not request the feasibility study or could deem unsatisfactory any feasibility study that Buyer received. However, the court held that the promise was not illusory because Buyer had to seek a feasibility

---

[19] 645 P.2d 727 (Wash. Ct. App. 1st Div. 1982).

study in good faith, and could reject it only if in fact the study was unsatisfactory. One might wonder how much of a constraint these clauses really represent. Can't Buyer always say that a study is unsatisfactory? But it is imaginable that a jury could hold that Buyer did not try hard enough to obtain a study in the first place (suppose Buyer did not try to hire anyone to perform the study) or that its rejection of the study was unreasonable (experts testify that the study showed the development was feasible) or in bad faith (Buyer's officers come across as liars on the stand).

Accordingly, we should keep in mind four categories: (1) deals or transactions that are not legally binding, (2) deals that are legally binding on only one party, (3) deals that are legally binding on both parties only after a certain event occurs, and (4) deals that are legally binding on both parties from the start. *Davis* fits in category (1). *Obering* and *Paul* fit category (3). *Wood* hovers between (3), (2), and (4). It fits (3) in the sense that Lucy's obligation is conditional on Wood's actions, but it fits (2) in the sense that the relevant act by Wood could be doing nothing. Well, Wood has to engage in best efforts — which sounds strenuous — but his best efforts could produce nothing in the form of evidence. But Wood could also fall into category (4) in the sense that Wood, like Lucy, has a legal obligation from the start — to engage in best efforts — though nothing is said in the contract about it.

Does Wood really have a legal obligation? We could imagine a future case in which the Lucy character respects the exclusivity provision and sues the Wood character for not engaging in best efforts. Suppose, for example, Lucy could prove that Wood never even tried to market her products. Wood testifies that he did not try to market her products because fashions had changed and, in his opinion, customers would not be interested in Lucy's styles. A court might very well agree. As noted before, one might believe that the contract, by making Wood's compensation a function of sales, gives him sufficient incentive to act even though he has no legal obligation. Here, the "best efforts" or "good faith" idea fills in for the consideration doctrine without actually creating a meaningful obligation.

But more likely, a court would be willing to hold Wood liable for insufficient efforts. We can see this happening in later cases. For example, in Feld v. Henry S. Levy & Sons,[20] Buyer (a baker) and Seller (a bread maker) entered an output contract under which Buyer agreed to buy all of the bread crumbs produced by Seller. Seller later dismantled the machinery it used to make bread crumbs to use the space for other purposes. Buyer sued, arguing that Seller breached the contract to sell its output. Seller replied with the seemingly reasonable defense that it did sell Buyer all its output — it's just that its output was zero. The court would have none of

---

[20] 335 N.E.2d 320 (N.Y. 1975).

that, and found Seller in breach, arguing that Seller did not act in good faith.

What is the good faith output of bread crumbs? The court drew a line at bankruptcy or "genuine imperiling of the very existence of [the] entire business."[21] But why draw the line there? The contract price was 6 cents per pound. Let us suppose that, at the time of contracting, the cost of production was 5 cents per pound. The cost of production can fluctuate, of course, and we can imagine Seller becoming more and more reluctant to sell as the cost rises above 6 cents. At some point (10 cents? 20 cents? 7 cents?), Seller will be driven into bankruptcy. The idea of good faith does not help much because Seller's motive for ending production would always be the same: to save costs and maximize profits. We might think that the hypothetical contract would draw the line at bankruptcy, but it could just as easily draw the line at the point where Seller begins to lose money, or draw no line at all (if the risk of bankruptcy is remote enough, Seller might be willing to take it in return for a price premium). Whatever one thinks of the case, the bottom line is that it shows that courts will treat indefinite promises as having limits, so that both sides of the contract have obligations.

Still, courts do not always decide that promises are definite; there is such a thing as a promise that is too indefinite. In Sun Printing & Publishing v. Remington Paper & Power,[22] the contract provided for the sale of paper, to be shipped monthly from September 1919 to December 1920. The price was fixed only until the end of 1919; for 1920, the parties were to negotiate a price no higher than that charged by the Canadian Export Paper Co. to its large customers. Seller sought to get out of the contract starting in 1920, arguing that it was "imperfect." Buyer argued that the contract was enforceable at the Canadian Export Paper rate. But the court held that it could not enforce the contract because the parties did not agree on the time period for the price. The Canadian Export Paper price could be one level for a year-long contract and another level for a monthly contract, and this was not specified.

The opinion is different in spirit from that of *Feld*. In *Feld*, the court bent over backward to find an enforceable term; in Sun Printing, the court bent over backward not to find an enforceable term. As the dissent pointed out, it would be easy enough to choose the monthly rate, given that the delivery was on a monthly basis. In any event, it will always be difficult to draw lines between definite and indefinite promises.

It is worth pointing out that the author of the majority opinion, Judge Cardozo, also wrote the opinion in Wood v. Lucy, Lady Duff-Gordon. In Wood, he was willing to hold that a contract existed because he used the implied good faith term to convert Wood's non-commitment into a promise. Why wouldn't he also have implied a good faith term in *Sun*? One

---

[21] Id. at 323.
[22] 139 N.E. 470 (N.Y. 1923).

answer is that Judge Cardozo had no problem with one-sided contracts, but otherwise insisted that parties be precise if they want obligations to be judicially enforceable. These positions are not inconsistent. The implied term of good faith is just a fiction that takes the place of consideration and does not itself create obligations.

A final example is Empro v. Ball-Co,[23] a case involving the sale of an entire business (Ball-Co). The case illustrates a common problem in contract law: two parties negotiate for a while, expecting to reach a deal, but only make a preliminary agreement, and then a dispute erupts. Is the preliminary agreement enforceable as a contract, or is it meant not to be legally enforceable? Representatives of the two companies wrote out an agreement, which they titled "Letter of Intent." The agreement provided many of the details of the transaction, including the nature of Ball-Co's assets and the price to be paid. These details all suggested a contract. But the phrase "letter of intent" is usually used to refer to an agreement that is not meant to be enforceable. And other language in the contract suggested some escape hatches. Most important, one clause provided that Empro's commitment was subject to approval of its shareholders and board of directors. The parties had also not resolved disagreement over whether Ball-Co would receive a security interest in the real estate.

As in *Wood*, the party without the escape hatch argued that the contract was not enforceable because the other party's promise was indefinite. Here, Ball-Co argued that the contract was indefinite because it was subject to approval by Empro's shareholders (and because of some other ambiguities and reservations). The court agreed. Unlike in *Feld*, the court was unwilling to argue that Empro was in fact bound by a good faith term, and therefore that the contract was not indefinite. The court sought to preserve the ability of parties negotiating complex deals to make preliminary promises that lay the groundwork for a final agreement without creating independent legal obligations.

§5.3   Promissory Estoppel

Promissory estoppel is an alternative route for enforcing a promise, used primarily when the conditions for an ordinary contract claim fail.[24]

---

[23] 870 F.2d 423 (7th Cir. 1989).

[24] See Restatement (Second) of Contracts §90 (1981):

(1) A promise which the promisor should reasonably expect to induce action or forbearance on the part of the promisee or a third person and which does induce such action or forbearance is binding if injustice can be avoided only by enforcement of the promise. The remedy granted for breach may be limited as justice requires.

(2) A charitable subscription or a marriage settlement is binding under Subsection (1) without proof that the promise induced action or forbearance.

If a promise is unenforceable on the contract theory because consideration is lacking, because the promise is insufficiently definite, because a writing is absent, or because of a similar problem, the promisee may argue that she nonetheless has a claim in promissory estoppel. Promissory estoppel remains a second banana because the promisee must prove, among other things, that he reasonably relied on the promise. By contrast, if a contract is valid, and the promisor breached, the promisee is entitled to expectation damages or another remedy regardless of whether she relied. The evidentiary burden for a breach of contract claim is less than the evidentiary burden for a promissory estoppel claim.

The main element of promissory estoppel is reasonable reliance. There are other things — the to-all-appearances meaningless requirement that enforcement of the promise be necessary to avoid injustice, for example — but reasonable reliance is the most important. It is also puzzling. As many scholars have noticed, justifying a legal claim on the basis of reliance appears to be circular. If reliance is reasonable, then the law should enforce the promise; but if the law enforces the promise, then reliance must be reasonable. (Contract law professors like to trap students in this circularity — it is an important element of their nonpecuniary compensation — so watch out!) But we can break out of this superficial circularity. To see how, imagine that Seller promises to install a machine on Tuesday. Buyer relies by shifting employees away from their ordinary workstations. Seller breaks its promise. Buyer can recover in promissory estoppel if the reliance was reasonable. Was it?

We can imagine a case in which Buyer relies too much. Suppose that Buyer did not need to move its employees to other workstations; this was unnecessary simply because installation of the machine would not have interfered with their ordinary work. Then presumably the promissory estoppel claim would fail. Suppose instead that the installation would have been worth a lot less to Buyer if it had occurred and Buyer had not moved his employees. The installation did interfere with their work, but less so if they were moved first. Then we might conclude that reliance was reasonable.

A numerical illustration might be helpful. In the table below, the first column shows how much money Buyer invests in anticipation of performance, from 0 to 100. The second column shows the value of performance as a function of investment. Note that the value of performance increases but at a decreasing rate. (The first 50 yields an increase in value of 100; the second 50 yields an increase in value of 50.) This is a typical pattern. Imagine that you want to sell your house. You can probably increase the sale price by painting the walls, fixing some broken door knobs, and so on, but as you look for more places to spend money, you will eventually be able to think only of improvements that are expensive and will increase the value only a little bit (for example, replacing slightly used floors). In the numerical example, the optimal investment is 50 because it generates a net benefit of 150 — the value of performance (200) minus the investment (50). By contrast, the net benefit of an investment of 100 is only 50.

Investment	Value of Performance	Net
0	100	100
50	200	150
100	150	50

It is possible, then, to identify the theoretically optimal investment for any contract; in a perfect world, courts would protect just that much reliance — by, for example, giving the promisee damages if and only if she engages in the optimal investment. If courts can do this, even roughly, promissory estoppel makes sense as a doctrine. But it may be doubtful that courts can reliably determine the optimal investment in any given contractual setting.

Enthusiasm over promissory estoppel among scholars is less pronounced today than it used to be. At one time, it was seen as a repudiation of the wooden rules of the consideration doctrine, as an effort to get at what really matters — the cost of reliance. But the consideration doctrine does protect reliance — as long as there was a formal offer and acceptance and a quid pro quo. The victim of breach obtains expectation damages, which will cover her reliance costs in normal cases. The real difference between the doctrines is that the promissory estoppel doctrine is more akin to a standard, while the consideration doctrine is closer to a rule. Under the promissory estoppel doctrine, courts can take into consideration more relevant factors — chiefly, again, the degree of reliance, plus perhaps the culpability on the side of the promisor in possibly making careless promises or representations — which is what distinguishes a standard from a rule. In cases like Goodman v. Dicker[25] and Hoffman v. Red Owl,[26] the promisor — franchisors in both cases — made a number of vague promises to the promisees that if they did certain things, they would eventually be granted a franchise. Both promisees incurred various expenses as a result. The franchisors did not make "offers" because the terms were never clearly spelled out. So the promisees could not accept, and there could not be a contract. To protect their reliance costs, the courts held that they reasonably relied on the promises.

---

[25] 169 F.2d 684 (D.C. Cir. 1948).
[26] 133 N.W.2d 267 (Wis. 1965).

§5.4   Promises for Benefits Received

Another category of cases is minor but receives inordinate attention in casebooks. These cases involve a promise that lacks consideration but is made in response to a benefit received. In Mills v. Wyman,[27] the father of a man who was helped by a Good Samaritan promised to pay the Good Samaritan's expenses after the help was rendered, then changed his mind. In Webb v. McGowan,[28] an employer promised to make payments to an employee for the rest of the employee's life after the employee saved the employer's life but was badly injured in the process and disabled from further work. The employer died and his estate refused to continue the payments.

The court in *Mills* refused to enforce the promise. The promise was not supported by bargained-for consideration: the father did not receive anything in return for his promise, given that the help was rendered before he made the promise.[29] The court in *Webb* came to the opposite decision for reasons that are not clear. To be sure, someone who confers a benefit is entitled to restitution unless he is a volunteer. The classic example is the doctor who helps an unconscious person and then demands his fee. If the patient promises to pay, the doctor is entitled to enforce that promise in court. This is a case of a promise for a past benefit being enforced (sometimes misleadingly called "past consideration"). But the doctor could obtain payment even if the patient did not make a promise, simply by suing for restitution.[30] So the promise does not do any legal work. In *Mills* and *Webb*, a court would not normally permit restitution because the benefactor is a volunteer. As noted above, there is no reason why the existence of a promise (in Webb) should change this outcome.

From the standpoint of policy, it may well make sense to enforce promises for past benefits. There are three well-established exceptions to the rule against past consideration: a promise to pay a debt that has been discharged in bankruptcy, a debt for which the statute of limitations has run, and a debt incurred during infancy. It is easy to see how these exceptions emerged. In an earlier era, business people would sometimes default on their debts, and then later try to enter business again. In order to persuade creditors to lend to them, such debtors need to reestablish a reputation for paying debts. They can do this by paying off the old debts even though they are not legally enforceable because the statute of limitations has run; if they do not have cash, however, the best they can do is promise to pay them off. By making those promises legally enforceable, the law gives

---

[27] 20 Mass. 207 (Mass. 1825).

[28] 168 So. 196 (Ala. Ct. App. 1935).

[29] Nor could the Good Samaritan have prevailed on a promissory estoppel claim. Because the promise came after the performance, the promisee could not have relied on it.

[30] See Section 8.8.

those debtors a mechanism for committing themselves to pay cash and hence reestablish their reputation.

Does this logic extend to *Mills* and *Webb*? Not really. The promises in those cases seem to have no purpose other than to convey wealth from one person to another. If courts believe there is no public policy reason to enforce ordinary gift promises, then they should not enforce this type either.

§5.5   Statute of Frauds

The Statute of Frauds provides that certain kinds of contracts are enforceable only if they are in writing, unless certain exceptions are met.[31] The most important contracts that must be in writing are contracts transferring interests in real property, service contracts that cannot be performed within one year, and sales of goods worth more than $500. The most important exception is the partial performance exception, according to which a promise is enforceable, even if not in writing, if the promisee has partly (or fully) performed her side of the bargain prior to breach. Note that parties may be able to evade the Statute of Frauds by pleading promissory estoppel[32] or by converting their contract claim into a tort claim (e.g., for fraud).

The original purpose of the Statute of Frauds was to prevent a certain kind of fraud. Suppose a stranger goes to a court and claims that I promised to buy pork belly options from him at a price that has since become highly favorable to him, and that I have breached my promise. The stranger persuades several friends to (fraudulently) testify that I made the promise; I cannot find anyone who can testify that I did not. (I would need someone who had observed me continuously, I suppose.) The Statute of Frauds discourages this kind of fraud by requiring the stranger to produce a document that I have signed. To be sure, the stranger and his friends could forge such a document, but forgery is a riskier proposition than perjury (I guess).

---

[31] See Restatement (Second) of Contracts §131 (1981):

> Unless additional requirements are prescribed by the particular statute, a contract within the Statute of Frauds is enforceable if it is evidenced by any writing, signed by or on behalf of the party to be charged, which
> (a) reasonably identifies the subject matter of the contract,
> (b) is sufficient to indicate that a contract with respect thereto has been made between the parties or offered by the signer to the other party, and
> (c) states with reasonable certainty the essential terms of the unperformed promises in the contract.

[32] See Riley v. Capital Airlines, Inc., 185 F. Supp. 165 (S.D. Ala. 1960) (determining that Riley is entitled to reliance damages even though the contract in dispute is void under the Statute of Frauds).

In solving one problem, however, the Statute of Frauds creates another. Sophisticated Seller promises to deliver widgets to unsophisticated Buyer at $10 each, one month hence. Seller insists on an oral contract. If the price declines in the meantime, Buyer — believing himself bound to the contract — will pay, but if the price declines, Seller breaches and hides behind the Statute of Frauds. Or both parties might be unsophisticated, neglect to use a writing; then after events change, one party hires a lawyer to get him out of the contract and the lawyer discovers the violation of the Statute of Frauds. The lesson is that formalities like the Statute of Frauds have to be costly enough, or extraordinary enough, that by conforming to them parties reveal their intention to be bound — but not so costly or strange that parties neglect to conform to them when they intend to be bound.[33] To avoid the bad results, courts cut back on formalities (as with the partial performance rule[34]), but in the process weaken the formality's capacity to deter fraud.

§5.6 Gifts

As we noted above, courts seem hostile to, or at least ambivalent about, contracts to give gifts. Contracts involving promises to perform ordinary commercial exchanges are presumptively enforceable. Gift promises are not always enforceable; even when they are, courts throw up hurdles. As we have seen, gift promises between family members are not enforced, even though contracts between family members are enforced. Charitable gift promises are frequently enforceable, but courts often demand formalities (such as writings) that are not required for the enforcement of commercial contracts.

What accounts for the special treatment of gift promises? We saw before that courts might believe that gift promises are less seriously given, or more susceptible to fraud, than ordinary promises are. These are concerns about process, and ought to be curable. In some countries, gift promises are enforceable as long as they are notarized. (Notarization in those countries is a more involved process than it is in the United States.) Yet American law goes further: A parent cannot make an enforceable gift promise to a child. The parent could set up a trust but would have to have assets on

---

[33] See Section 2.3.

[34] This rule provides that if the promisee partly performs, then he can enforce a contract even though it is not in writing and is covered by the Statute of Frauds. If the promisor observed partial performance by the promisee and did not try to stop it, that provides evidence that the promisor himself believed that the parties had a contract, in which case the promisor's claim that a contract exists is not fraudulent.

125

hand to put in the trust; the parent couldn't make an enforceable promise to pay out of assets acquired in the future.

This rule is puzzling since it is clear that reliance can be value-enhancing for the promisor and promisee of a gift just as it is for the promisor and promisee in a commercial exchange. Grandfather wants his granddaughter to stop working. She won't unless she has a guaranteed source of income; otherwise, she might not be able to regain her position if the flow of funds is turned off.[35] If he can make a legally enforceable gift promise, he can achieve his end. If he cannot make such a promise, his goal is frustrated.

One sometimes hears that a gift promise is "sterile" — that it has no social utility. Recall that a contractual exchange produces value $v - c$: Buyer gains v, at a cost, c, to Seller. Now consider a gift of \$100 from Donor to Recipient. Recipient gains \$100 while Donor loses \$100, so it is a wash.

However, this argument does not bear scrutiny. If Recipient is poor and Donor is rich, Recipient will value the \$100 more than the Donor does, so the transfer enhances social welfare. This is even more clear with objects: Donor gives away an old television set to Recipient, who doesn't have one. There is nothing sterile or objectionable about gift giving, and so the legal skepticism about it remains puzzling.

Some economists claim that gift giving is objectionable because the recipient almost always prefers cash to goods.[36] If your uncle gives you a paisley scarf that costs \$50, you probably would prefer the \$50 in cash so you could buy something you really want. Even if the paisley scarf is at the top of your wish list, it couldn't be worth more than \$50 to you. So the uncle can do no better, and will probably do worse, by giving you the scarf rather than the cash. This creates a deadweight loss, which could be eliminated if people would only give each other cash rather than goods. Where gift giving is reciprocal, one could just make bookkeeping entries. For example, if I give my wife \$100 and she gives me \$150, then we just agree that she owes me \$50 — and perhaps we will abandon the whole pointless exercise if we have a joint checking account.

There is a lot that is wrong with this thinking. People give gifts to each other for various reasons, not always just to transfer wealth. But for our purposes, this theory does not explain the law. After all, the law does not treat cash gifts better than non-cash gifts. And the law allows people to make gratuitous transfers, which are treated the same as transfers that are made as part of an exchange. If you hand \$100 to someone, the property interest in the cash is conveyed, and you can't get it back. It doesn't matter whether you hand the cash over in order to obtain goods in return

---

[35] Ricketts v. Scothorn, 77 N.W. 365 (Neb. 1898). Unusually, in this case the court enforced the promise.

[36] Joel Waldfogel, Scroogenomics: Why You Shouldn't Buy Presents for the Holidays (2009).

or not. The puzzle is that while gratuitous transfers are treated the same as transfers that are part of an exchange, gratuitous promises are given less protection than promises that are part of an exchange.

§5.7 Summary

We have followed the convention of casebooks and treated the rules governing "which promises are enforced" as a separate module in contract law. But these rules could just as accurately be treated as contract formation rules. Recall that contract formation rules attempt to ensure that the parties consented to the contract. The consideration doctrine can similarly be understood as a formality that distinguishes contracts to which promisors normally consent (those involving a quid pro quo) from those to which promisors normally do not consent, at least in the sense of agreeing to be legally bound (those that are gratuitous). But the rules can also be understood in a more substantive sense, as reflecting a public policy against enforcing certain types of promises.

Chapter *6*

Contract Interpretation

§6.1   In General

Suppose X sends a note to Y saying, "I'll meet you at the corner of Fourth and Pine at 8." We can distinguish two ways of interpreting this statement. The *subjective meaning* consists of the information that X intended to convey to Y. The *objective meaning* consists of how a "reasonable person" (to be defined later) would interpret this statement. For example, suppose X's note is a response to an earlier suggestion from Y that they meet for breakfast. The objective meaning is that they will meet at 8 *A.M.* However, it is possible, especially if X is absent-minded or peculiar, that X really intended 8 *P.M.* We can argue endlessly about what the real meaning of the statement is. For our purposes, it is sufficient to stipulate that the meaning is X's intention. After all, when deciding when to meet X, Y cares about what X intends, not what the reasonable person would interpret the statement to mean. So if Y knows that X is absent-minded, and also that X does not like getting up early, he could divine X's meaning. The objective meaning matters too, however. We are likely to be irritated with X even if X can prove her real meaning, because we think X should have known how her statement was likely to be interpreted, and taken more care to avoid confusion.

Consider now Seller's promise to deliver a batch of chickens next Thursday in return for $100.[1] Thursday arrives, and Buyer rejects the delivery, arguing that the chickens are substandard. Buyer says that the chicken that were delivered were old and scraggly, suitable only for stews, whereas Buyer expected "broilers," which are young and juicy chickens. Seller has two strategies: to argue that the chickens comply with the contract, in which case Seller seeks enforcement of the contract, accuses Buyer of breach, and asks for expectation damages; or to argue that the parties never reached agreement, in which case Seller seeks rescission of the contract and does not ask for damages. Both of these strategies can be interpreted "subjectively" or "objectively," though little turns on this distinction, as we will see.

To argue that Buyer has breached the contract, Seller must persuade the court that "chickens" means stewing chickens, or generally means *either* stewing chickens *or* broilers (that is, Seller has the choice). From the subjective perspective, Seller must show the court that Seller and Buyer understood "chickens" in this way; that is, both believed at the time of contract that Seller would deliver stewing chickens or had the right to deliver broilers or stewing chickens. From the objective perspective, Seller must show the court that a "reasonable person" — the poultry trade — interprets "chickens" in this way.

To argue that no contract exists, Seller must persuade the court that, in essence, the word "chickens" is ambiguous. From the subjective perspective, Seller must show that she meant stewing chickens and Buyer meant broilers. From the objective perspective, Seller must show that a reasonable person would simply not know whether a person using the word "chickens" was referring to broilers or stewing chickens, or both. There are also cases in which a party argues that he meant the contract as a joke — that he never intended to enter it in the first place, and the other party should have understood this.

At one time, commentators and judges believed that the choice between the objective theory and the subjective theory mattered. The subjective theory seems to imply that the court defers to the wishes of the parties, and it will not intervene and coerce someone to pay damages or perform unless that person has volunteered to be subjected to such coercion, by freely entering a contract at an earlier time. The objective theory seems to imply that the court does not care much about what the parties intended to do, and will hold them against their will — to some community standard of reasonableness. To some the objective theory stinks of coercion, while the subjective theory seems to submit courts to the non-coercive role of carrying through the intentions of parties.

---

[1] This example is based on Frigaliment Imp. Co. v. B.N.S. Int'l Sales Corp., 190 F. Supp. 116 (S.D.N.Y. 1960).

In truth, judicial enforcement of contract is a complex mixture of coercion and non-coercion. On the one hand, the parties intend certain outcomes — Seller will deliver, Buyer will pay — and courts generally respect their agreement. On the other hand, the parties cannot render their intentions perfectly transparent. Words have multiple meanings, and any transaction potentially involves an indefinitely large number of contingencies that the parties cannot anticipate or reach agreement on. By devoting a great deal of time and effort, the parties can narrow the range of meanings that a contract might be subject to, but they will stop at the point of diminishing returns.

Seller and Buyer might not realize that "chicken" has a certain trade usage; or they might realize that "chicken" could have many meanings, but not have enough time to discuss all the possible meanings and nail down a precise specification in this particular contract. Inevitably, then, parties use words in their contracts that are susceptible to multiple interpretations; they "voluntarily" use these words, knowing that a court will have to assign meanings to them, and meanings the parties might not have intended. Consequently, when the court enforces its interpretation of the contract, it might end up coercing a party, in the sense of requiring it to act in a way that it never agreed to.

So what do courts do? On my reading of the cases, they do the following. First, they try to determine what each party intended, if their intentions are likely to encompass the contingency that gave rise to the dispute. If Seller and Buyer meant the same thing by "chicken," and this can be proved, then their meaning prevails over some "objective" meaning — the meaning held by the "average" third party. However, if the delivery of a stewing chicken was due to, say, an unexpected pestilence that affected only broilers, and the parties did not anticipate this pestilence, then the court cannot resolve the dispute by appealing to the parties' intentions, and must use some other doctrinal device — maybe the impossibility doctrine, which we will discuss later.[2] How does the court determine what the parties' intentions were? Aren't these invisible, no longer accessible? This requires evidence, of course; there might be the statements from witnesses, memos, and — here the objective theory reappears, though domesticated somewhat — testimony about trade customs and conventional usages, on the assumption that, in the absence of evidence to the contrary, people in the trade use terms in the same way. Usually dictionary definitions and trade usages are so powerful that we simply do not believe that the parties attached to their terms the peculiar meanings they insist on during litigation; that is probably why courts and scholars often say that the objective theory has prevailed over the subjective theory.

---

[2] See Section 7.5.

If Seller and Buyer did not mean the same thing by "chicken" — that is, the evidence proves that the parties assigned different meanings to the word — then the court must enforce one meaning or the other, or rescind the contract. Often, one party is in a better position to anticipate and correct a misapprehension by the other or, what roughly amounts to the same thing, one party uses language carelessly — that is, speaks imprecisely even though precision would require little additional effort. Courts will use the meaning of the careful party if the other party is careless. If both parties are careful and nevertheless use different meanings, or if both parties are careless, the court might rescind the contract, letting the loss lie where it falls.[3]

	Buyer is careful	Buyer is careless
Seller is careful	Contract is rescinded	Seller's meaning enforced
Seller is careless	Buyer's meaning enforced	Contract is rescinded

This doctrine should remind you of tort law. Imagine two drivers crashing their cars together. If both drivers are careless or both are careful, courts will not attempt to transfer value from one driver to the other: the losses lie where they fall. Similarly, if contracting parties are both careful or both careless, courts will refuse to enforce the contract. Although either party is entitled to restitution, so long as there is reliance there is a loss, and that loss will be absorbed by whichever party incurred it (generally speaking). To continue with the analogy, if only one driver is careless, that driver either will not recover damages or will have to pay damages to the other. If one of the contracting parties is careless, the other party's meaning will prevail. The doctrine we have been discussing gives parties the incentives to draft their contracts with precision.

It should not be surprising that tort principles govern these circumstances. Though technically a contract issue, the parties meet as strangers — much as two drivers do — and can injure each other through careless language.

§6.2   Mutual Assent Revisited

Section 3.1 introduced the concept of mutual assent, and noted that its implication that people must fully agree — that they enjoy a "meeting of the minds" — is inaccurate. Contract law does give people the tools to

---

[3] See Section 4.1.

enter voluntary cooperative arrangements. But one can find oneself bound to a contract against one's will. Some examples follow.

- A person who speaks carelessly, or even carefully but contrary to linguistic or trade conventions, can be held to have made an offer, or to have accepted an offer, even though he did not intend to do so. The employer who says to an employee, "Get your men out" might not have intended to make or accept an offer, but the court says that a reasonable person would interpret his statement in that way, and the court does not pay attention to the employer's disavowal of any such intention.[4] The person who makes an offer as a joke also can find himself bound against his intention, if the joke would not be apparent to a reasonable person.

- It also seems clear that courts sometimes bind individuals who do not make formal offers, and do not intend to make formal offers, but make statements intended to dupe unsophisticated people. The advertisement with fine print or confusing language, designed to lure consumers to the store, might be converted into an offer by a court, with the result that the seller is bound to a contract he never intended to enter.[5]

- An offeror who revokes his offer no longer intends to enter a contract, and in normal cases the person who received the offer cannot bind the offeror by purporting to accept. But if the revocation occurs after the offeree has put his acceptance in the mail, the offeror can be bound to a contract, against his will.[6]

- A person who makes a firm offer can end up being bound to a contract against his will. If he changes his mind and attempts to revoke, the law stops him, and the offeree can accept an offer that is no longer intended.

- One can be found to have accepted an offer, even though one has not intended to enter a contract, just because one's behavior conforms to the offer's terms or because one has accepted an offer silently before.[7] Technically, an intention to accept is required. In practice, courts read an intention into behavior even though the behavior is consistent with lack of intention. In Russell v. Board of County Commissioners, for example, the offeree's trespass on the offeror's property was deemed to be an acceptance of an offer that said it could be

[4] See, e.g., Embry v. Hargadine, McKittrick Dry Goods Co., 105 S.W. 777 (Mo. App. Ct. 1907).

[5] See, e.g., Lefkowitz v. Great Minneapolis Surplus Store, Inc., 86 N.W.2d 689 (Minn. 1957); Carlill v. Carbolic Smoke Ball Co., 1 Q.B. 256 (Cal. 1892).

[6] See, e.g., Adams v. Lindsell, 1 B & Ald 681 (K.B. 1818).

[7] Smith-Scharff Paper Co. v. P.N. Hirsch & Co., 754 S.W.2d 928 (Mo. App. Ct. 1988); see also Hobbs v. Massasoit Whip Co., 33 N.E. 495 (Mass. 1893).

accepted by continued trespass.[8] The offeree clearly intended to trespass, but did not clearly intend to accept the offer *by* trespassing.

In sum, the respective intentions of the offeror and the offeree don't necessarily control whether the law finds that an offer and acceptance exist, thus creating a contract. Again, I want to stress that this does not mean that intention is not relevant; it clearly is. But intention is not controlling, and so the statement that mutual assent — or a meeting of the minds — is a necessary condition for the finding of a contract is false.

§6.3   Hypothetical Bargain

Courts take two approaches to interpretation. In what I call the ordinary-language approach, the court interprets the disputed terms in the same way that an ordinary person interprets any ordinary statement. Our usual bag of interpretive tools, the ones we use every day as we negotiate signs, instructions, and other texts, are used by the courts to interpret contract terms. It is very hard to generalize about this process, but a few words may be helpful. When we interpret texts, we approach them with a number of assumptions. We assume that words are used consistently; that they are used in their ordinary sense rather than in esoteric ways, but that their ordinary sense is a matter of context and convention; that every word or statement has a purpose and redundancies have been avoided; that text written with care is more important than text that is written carelessly; and so on. All of these assumptions are subject to revision for good reason; for example, we might take more seriously terms of art used by professionals than the same terms used by amateurs. The ordinary-language approach sometimes tends toward literalism, because even in ordinary language we use words with more care — defining them, using them more consistently, choosing clear words over ambiguous words — when we seek to make our intentions clear, such as when we give instructions; then a literal interpretation is more appropriate than in other contexts.

According to the hypothetical bargain approach, the court interprets the contract by asking, "what would the parties have said if they had anticipated this dispute?" This approach, like the ordinary-language approach, relies on the tools of interpretation but goes a step further, requiring the court to reconstruct the reasoning process used by the parties. The hypothetical bargain — what the parties would have wanted — might be understood as the purpose of the contract, and a reasonable guide to the purpose

---

[8] Russell v. Bd. of County Comm'rs, 952 P.2d 492 (Okla. 1997).

of a contract will be those terms that minimize the joint cost (or maximize the joint value) of the contract. This leads to a subsidiary principle: the responsibility for a contingency should fall on the shoulders of the party that could more cheaply have anticipated and avoided it — that is, the "cheaper cost-avoider." The idea is that if the parties had anticipated a contingency and drafted a term to cover it, that term would have made the cheaper cost-avoider liable in case that contingency occurs. They would have done this because the efficient allocation of risk generates value, which can then be divided by the parties.

For example, suppose that Seller agrees to sell a widget to Buyer for $100, which Buyer pays in advance. The widget is destroyed during delivery, and the contract omits a term assigning the risk of loss. Buyer sues Seller for damages and argues that because the widget never arrived, Seller has breached the contract. Seller responds that she discharged her contractual obligations by handing the widget over to the delivery service (which we will assume is not contractually obligated to supply insurance against the loss).

The hypothetical bargain approach asks how the parties would have allocated the risk if they had anticipated it. Imagine that Seller regularly makes deliveries and thus has experience with different carriers and is in a better position than Buyer to evaluate them. We can assign some numbers for illustrative purposes. It would have cost Seller $10 to find a low-risk carrier, while it would have cost Buyer $20 to find such a carrier. Since Seller can find the low-risk carrier more cheaply, she should be held liable for the loss.

The parties would have ("hypothetically") made such an assignment of risk in order to minimize their joint costs. Seller would have passed on the cost to Buyer, so in the end this allocation means that Buyer pays Seller $10 to find the best carrier rather than pay $20 to find the carrier himself. If in this particular contract, the price did not reflect this allocation of risk, a rule that puts the risk on the cheaper cost-avoider will reduce the cost of future contracts. Parties will know that the low-cost agent will bear the risk of loss, and thus they do not need to go to the trouble of agreeing on risk allocation and writing it into the contract in advance, which saves transaction costs.

It should be emphasized that courts rarely discuss their interpretive methods, and indeed that one court might switch back and forth between the ordinary-language and hypothetical bargain approaches. But it is clear that courts are sometimes more aggressive and sometimes less aggressive in their interpretations, insofar as they rely on their judgment about the purpose of the contract rather than defer to the (oral or written) text of the contract; the hypothetical bargain idea captures their more aggressive mood, and the ordinary-language idea captures their less aggressive mood. Most readers will notice the parallel to statutory interpretation, where the less aggressive approach is known as textualism and the more aggressive approach relies more on divining the purpose of the legislature with the help of legislative history.

Courts and scholars often talk as though contract interpretation is not an issue unless there is a "gap" in a contract; otherwise, the court should simply follow the terms of the contract. This is a misleading way of thinking about this subject.[9] To see why, start by observing that the term "gap" is used to refer to the failure of a contract to contain a term that clearly governs the contingency that produced the legal dispute. The contract does not say whether Seller or Buyer bears the risk of loss during transit. The train derails, the goods are destroyed. Now, Seller will argue that there is a gap in the contract — it does not say what happens if the goods are destroyed — and Seller will further argue that the gap should be filled with an "implicit" term putting the risk of loss on Buyer or perhaps dividing it up, depending (say) on the custom of the industry. Buyer, by contrast, will not concede that there is a gap, but will argue that the contract is "complete" (that is, gapless): the contract, after all, says that Seller must deliver the goods to Buyer by a certain date. The date has passed, and the goods have not arrived. Therefore, Seller has breached the contract.

The existence of a gap is thus contested, and determination of whether a gap exists is itself a matter of contract interpretation. The better way of thinking about contract interpretation is to note that inevitably one can identify some contingency that causes the dispute: the destruction of the goods in transit, a strike, a change in the price of inputs, a decline in demand. This contingency makes performance unattractive to the promisor (that is, the party who, because of the contingency, no longer wants to perform if the original terms are literally enforced). The promisor argues that the contract should be interpreted to release him from his obligation if this contingency occurs. The promisee argues that the contractual obligation is unaffected by the occurrence of the contingency. The promisee thus usually argues that some general term ("promisor will deliver X") should be interpreted broadly to mean, "even if the relevant contingency occurs." The promisor argues that this term is circumscribed, either by other terms in the contract, or more usually, by the purpose of the contract — the parties would not have required the promisor to perform if that contingency had occurred, because performance would have cost the promisor more than it would have benefited the promisee. In cases such as these, the promisor prefers courts to take the hypothetical bargain approach, while the promisee wants courts to take the ordinary-language approach.

---

[9] See Richard Craswell, Do Trade Customs Exist?, in The Jurisprudential Foundations of Corporate and Commercial Law (Jody S. Krauss & Steven D. Walt eds., 2000).

Which approach to contractual interpretation is superior? I am tempted to think that this question cannot be answered, or that the answer does not much matter. But let me make some general observations.

The answer depends on one thing: how much confidence we should have in the ability of courts, ex post, to determine the optimal contract in ex ante terms. Suppose that courts have perfect information about the economics of the transaction. They know Buyer's ex ante valuation, Seller's cost, the contingencies that could arise and their effect on the valuation and cost, the parties' outside opportunities, and so forth. On the basis of this heroic assumption, the court should use the hypothetical bargain method. The reason is simple. The parties cannot write down the optimal terms given every possible future contingency, and even to anticipate, bargain about, and write down a few terms can be quite expensive. If courts, ex post, can be anticipated to fill in the optimal terms, then the parties can save vast expense on transaction costs. Contracts would be exceedingly simple — maybe just the identities of the parties and a brief identification of the goods — and parties would then either rely on courts to fill in the terms, or more likely bargain again after the relevant contingency has occurred in light of their expectations about a court's determinations in case of a lawsuit.

Skepticism about hypothetical bargaining is based on skepticism about the ability of courts to determine the optimal terms ex post. If they are so great at choosing terms, why should they ever defer to what the parties write down? Why should they defer to the price, for example? Indeed, why have contracts at all? Why not direct courts to allocate resources directly, as in a socialist state?

But if you go the other direction, similar problems arise. If courts cannot reliably reconstruct the hypothetical bargain, then it must be because the purposes of the contract are hidden, and the parties' aims, valuations, costs, and so forth cannot be ascertained. And yet how realistic is it to suppose that courts can interpret the terms of the contract, even using the ordinary-language method, without having a sense of what the parties were trying to accomplish? When we interpret signs, instructions, and other texts, we cut through ambiguities by thinking about the purpose of the author. If courts cannot do this, can one really believe that they can interpret the terms of the contract in a non-arbitrary way? If not, then what does the judicial system accomplish?

The puzzle becomes more complex as we turn from theoretical considerations to the practices of sophisticated contract makers. On the one hand, contracts frequently include terms designed to cabin the discretion of judges, including merger clauses, which direct courts not to consider extrinsic evidence. And parties frequently revise contracts in order to counteract judges' implications of new terms. On the other hand, contracts have vague terms — not just words that are inherently vague because they are used in multiple ways, but phrases like "best efforts," "good faith," and "reasonable," which seem to be invitations to judges to read terms into the contract if a dispute arises.

§6.4   On Literalism and Formalism

Interpretation plays a central role in contract law, indeed in all of law, but it is difficult to understand at a theoretical level. Nobody has developed rules of interpretation that reliably guide the reader. Judges fall back on unhelpful generalizations, typically arguing that the interpretation they favor is "reasonable" or a matter of "common sense." They also rely on various maxims (discussed in the next section), but these rules are, as we shall see, of limited value.

Fortunately, interpretation is something we all do — all the time, in our everyday lives — and so everyone has a sense of how to do it, though some people are better at it than others. Let me use a homespun example. Suppose that you buy a piece of furniture — say, a desk — that you must construct at home. You open the box and out fall the directions, often badly translated from a foreign language.

You note that you construct the desk by sticking wooden pegs into holes on the pieces. There are two types of pegs: big and small. So far, so good. You pick up the instructions and you read that you are to put "a peg in each of the holes on the top of the desk." You identify the top of the desk but you realize that the instructions are vague: they don't tell you whether to put the big pegs or small pegs into the holes on the top of the desk.

Fortunately, this interpretive problem is easy to solve. You try out each peg and discover that only the small pegs fit into the pre-drilled holes. You also notice that if you jammed the big pegs into those holes, you wouldn't have enough big pegs for the other big holes and you would have too many small pegs. Notice how you interpret the instructions by going back and forth between the literal language and the purpose of the instructions, which is to enable you to build the desk, while also relying on some background knowledge — for example, that the manufacturer would supply you with the right number of big and small pegs for the product rather than force you to order more.

Now suppose that the instructions tell you to "insert big pegs into the holes on the legs." You try to do this and discover that they don't fit. The small pegs, however, fit perfectly. Here, you would ignore the literal meaning of the instructions, reasoning that the manufacturer or translator made a mistake. Again, you are guided by the purpose of the instructions and your background knowledge.

When judges interpret contracts, they follow a similar process. They go back and forth between the purpose of the contract and the literal terms, where "literal" refers to something like the dictionary definition and/or the judge's background knowledge of the meanings of words. Judges may permit the apparent purpose of the contract to resolve ambiguities and even to override terms that would otherwise appear to suggest absurd or implausible results.

People known as formalists believe that judges should pay more attention to words and less to purpose. In our example involving the desk, this view makes little sense. Should I jam the big peg in the small hole even though the resulting desk does not stand up? But contracts are different in this respect from instructions. Suppose that courts have trouble discovering the true purpose of a contract — it is harder for them to understand the diverse purposes of the multitude of contracts to which they are exposed than it is for me to understand instructions for building furniture. And recall that parties have the power to write a more explicit contract. By enforcing contracts literally, without paying attention to possible purposes, courts would encourage parties to write clearer and more explicit contracts. Whether this course of action is the right one is an empirical question: it depends on how good or bad judges are at discerning the purposes of contracts, and how easy or hard it is for parties to write their contracts clearly. When judges are bad at interpretation, and parties can easily draft clear contracts, the case for formalism is stronger.[10]

§6.5 Canons of Interpretation

Courts may follow certain canons or maxims when a contract is ambiguous.[11] Most of them are self-explanatory. Contracts are assumed to be consistent, and words that appear more than once are assumed to have the same meaning. An ambiguous contract is interpreted against the drafter ("contra proferentem") — meaning that if a term has two meanings, one favoring the drafter and the other favoring the non-drafter, the court chooses the meaning that favors the non-drafter — because the drafter is in the better position to eliminate ambiguities. An ambiguous insurance contract is frequently interpreted against the insurer for the additional reason that people depend heavily on insurance. An ambiguous contract is interpreted to avoid forfeiture, either because parties usually do not agree to forfeitures or courts disapprove of them. More generally, ambiguous

---

[10] For a defense of formalism, see Alan Schwartz & Robert E. Scott, Contract Interpretation Redux, 119 Yale L.J. 926 (2010).

[11] For a brief, helpful summary, see E. Allan Farnsworth, Contracts §7.11 (4th ed. 2004).

contracts are interpreted so as to prevent conflicts with public policy, which may be embodied in related statutes.

§6.6 Course of Dealing, Trade Usage, and Course of Performance

When contracts are ambiguous — and even when they are clear — courts use various types of extrinsic evidence to interpret a contract. "Course of dealing" refers to "a sequence of conduct concerning previous transactions between the parties to a particular transaction that is fairly to be regarded as establishing a common basis of understanding for interpreting their expressions and other conduct."[12] "Trade usage" refers to "any practice or method of dealing having such regularity of observance in a place, vocation, or trade as to justify an expectation that it will be observed with respect to the transaction in question."[13] Course of performance refers to "a sequence of conduct between the parties to a particular transaction that exists if: (1) the agreement of the parties with respect to the transaction involves repeated occasions for performance by a party; and (2) the other party, with knowledge of the nature of the performance and opportunity for objection to it, accepts the performance or acquiesces in it without objection."[14] The definitions are taken from the U.C.C., but similar ideas can be found in the common law.

The explanations for these rules are straightforward. Take course of dealing. When people speak to each other, they often use shorthand based on past experience or the activities of others. Suppose that two parties, Seller and Buyer, have a long-term continuing relationship. They have entered and executed dozens of contracts for the sale of widgets. In the latest contract, Seller delivers widgets that Buyer rejects. Buyer argues that the widgets do not conform to the contract, but the contract refers only to "widgets" and does not have any specifications. The parties can plausibly argue that the meaning of "widget" in the latest contract is the same as the meaning in earlier contracts, and one can discover that meaning by examining the widgets that Buyer accepted. If the most recent batch is identical to the previous batch, then Seller has complied with the contract; if not, then Seller has breached.

Reliance on trade usage reflects a similar logic, though there is a twist. Suppose General Contractor and Subcontractor enter a contract requiring Sub to paint apartment "units." Sub paints the interior walls, and General argues that Sub has an obligation to paint the exterior walls — painting

[12] U.C.C. §1-303(b).
[13] U.C.C. §1-303(c).
[14] U.C.C. §1-303(d).

"units" means painting both types of wall. There is no course of dealing but it turns out that if one observes the contracts between other generals and subs, the subs always paint both exterior and interior walls when the contract calls for painting of "units." In the trade, "unit" means both types of wall, just as in the bakery trade a dozen means 13. In such a case, a court might reason that General and Sub actually agreed to both types of walls — and Sub is now trying to back out of the agreement.

But not all subs know the terms of trade. People who enter the trade for the first time may be unfamiliar with trade usage. In such cases, courts do not usually bind the ignorant party to the trade term, holding instead that there is a misunderstanding and the contract is void.[15] One might argue that courts should hold the neophyte to the trade usage on the ground that neophytes should be given an incentive to learn the trade usage, just as they should be given an incentive to learn local regulations (and ignorance of the law is not an excuse if they violate those rules). A possible counter-argument is that courts should encourage the informed party to provide information about trade usage to neophytes — at least if it is obvious that the neophyte is in fact a newcomer.

Course of performance provides a slight variation. Consider the earlier widget example but suppose that the parties enter a single long-term contract for the first time, under which Seller makes periodic deliveries to Buyer. Buyer accepts the first n batches of widgets without complaint, then argues that batch $n + 1$ is substandard. If the last batch is identical to earlier batches, Seller could argue that Buyer's acceptance of the earlier batches shows that the quality of the last batch conforms to the contract; if Buyer really believed that the widgets did not conform, he would have complained at the start.

As noted earlier, these rules permit evidence to "vary" the terms of the contract. The phrase is misleading. Suppose that a contract between a baker and a customer calls for a "dozen" rolls. The word "dozen" does not seem ambiguous: it means 12. However, a baker's dozen is 13. You might argue that "dozen" is ambiguous but it is not really: in this context, a dozen means 13 and that is perfectly clear. This phenomenon — where a term that has a clear meaning in common speech but a different meaning within a trade — is quite common. It has been suggested that in the mists of time, bakers began adding an extra roll or loaf in order to avoid draconian punishments against cheating customers by supplying less than they ordered, or that thirteen baked goods fit into a box more snugly than twelve.[16] Whatever the case, the important thing to understand is that language evolves in complex ways, and can evolve in different directions in separate communities or trades.

---

[15] See Flower City Painting Contractors, Inc. v. Gumina Const. Co., 591 F.2d 162 (2d Cir. 1979).

[16] See Wikipedia, Baker's Dozen, http://en.wikipedia.org/wiki/Baker's_dozen.

§6.7   Plain Meaning Rule

Many contracts are ambiguous, and we have seen how contract law attempts to address ambiguity: with the reasonable person standard. Remember that a contract can be oral as well as written, and words, whether spoken or written, can always be ambiguous. Courts resolve ambiguity by asking how a reasonable person would understand the words (or actions) in dispute. Sometimes, as in Raffles v. Wichelhaus,[17] the reasonable person would simply be confused, unable to distinguish two or more possible interpretations of the words. In that case, no contract exists. More often, one of the multiple interpretations being offered is more plausible than the others. A reasonable person would adopt that more plausible interpretation, and the contract is enforced accordingly.

Written contracts provide a new set of issues. Courts give extra weight to the writing because they believe that parties are more likely to write carefully than to speak carefully. Oral contracts emerge from hasty conversations. Written contracts follow often lengthy negotiations and are (in theory) read by both parties before signature. Or written contracts are based on forms that have been drafted after much debate. With these considerations in mind, courts are often tempted to enforce written contracts "on their face," that is, based on the writing, without any attention to oral discussions, letters, e-mails, or other writings may have preceded the final writing.

There is an advantage to such an approach. When contractual interpretation is based solely on the writing, litigants can simply hand over the contract to the court and ask for an interpretation. Litigation involving oral contracts is not so simple. The parties must testify as to what they remember, and invariably they remember different things. Other witnesses are called. The jury must sort out the testimony, and this can be hard to do.

However, written contracts can be ambiguous — indeed, often are ambiguous. However hard parties try to be clear in writings, it often turns out that they were not clear enough. The plain meaning rule says that the meaning of the contract, for judicial purposes, is based on the writing, unless the writing (that is, the relevant provisions of the writing) is ambiguous, in which case the court can look at "extrinsic evidence" — documents or testimony that disclose what the parties thought they were agreeing to.[18] In this way, the plain meaning rule continues to give primary weight

---

[17] See Section 4.1.
[18] See Restatement (Second) of Contracts §201 (1981):

> (1) Where the parties have attached the same meaning to a promise or agreement or a term thereof, it is interpreted in accordance with that meaning.
> (2) Where the parties have attached different meanings to a promise or agreement or a term thereof, it is interpreted in accordance with the meaning attached by one of them if at the time the agreement was made

to the writing. Parties cannot offer extrinsic evidence about the meaning of the contract if the writing is clear, even if the extrinsic evidence says something different. But if the writing is unclear, then extrinsic evidence is admissible.

Many courts have rejected the plain meaning rule, arguing that extrinsic evidence is always relevant in interpreting a contract.[19] A contract that appears clear to a judge may actually have a different meaning from the one the judge assigns to it. When people interpret texts, they bring to bear certain assumptions that are based on their own experiences. A judge may not understand that a contract written by olive merchants might reflect the assumptions of olive merchants, which are different from the assumptions of judges. Now this point is reflected in doctrines that we have already seen — the admissibility of trade usage and course of dealing, for example. Judges who apply the plain meaning rule permit such evidence even though it might contradict what appears clear in a writing. The critics of the plain meaning rule argue that specialized language might go deeper, showing up in all sorts of linguistic conventions of which the judge is unaware.[20]

Let's consider some examples, which will help clarify what is at stake. In W.W.W. Associates v. Giancontieri,[21] Sellers agreed to sell some real estate to Buyer. The contract included a reciprocal cancellation provision, which noted that litigation existed against the property at the time of the contract and that either party has the right to cancel the contract if the litigation was not concluded by June 1, 1987. The litigation did not conclude by that date, and Sellers canceled the contract on June 2. Buyer sued to enforce the contract, arguing that the clause had been added for Buyer's benefit alone. Only Buyer needed that protection because Buyer would not want to purchase the real estate if it could not secure construction financing — but in fact it did secure the financing. Sellers canceled the contract because they realized they could get a higher price from someone else.

The court rejected the argument, stating that "when parties set down their agreement in a clear, complete document, their writing should as a

---

(a) that party did not know of any different meaning attached by the other, and the other knew the meaning attached by the first party; or

(b) that party had no reason to know of any different meaning attached by the other, and the other had reason to know the meaning attached by the first party.

(3) Except as stated in this Section, neither party is bound by the meaning attached by the other, even though the result may be a failure of mutual assent.

[19] See, e.g. Weinberg v. Edelstein, 110 N.Y. Supp. 2d 806 (1952) (defining "dress" in a contract by relying on practices and customs of the women's fashion industry rather than the dictionary definition).

[20] See, e.g,. Pacific Gas & Elec. Co. v. G. W. Thomas Drayage & Rigging Co., 442 P.2d 641 (Cal. 1968).

[21] W.W.W. Associates, Inc. v. Giancontieri, 566 N.E.2d 639 (N.Y. 1990).

rule be enforced according to its terms. Evidence outside the four corners of the document as to what was intended but unstated or misstated is generally inadmissible to add to or vary the writing."[22] However, the court added that the reciprocal cancellation provision was supported by logic. Sellers received a security interest in the property; this would secure their loan to Buyer (Buyer bought the property partially on credit from Sellers). If the property continued to be subject to litigation, that security interest would be vulnerable to litigation; therefore, Sellers might prefer to reserve the right to sell for cash until the last moment.

In Pacific Gas & Electric v. G.W. Thomas Drayage & Rigging Co.,[23] Contractor entered into a contract with Owner under which it agreed to replace the cover of Owner's steam turbine. Contractor agreed to "indemnify" Owner against losses arising from performance of the contract. While Contractor was performing the contract, the cover fell and damaged the turbine. Owner sued for damages, arguing that Contractor had indemnified Owner against all losses, which must include the damage to the turbine. Note that if the contract did not assign liability to Contractor, Owner could only recover in tort, and apparently that theory was not likely to succeed — perhaps the cover fell because of the negligence of Owner, whose employees may have been involved in the work or may have secured the original cover improperly.

The court rejected the "four corners" rule applied in *Giancontieri*. "The fact that the terms of an instrument appear clear to a judge does not preclude the possibility that the parties chose the language of the instrument to express different terms."[24] The court actually expressed doubt that the word "indemnity" is unambiguous, noting that the word is used in two senses — to mean the obligation to cover *any* loss and the obligation to cover only losses caused by third parties. In *Pacific Gas & Electric*, the first meaning implies that Contractor must cover the loss; the second meaning implies that Contractor does not have to cover the loss (because it was not caused by a third party). However, this is all left to a footnote. The court held that the trial court should have admitted evidence suggesting that the parties meant the clause to cover only third-party losses.

The rule is expansive. "The test of admissibility of extrinsic evidence to explain the meaning of a written instrument is . . . whether the offered evidence is relevant to prove a meaning to which the language of the instrument is reasonably susceptible."[25] But it is itself ambiguous. What does it mean to say that language is "reasonably susceptible" to a meaning? The

---

[22] Id. at 642.
[23] Pacific Gas & Elec. Co. v. G.W. Thomas Drayage & Rigging Co., 442 P.2d 641 (Cal. 1968).
[24] Id. at 645.
[25] Id. at 646.

Court believed that "indemnify" was susceptible to the third-party interpretation, but why exactly? In *Giancontieri*, would the reciprocal cancellation clause be susceptible to the interpretation that limited the right to cancel to the buyer? The clause says explicitly that both parties had the right to cancel; it is not clear whether the narrower interpretation would be excessively in tension with the literal meaning.

Pacific Gas & Electric is famous for its skeptical comments about the determinacy of language. The court said that the "four corners" rule "reflects a judicial belief in the possibility of perfect verbal expression. . . . The belief is a remnant of a primitive faith in the inherent potency and inherent meaning of words."[26] More: "If words had absolute and constant referents, it might be possible to discover contractual intention in the words themselves and in the manner in which they were arranged. Words, however, do not have absolute and constant referents."[27] There is a great deal of nonsense mixed in with a reasonable point. The court confuses words and written words. The court does not deny that one can discover contractual intention by interpreting words in general. The court's skepticism is directed toward reliance on the *writing*, which will inevitably leave out aspects of the bargain that the parties discussed or that can be inferred from their conduct. The Court fears that judges will assume that a term is clear because of their own background assumption about what it means, when in fact the term means something different within the specialist community of the bargainers.

A "four corners" advocate would reply that the parties can anticipate the ignorance of courts and provide definitions in the written contract, as parties so frequently do. The controversy boils down to an empirical question about whether parties are sufficiently sophisticated (and can anticipate and provide for future judicial confusion) and whether courts are sufficiently sophisticated (and can sort between opportunistic and honest proffers of extrinsic evidence suggesting that terms have special meanings). The more sophisticated the parties are and the less sophisticated judges are, the better the case is for the four corners rule.

§6.8 Parol Evidence Rule

The parol evidence rule resembles the plain meaning rule. But whereas the plain meaning rule address contractual *ambiguity*, the parol evidence rule address contractual *incompleteness*. These two concepts overlap, as we will see later in this section.

---

[26] Id. at 643-644.
[27] Id. at 645.

The parol evidence rule says that when a contractual writing is incomplete, the court may admit extrinsic ("parol") evidence to fill in the gaps; when the writing is complete, the court may not admit extrinsic evidence.[28] Extrinsic or parol evidence may consist of letters, memos, e-mails, oral statements, and other evidence of promises made before the contract was entered, just as in the case of the plain meaning rule. If the writing is complete, the extrinsic evidence can only be redundant (if it is consistent with the writing) or contradictory (if it is inconsistent with the writing). Redundant evidence can obviously be ignored. When the extrinsic evidence is contradictory, then one must decide whether to give priority to the writing or to the extrinsic evidence. As we noted in the last section, courts assume that the parties take writings more seriously than oral or other types of representations not included in the final writing — in the sense that the parties are more likely to intend the terms of the deal embodied in the final writing than in other sources.

The parol evidence rule and the plain meaning rule reflect a trade-off. On the one hand, one might think that more evidence is always better. It is a cliché that one cannot understand a statement without knowing its context. Admit extrinsic evidence, weigh it against the writing, and make an all-things-considered judgment. On the other hand, it is clear that parties often do not want courts to consider the extrinsic evidence. Why not? The answer is that the negotiations that lead up to writings often involve give-and-take and take-back. A party might offer a particular term X and then retract it when it appears that the other party will not reciprocate by offering a term that the first party seeks. Courts that go back and look at the record of negotiations — often relying on the parties' fallible memories — might mistakenly believe that term X was agreed to as part of the contract. The parol evidence rule, like the plain meaning rule, reflects doubts about judicial ability to understand the record of the negotiations. The parties seek to control the materials that judges can examine after a dispute arises, because they believe that otherwise judges will make mistakes after relying on the wrong information.

This explains the popularity of "merger" or "integration" clauses, which one can find in virtually every form contract, and many other contracts as well. A typical merger clause states:

---

[28] See Restatement (Second) of Contracts §213 (1981). The U.C.C.'s version of the rule is less confusing; see U.C.C. §2-202 (prohibiting extrinsic evidence, except to supplement with evidence of "(a) course of performance, course of dealing, or usage of trade" and "(b) consistent additional terms unless the court finds the record to have been intended also as a complete and exclusive statement of the terms of the agreement"). Some commentators believe the U.C.C. provision is more liberal than the common law provision, but it is just not clear. See, e.g., Avery Wiener Katz, The Economics of Form and Substance in Contract Interpretation, 104 Colum. L. Rev. 496, 517 (2004) (contrasting the approach taken under U.C.C. §2-202 "with the traditional common law, which took a stricter stand on the admission of parol evidence and did not explicitly confer official status on course of performance").

The foregoing contain the whole agreement between the parties to this contract and they, and each of them, shall be stopped from asserting, as an inducement to make said contract, any misrepresentation upon the party of either of the parties hereto, or any agent or servant of either of the parties hereto.[29]

The clause implicitly invokes the parol evidence rule, instructing the court that because the writing is complete, the court should resist the temptation to examine extrinsic evidence.

All of this should seem straightforward, but it is evident that courts often believe that they cannot trust parties to put the complete contract in the writing. At the heart of the parol evidence rule is a paradox. Recall that "completeness" means that the contract anticipates every possible future contingency. But that is impossible: the parties cannot anticipate every contingency. When parties write that the contract is complete, they are just guessing that they have anticipated every contingency, or enough contingencies that judicial reliance on extrinsic evidence will do more harm than good. By the time that a case arises, the future has unfolded, and the court knows–or thinks that it knows — that the parties failed to anticipate whatever contingency gave rise to the dispute. Thus, courts have continued to create exceptions to the parol evidence rule, and the parties have then tried to evade these exceptions, the result being a complex series of rules and exceptions.

Let us start with what one might call the first iteration of the rule: the basic idea that a complete contract cannot be revised with extrinsic evidence. Well, how does the court know whether a contract is complete or not? We immediately confront a possible problem of circularity. The court could examine the extrinsic evidence to determine whether the contract is complete. If the extrinsic evidence includes only terms that are the same as those that are in the writing, then we know the contract is complete. If the extrinsic evidence includes terms that are different from those in the contract, then we know the contract is incomplete. But if we take this approach, then the parol evidence rule would have no force: we are just using whatever extrinsic evidence that exists. For the parol evidence rule to mean anything, we must ignore contrary extrinsic evidence.

There are a couple ways to break out of this circularity. One is to look at the writing itself for clues regarding completeness. If the writing looks complete — if it is long and detailed, and seems carefully drafted — then we treat it as complete. If the writing does not look complete — it is short, brief, and carelessly drafted — then we treat it as incomplete.[30] Another approach is to look at the extrinsic evidence only for clues about whether

---

[29] LaFazia v. Howe, 575 A.2d 182 (R.I. 1990).
[30] See, e.g., Hatley v. Stafford, 588 P.2d 603 (Or. 1978); Mitchell v. Lath, 160 N.E. 646 (N.Y. 1928).

147

the parties intended for the writing to be complete. In this latter approach, we would have to ignore contrary extrinsic evidence unless it reveals something about the parties' desire to draft a complete contract. Of course, the fact that extrinsic evidence includes terms contrary to the writing might seem to constitute just such evidence; if contrary evidence exists, maybe this suggests that the parties did not mean the writing to be complete. But then we have again undermined the parol evidence rule.

These two approaches have emerged as the dominant alternatives in the law. The first, where one inspects the writing for clues as to completeness, is the more formalistic approach, and corresponds to the four corners (plain meaning) rule.[31] The second, where one considers extrinsic evidence for the purpose of making the determination as to completeness, corresponds to the weaker interpretation rule advocated by Justice Traynor in *Pacific Gas & Electric*.[32] Which rule is better? It depends on how much one trusts judges to interpret extrinsic evidence properly. If judges are sophisticated enough, they may be able to read the evidence properly. If they are not, then it would be better to require them to rely on the writing. The logic of the argument is the same as in the controversy over the plain meaning rule.

As noted earlier, parties frequently use merger clauses to prevent judges from admitting extrinsic evidence. And judges in both types of jurisdictions give some deference to merger clauses. The ubiquity of merger clauses suggests that contract parties, at least, do not expect judges to interpret extrinsic evidence correctly and for that reason want them to exclude extrinsic evidence from consideration. In any event, when merger clauses are used, the practical difference between the two types of jurisdictions may be minimal.

Even in jurisdictions with the more formalistic parol evidence rule, courts have continually recognized exceptions that reduce its force. All of these exceptions reflect the paradox that constantly threatens to undermine the rule — that a tempting way to determine whether the writing reflects the parties' intentions is to look at the extrinsic evidence that the writing might be meant to exclude.

Consider, for example, the fraud exception to the parol evidence rule. Seller asks Buyer to sign a petition for the nomination of a political candidate. Buyer signs without reading the document that Seller hands him, which turns out to be a contract for the purchase of Seller's stuffed albatross for a below-market price. The contract has a merger clause. When Buyer sues for rescission, Seller points to the merger clause and argues that the court should not permit Buyer to introduce extrinsic evidence of fraud — namely, Buyer's testimony that Seller had lied to him about the content of

---

[31] See Restatement (Second) of Contracts §201 (1981).

[32] Pacific Gas & Elec. Co. v. G.W. Thomas Drayage & Rigging Co., 442 P.2d 641 (Cal. 1968).

the document. The court would admit the extrinsic evidence. Buyer could have protected himself by reading the document, but it is cheaper and easier for people to rely on representations made by others. The rule does not give Buyer a chance to opportunistically introduce extrinsic evidence when fraud has not occurred because the only relevant evidence would concern the question of whether the document was authentic. Buyer would not be able to introduce extrinsic evidence that the price was higher than what was written on the contract.

But here is a harder case. Buyer claims that Seller told Buyer that if Buyer buys her car, Seller will give him a year's free supply of gas. Now Buyer is claiming that Seller's fraudulent promise induced him to enter the contract. What should the court do? If Buyer's claim is true, then Buyer never sought to enter the contract and, a fortiori, did not agree that the writing was complete. But if Buyer's claim is accepted, then the extrinsic evidence can be used to vary the terms of the contract. What appears on its face to be a contract that provides only for the exchange of a car for cash, is now interpreted as a contract that provides for the exchange of a car for cash and gas. Nonetheless, courts often admit the extrinsic evidence.[33] This exception does not entirely undermine the parol evidence rule, because Buyer must prove fraud — meaning that Seller intentionally misled him — and that can be difficult. But the rule is hollowed out.

Other exceptions are also made. Suppose Buyer claims that the contract rests on mutual mistake: extrinsic evidence can be admitted to prove mistake.[34] Or suppose Buyer claims that extrinsic evidence proves that the contract was conditional on some event — for example, that Buyer's commitment to enter the contract was conditional on Seller's supplying Buyer with gas.[35] Courts will admit extrinsic evidence of the condition.

The difficulty in all these cases is that Buyer can use these exceptions to defeat the purpose of the rule. If Buyer had merely argued that the parties had agreed that Seller would supply gas but neglected to put this term in the writing, the parol evidence rule would bar admission of that evidence for the purpose of varying the terms of the contract. But if Buyer instead argues that the extrinsic evidence showing that Seller promised gas proves that Seller engaged in fraud, or there was a mistake of some sort, or the contract was subject to a condition, then Buyer achieves more or less the same outcome. As noted, courts sometimes impose higher evidentiary requirements or additional elements (as in the case of fraud) in order to maintain the spirit of the rule.

---

[33] See, e.g., Lipsit v. Leonard, 315 A.2d 25 (N.J. 1974).
[34] See, e.g., Hoffman v. Chapman, 34 A.2d 438 (Md. 1943).
[35] Cf. Long Island Trust v. Int'l Inst. for Packaging Educ., 344 N.E.2d 377 (N.Y. 1976).

§6.9   Summary

Rules governing contractual interpretation reflect a basic trade-off. On the one hand, courts try to interpret contracts so as to maximize the value of the transaction for the parties — as illustrated most clearly by the hypothetical bargain method, but also by rules that give weight to trade usage and similar forms of evidence. If parties expect courts to do this, they can write brief, incomplete contracts — thus minimizing bargaining or transaction costs — with the expectation that a court will fill the gaps if a dispute ever occurs.

On the other hand, courts try to give parties incentives to disclose information about the transaction in a clear way. The bias in favor of writings illustrates this idea. If parties know that unwritten terms will not be enforced, they are more likely to put terms in the writing, which is relatively easy for courts to interpret and enforce — as opposed to taking testimony on oral statements, evaluating the credibility of witnesses, and the like. The focus here is on minimization of judicial decision costs. This approach, unlike the first, assumes that courts (judges and juries) are not very good at understanding contracts, or are likely to let their biases creep in.

The formalism of the second approach has the most to recommend it when parties are sophisticated and judges are not. But it is hard to generalize. Sometimes parties are sophisticated, sometimes not; the same can be said about judges, and the relative sophistication may depend on the type of transaction.

Chapter *7*

Performance or Breach

§7.1 In General

Contract disputes usually boil down to whether the promisor breached or complied with the promise. This inquiry involves two questions. First, what exactly does the promise mean? That question is answered through interpretation of the contractual materials — the writing, if any, and any admissible oral statements, as well as contextual evidence. Second, what did the promisor actually do? Here, the factfinder must examine evidence touching on the promisor's actions. Was delivery on time? Did the goods conform to specifications?

Performance must always be exact. If a deviation from the promise occurs, however small, a breach exists and the victim is entitled to damages. In practice, slight deviations are often tolerated; they are inevitable and not enough money is at stake to justify a lawsuit. However, sometimes a slight deviation matters a great deal. As we discuss below, in sales of goods Buyer may reject goods that fail to conform exactly to the contractual specification. By contrast, in other types of contracts Buyer may not reject performances that fall short of perfection but substantially conform to the contract — but still may sue for damages.

§7.2 Anticipatory Repudiation

Suppose that Buyer and Seller agree that Seller will deliver goods to Buyer in one month and Buyer will pay on delivery. Two weeks before the date of delivery, Seller informs Buyer that she will not deliver. In a literal sense, Seller has not breached the contract. The contract gives her two more weeks until delivery; breach cannot actually occur until the date of delivery arrives and the delivery itself does not. However, courts treat Seller's announcement as equivalent to a breach under the doctrine of anticipatory repudiation.

The rule makes a great deal of sense. If Seller does not intend to perform, then Buyer should not be forced to wait and see if Seller changes her mind. In the meantime, Buyer can take actions that mitigate the loss from breach. In Rockingham County v. Luten Bridge, for example, the contractor should have stopped working on the bridge when the County announced that it would not honor the contract. In the absence of the doctrine of anticipatory repudiation, the contractor would need to complete the bridge so as to be able to demand payment.[1] Thus, the doctrine of anticipatory repudiation works with the mitigation doctrine[2] to ensure that resources are not wasted on unwanted performances.

The larger point in these cases is that between entry into a contract and the time of performance (or completion of performance), one party may come to believe that it no longer stands to benefit from the contract. But it may not be sure — in which case it may be tempted to hold off breaching until later. The doctrines of mitigation and anticipatory repudiation encourage that party to announce its intention to breach early, to permit the other party to mitigate the loss, which minimizes the damages that the first party will need to pay for breach of contract.

§7.3   Conditions: Definitions and Consequences

Many promises are contingent on certain events (including the performance of other promises).[3] These promises are called "conditional" (or sometimes "dependent") promises. They can be contrasted with "unconditional," "absolute," or "independent" promises, or "covenants." When a promise is absolute, a person must perform or pay damages. When a promise is conditional, a person must perform only if the event takes place.

It matters a great deal whether a promise is conditional or absolute. Consider an insurance contract. Insurer promises to pay for a new house if Client's house burns down. Insurer's promise to pay is conditional on

---

[1] See Rockingham County v. Luten Bridge, 35 F.2d 301 (4th Cir. 1929). Because the contractor in fact did complete the bridge after the anticipatory repudiation, it violated its duty to mitigate.

[2] See Section 8.10.

[3] See Chapter 3.

Client's house burning down. Thus, if Client's house does not burn down, Insurer need not pay. So far this is straightforward.

Now consider a clause providing that Client must give notice to Insurer within X days of the fire, and then Insurer must make the payment. Such clauses are common. Insurers want to be able to inspect the premises to confirm that the insured event has actually taken place (rather than arson or some other event). If Insurer's obligation to pay is conditional on Client's giving notice within X days of the fire, and Client fails to give notice, Insurer has no obligation to pay. If Insurer's obligation to pay is unconditional, and Client fails to give notice, Insurer has an obligation to pay. Client's right to receive the insurance payment and ability to build a new house depend on whether Insurer's promise is conditional or absolute.

Frequently, courts can easily make this determination. If the insurance contract is explicit — "it shall be a condition to the payment of any loss that Client give notice to Insurer within X days of the accident" — the court merely follows the contract's lead. But interpretation is not always easy.

In many cases, courts determine whether promises are conditional or not by applying rough default rules or interpretive canons, or by adverting to the purpose of the contract. In both situations, the reasoning appeals to general features of conditions and their role in contracts.

Conditions are attractive for three reasons. First, they create knife-edge incentives. Contractor enters a contract to build a house where Owner promises to pay the entire contract price when the house is completed. Contractor stops construction before installing the roof. If Owner's promise is absolute, Owner must (in effect) pay Contractor the price and sue for damages. If Owner's promise is conditional, Owner may simply refuse to pay. (Owner can also sue for damages.) Contractor may sue for restitution for the work performed.[4] But the burden will be on Contractor. Courts tend to undercompensate because the plaintiff bears the burden of proof: it will be harder for Owner to prove damages for noncompletion (for example, by calculating losses from delay) and harder for Contractor to prove the cost of work performed (for example, by calculating the share of overhead). By making his obligation to pay conditional on Contractor's performance, Owner throws the burden of proof onto Contractor, which creates a risk that Contractor will not be fully compensated, and hence strengthens Contractor's incentive to perform.

Second, conditions can protect parties from problems of proof. Consider another version of the insurance example. Insurer argues that its promise to pay crop insurance is conditional on Farmer not plowing over the field.[5] Insurer fears that if Farmer can claim insurance after plowing over the field, then Farmer will be able to hide the cause of the loss and possibly demand payment for a loss that the insurance does not cover (for

---

[4] See Section 8.8.
[5] See Howard v. Fed. Crop Ins. Corp., 540 F.2d 695 (4th Cir. 1976), which held otherwise.

example, crop destruction from locusts rather than rain). The condition forces Farmer to keep the field available for inspection. By contrast, if Insurer's promise is absolute, Insurer can only sue Farmer for damages, and it will be impossible to prove that if Farmer had left the field alone, Insurer would have discovered that an uninsured event caused the loss.

Third, conditions can protect a party from insolvency risk (sometimes called "credit risk"). Suppose Owner fears that Contractor will complete the house but do a shoddy job. If Owner's promise to pay is absolute, Owner can sue for damages; but if, in the meantime Contractor has entered bankruptcy, Owner will not be able to recover full compensation. (Owner will have a claim in bankruptcy, but will share with other creditors.) If Owner's promise to pay is conditional, Owner can simply withhold payment for the house. Again, Contractor may be able to obtain restitution (or maybe not); whatever the case, Owner does not need to worry that he will not receive the full benefit.

If conditional promises have so many advantages, they nonetheless come with a significant disadvantage — namely, the prospect that the promisee pays in advance and receives nothing in return (the insurance case) or that the promisee does work in advance and receives nothing in return (the construction case). Thus, promisees will be reluctant to accept conditions in many instances or will demand more money from the other side in return for accepting them. This is the problem of forfeiture.

Courts address the forfeiture problem in several ways:

1. *Interpretation.* Courts will sometimes interpret a clause as an absolute promise rather than a conditional promise in order to avoid forfeiture. For example, in Howard v. Federal Crop Insurance Corp.,[6] the court interpreted a clause requiring a farmer not to plow over a ruined crop before the insurer inspection as creating a promise (so the insurer must pay the insurance) rather than a condition (where the insurer would not have to pay the insurance). In other cases, courts will interpret conditions narrowly rather than broadly. For example, in Grenier v. Compratt Construction Co., the court interpreted a clause conditioning payment for the construction of roads on approval by the City Engineer as requiring approval by any relevant official with the proper authority, when it turned out that the City Engineer did not have the power to approve roads.[7]

2. *Impossibility.* Where it is impossible to comply with a condition, the party is excused from compliance. In Royal-Globe Insurance v. Cravin,[8] for example, the client's right to the insurance payout was conditional on her giving notice within 24 hours of an accident.

[6] 540 F.2d 695 (4th Cir. 1976).
[7] 454 A.2d 1289 (Conn. 1983).
[8] 585 N.E.2d 315 (Mass. 1992).

Because she was unconscious during that period, she was excused from giving notice as long as she did so within a reasonable time after she regained consciousness and the capacity to communicate with others.

3. *Substantial performance.* For contracts not involving sales of goods, the party protected by a condition cannot reject the performance of a promisor who substantially (but not perfectly) complies with the condition. The party can still sue for damages. For example, in Jacob & Youngs v. Kent,[9] a contractor constructed a building properly but installed the wrong pipes. Because the wrong pipes were very similar to the correct pipes, the performance fell short to a trivial degree. The court held that the owner could not withhold the final installment payment but could only sue for damages.[10] Note that for sales of goods, the perfect tender rule applies: buyers can reject goods that do not perfectly conform with specifications. Because the seller retains the goods (unlike the contractor, whose work remains on someone else's property), the forfeiture problem is absent.

4. *Restitution.* Some jurisdictions do not recognize the substantial performance doctrine or put limits on it. But in those jurisdictions, the party subject to the condition can sue for restitution. Consider again the facts of *Jacob & Youngs*. If Contractor finishes a house but does not receive the last installment payment because of a minor defect, Contractor cannot sue on the contract, but she can sue for restitution. The court will evaluate the benefit Contractor conferred and award her damages.[11]

5. *Good faith.* Contracts sometimes provide that Buyer may reject a performance if it does not "satisfy" him. These clauses could be read to give Buyer complete discretion; but if Buyer has complete discretion, then Buyer can turn down a "perfect" performance — for example, because he has since found a better deal elsewhere. Courts restrict satisfaction clauses by requiring Buyer to act in good faith. When the performance is relatively mechanical and routine, like repairing machinery, Buyer may reject it only when it does not conform to an "objective" standard — when a reasonable person would approve of it. When the performance requires idiosyncratic talent, such as painting a portrait, Buyer may reject it as long as his rejection is honest.[12] Proving that Buyer did not act honestly may be difficult, but from Seller's perspective this restriction is better than

---

[9] 129 N.E. 889 (N.Y. 1921).

[10] See Section 8.9.

[11] See 129 N.E. 889, 891-892 (N.Y. 1921).

[12] See Fursmidt v. Hotel Abbey Holding Corp., 200 N.Y.S.2d 256 (N.Y. Sup. Ct. App. Div. 1st Dept. 1960).

nothing. The doctrine reflects a familiar trade-off between judicial error costs and the risk of holdup (or opportunism). When performance is easily evaluated by a court, restrictions on Buyer's behavior limit the risk that Buyer will feign dissatisfaction in order to obtain a better deal or to contract with someone else. But when performance is not easily evaluated, this risk of opportunism cannot be prevented through judicial review. Seller can only protect herself ex ante by charging a higher price.

6. *Prejudice.* Recall that conditions serve certain purposes — for example, to enable the protected party to secure evidence. The insurer requires the insured to give notice promptly after the accident so that the insurer can obtain evidence, interview witnesses, and intervene in legal disputes. However, it is always possible that, in a particular case, the condition is violated but the insurer is not harmed by the violation. In Murphy v. Aetna Casualty & Surety Co.,[13] a dentist damaged the premises of his office and was sued by the owner of the building. The dentist filed a claim with his liability insurer years after the incident. The insurer denied the claim because of its tardiness, but the court gave the dentist a chance to show that the insurer had not been prejudiced by his tardiness. Such a showing would be difficult but not impossible. If the dentist had complied with the condition, the insurer would have had the opportunity to inspect the damage and so be able to protect itself from an exaggerated claim from the building owner. But suppose that an independent and reliable third party carefully documented the damage; then the dentist would be able to argue that the insurer was not hurt by his tardiness. The burden is on the dentist, however, and proving lack of prejudice may be difficult.

But it is not clear that the forfeiture problem is really a problem. If parties are sophisticated and informed, the party subject to the risk of forfeiture will be compensated for that risk. Sophisticated parties are well aware of the risks, and frequently design contracts to address them.

The installment contract is the classic example. In a non-installment contract, Contractor promises to build a house over (say) twelve months for a total price of $120,000. In the installment contract, Contractor promises to build the same house in the same time period, but Owner must pay Contractor $10,000 at the end of each month of work. (Or, more likely, somewhat less than $10,000 plus a final payment at the end that makes up the difference: for example, $9000 per month and then a final payment of $21,000. This gives Owner a little more leverage.) Under the installment

---

[13] 955 S.W.2d 949 (Mo. Ct. App. 2d Dist. 1997).

contract, Contractor need not risk doing twelve months' work and receiving no pay, aside from what she can get through a restitution claim. By the same token, Owner loses some leverage. He cannot threaten to withhold $120,000 if Contractor does a bad job; he can threaten only to withhold $10,000 on a monthly basis. Nonetheless, this compromise might work out best for both parties. Contractor need not fear a catastrophic loss of $120,000 for a year's work and can minimize the cost of financing the construction (because she needs to borrow only $10,000 month to month rather than $120,000 by the end of the term); and Owner may retain sufficient leverage to ensure that Contractor does work on time and in an adequate manner.[14]

§7.4 Conditions: Timing Issues

There is a huge class of cases where parties fail to designate promises as conditional and yet courts treat them as conditional. When parties promise to perform simultaneously, each promise is treated as conditional on the performance of the other promise. When parties promise to perform sequentially, each promise is treated as conditional on the immediately preceding promise's (from the other side) being performed.[15] These (very rough) generalizations are, of course, subject to the explicit (or implied) language of the contract.

What accounts for these rules? Let us start with the sequential case. Buyer and Seller agree that Buyer will pay in advance, and then Seller will deliver a custom-built boat. Under the rule, Buyer's obligation is unconditional, and Seller's obligation is conditional on payment by Buyer. We can imagine the alternative where Seller's obligation is also unconditional. That would mean that if Buyer refused to pay, Seller would be required to deliver the boat and then sue for the price. It is easy to see why the alternative rule is not in place. If Seller must deliver, then Seller runs the risk

---

[14] Courts recognize installment contracts only when parties explicitly create them; the default rule is roughly that Buyer pays upon completion. See Stewart v. Newbury, 115 N.E. 984 (N.Y. 1917). Courts sometimes make an exception when the performance can easily be broken down into steps that can be easily valued — for example, where identical goods are shipped in lots. See U.C.C. §2-612 (permitting buyer to reject any installment which is nonconforming "if the non-conformity substantially impairs the value of that installment and cannot be cured or if the non-conformity is a defect in the required documents").

[15] See Restatement (Second) of Contracts §225(1) (1981) ("Performance of a duty subject to a condition cannot become due unless the condition occurs or its non-occurrence is excused."). Classifying an exchange as simultaneous or sequential can be tricky since in many cases the timing of each performance may be vague or discretionary. See, e.g., Price v. Van Lint, 120 P.2d 611 (N.M. 1941); Wholesale Sand & Gravel, Inc. v. Decker, 630 A.2d 710 (Me. 1993).

that Buyer will be insolvent (or judgment-proof in other ways) and that Seller will not be able to retrieve the boat (or perhaps it will be damaged or used). If Seller has the option to terminate the contract, she can protect herself from this insolvency risk. Now let us look at Buyer's side. Buyer certainly does better if Seller's obligation is unconditional; then Buyer has a chance to obtain the boat without paying for it. But Buyer will have to pay in advance for this option through a higher price, and otherwise does not gain. Giving Seller the option to terminate prevents waste — damage to the boat, its transportation back and forth, and so forth — without producing any offsetting harm. The parties can divide these savings ex ante by adjusting the price term.

The logic can be extended to the case of simultaneous exchange. Buyer and Seller agree that Buyer will pay at the time of delivery. Suppose now that either (1) Seller does not deliver but demands payment, or (2) Buyer refuses payment but tries to take the boat. We could force the victim to go through with the transaction and then sue for damages. But what would be the point of this? Again, the wrongdoer would get something (the boat, money), which he might waste or squander while the victim goes to court. It is more convenient to allow the victim to terminate the contract.

But what if the breach is trivial? Consider the sequential case. Contractor agrees to build a driveway for Owner. Early in the construction, Contractor's bulldozer causes minor damage to Owner's house. The accident breaches the obligation to perform in a workmanlike manner, and Owner attempts to terminate the contract.[16] However, courts hold that Owner cannot terminate on the basis of a "partial" (as opposed to "total") breach.[17] Such a right would make it too easy for parties to escape contracts that they have decided, for other reasons, do not serve their interests. In this case, for example, Owner might seek to escape the contract because he has discovered another contractor who is cheaper. When breaches are not total, parties may in some cases suspend their own performance and demand performance ("cure") from the other;[18] in other cases, they must go through with their own performance. In both situations, they are entitled to sue for any damages.

---

[16] Cf. K&G Constr. Co. v. Harris, 164 A.2d 451 (Md. 1960), where, however, the damage done was substantial enough to give the victim the right to terminate.

[17] Restatement (Second) of Contracts §224 (1981) ("Except as stated in §240, it is a condition of each party's remaining duties to render performances to be exchanged under an exchange of promises that there be no uncured material failure by the other party to render any such performance due at an earlier time.").

[18] Restatement (Second) of Contracts §245 (1981) ("Where a party's breach by nonperformance contributes materially to the non-occurrence of a condition of one of his duties, the non-occurrence is excused.").

158

§7.5 Impossibility / Impracticability / Frustration

When two parties enter a contract, either can be disappointed (or, in rare circumstances, both can, but then they can easily renegotiate). Seller expects her cost to be $100, but instead her cost rises to $200, or $1000, or $10,000. Indeed, sometimes it may be impossible for her to perform. Buyer expects that she will value the performance at $200, but instead she turns out to value it at $150, or $100, or even $0. An intervening event has radically changed one or the other party's valuation; that party now wants to void the contract so that she (Seller) does not have to perform at high cost or he (Buyer) does not have to pay for something he does not want.

Contract law presumptively disapproves of these arguments. Buyer and Seller voluntarily took the risk that their valuations will change as a result of unforeseen or low-probability events. One might argue that performance would be inefficient in these cases, or in at least some of them. Consider a contract in which Seller sells a widget for $100. Buyer's valuation is $200. If Seller's cost increases to $150, performance is still efficient; but if Seller's cost increases to $250, performance is inefficient. One might argue that the law should compel enforcement in the first case and not in the second case.

But we already have a system of damages that ensures this result. Contract law provides that Seller must either perform or breach and pay damages. In both cases, the contract is enforced, in the sense that Buyer either receives what he contracted for or obtains compensation. Expectation damages ensure that Seller performs if and only if performance is efficient, in the sense of making Buyer better off more than Seller is made worse off.[19]

Nonetheless, sellers can sometimes escape their obligation to perform when the cost of performance rises too high, and buyers can sometimes escape their obligation to pay when their valuation sinks too low. The circumstances under which they may escape their obligations are governed by the impossibility and impracticability doctrines,[20] and the frustration doctrine.[21] Because impossibility is a subset of impracticability, I will

---

[19] See Section 8.4.

[20] See Restatement (Second) of Contracts §261 (1981) ("Where, after a contract is made, a party's performance is made impracticable without his fault by the occurrence of an event the non-occurrence of which was a basic assumption on which the contract was made, his duty to render that performance is discharged, unless the language or the circumstances indicate the contrary.").

[21] Restatement (Second) of Contracts §265 (1981) ("Where, after a contract is made, a party's principal purpose is substantially frustrated without his fault by the occurrence of an event the non-occurrence of which was a basic assumption on which the contract was made, his remaining duties to render performance are discharged, unless the language or the circumstances indicate the contrary.").

henceforth refer only to the impracticability doctrine. The impracticability and frustration doctrines overlap and are not always used consistently, but there is a rough conceptual difference: Seller generally invokes impracticability because performance becomes too costly for her (performance is "impracticable"); Buyer generally invokes frustration because performance loses its value to him (its purpose is "frustrated").[22]

The courts labor hard to assert that impracticability does not just mean "too costly." Instead, they emphasize that the event that renders performance impracticable is unforeseeable; its occurrence was a basic assumption of the contract. Frustration also rests on unforeseeability: the event that frustrates the contract is unforeseen or unforeseeable. But these concepts do not always distinguish the cases. The owner of a music hall, and the performers who pay to use the building, can surely foresee that it might burn down. Buildings burn down all the time. Yet the contract is avoided under the impossibility doctrine.[23] The lessor and lessee of a building to house a roller skating rink probably could not foresee that a crisis in liability insurance would make it impossible for the lessee to obtain such insurance as required by the contract, yet the contract is enforced.[24] If a contract takes place between parties in an industry where labor disputes are common, a labor dispute will not excuse performance; whereas if labor disputes are uncommon in another industry, a labor dispute may excuse performance.[25] But how frequent do labor disputes need to be before they become common? Surely everyone by now knows that a labor dispute is possible even in an industry where they do not happen every day. Foreseeability is a slippery concept because the supervening event can be defined at different levels of generality. At the highest level of generality, everyone can foresee that costs may increase and valuations may decline.

To make progress with the doctrines, let us focus on Seller. Seller enters a contract and knows that her costs might increase. The baseline idea in contract law is that Seller bears the risk of any cost increase. The reason is that Seller is in a better position than Buyer to minimize this risk because Seller has possession of the goods and usually knows the market better than Buyer does.

Suppose, for example, that Seller is a contractor who agrees to build a house for Buyer. Seller knows that her labor or material costs might increase, or that the government might issue regulations that increase the cost of building the house. Seller will take these risks into account when calculating her bid; she will also arrange her operations so as to minimize

---

[22] See, e.g., Krell v. Henry, 2 K.B. 740 (1903), where it was possible for Seller (the owner of the apartment) to supply the premises, but Buyer no longer attached any value to occupying the flat because the parade had been canceled.

[23] Taylor v. Caldwell, 122 E.R. 309 (K.B. 1863).

[24] Kel Kim Corp. v. Cent. Mkts., Inc., 519 N.E.2d 295 (N.Y. 1987).

[25] See Mishara Constr. Co. v. Transit-Mixed Concrete Corp., 310 N.E.2d 363 (Mass. 1974).

the risks — for example, arranging to rent labor-saving machinery if labor costs rise, and to hire more workers if the cost of renting equipment rises. Buyer is in no position to make these calculations and preparations.

Let us distinguish these run-of-the-mill calculations with the risk that an asteroid will strike and destroy the worksite after Seller has nearly finished the house. The asteroid poses a risk of loss (albeit a small one) in the same way that the labor market poses a risk of loss. But Seller is in no better position than Buyer to prevent an asteroid from striking; nor is it sensible for Seller to take precautions against asteroid strikes (for example, by keeping work material away from the worksite until it is needed) given their low probability.

It is not as obvious that Seller should bear the risk of the asteroid strike as it is that Seller should bear the risk of labor market fluctuations. But what should the law do? We can imagine three basic positions. First, Seller bears the risk — which means that she must rebuild at her own expense or pay damages for breach of contract. Second, Buyer bears the risk — which means that he must pay Seller for her work plus lost profits even though he never obtains a house. Third, the risk could be split. For example, Seller could be compensated for work that she has done, but not be given any profits.[26]

When courts invoke the impracticability doctrine, the third outcome is the usual result. Is it the right result? The answer turns out not to be clear. Imagine that Buyer values the new building at 100, and the cost of performance (barring an asteroid strike) is 75. If the asteroid strikes, Seller must start over and build a second building at a cost of 75, so in the end Seller spends 150 to obtain the price of 100. The asteroid strike produces a loss of 75 (the value of the building that was destroyed), and this loss must be allocated. As we saw above, this can be done in three ways. If Buyer bears the risk, he must pay Seller 175 (the purchase price plus compensation for constructing a second building). If Seller bears the risk, Buyer pays Seller only 100. The loss could also be divided in any way; for example, Buyer could pay Seller an extra 37.50, so they split the loss.

If Seller bears the risk, how will this affect the original purchase price? If the parties can anticipate the asteroid strike, Seller will demand an extra 75 multiplied by the probability of the asteroid strike. This amount will compensate Seller in advance for the risk. For example, Seller could give this amount to an insurance company in return for insurance against the loss. The question, then, boils down to whether Buyer would be willing to pay Seller this amount for insurance. Not necessarily: Buyer could instead directly pay the insurance company himself. If the insurance company offered Buyer a better deal than it offered Seller, then Buyer would refuse to pay Seller extra so that Seller can buy more expensive insurance.

---

[26] Cf. Carroll v. Bowersock, 164 P. 143 (Kan. 1917).

These considerations have led scholars to argue that the impossibility and frustration doctrines should be understood as devices for allocating the cost of insurance to the party that can more easily buy insurance against, or otherwise absorb low-probability risks of, loss that the parties cannot avoid by taking precautions. If Seller is the cheaper insurer, then the contract should be enforced even when the asteroid strikes. If Buyer is the cheaper insurer, then the contract should be rescinded on grounds of impossibility when the asteroid strikes.

Unfortunately, it will rarely be obvious who is the cheaper insurer. Both parties could buy insurance against asteroid strikes for — one suspects — the same price. However, in other cases the answer will be clearer. When partially completed structures on a building site are destroyed by fire, it makes sense to enforce the contract because the contractor will usually be in the better position to buy insurance against such risks. Insurers would rather deal with the party in control of the structure than the party that does not control the structure, so that its client will be able to implement its annoying injunctions to install smoke detectors and the like. But when a builder does work on a structure that remains in control of its owner — such as when a contractor engages in repairs — the analysis is different. If the entire structure burns down, preventing the contractor from continuing with the repairs, surely the contractor should be released from its obligation to finish the repairs, and should be compensated for the work that it has done. Here, the owner is the superior insurer.

For another example, consider Kel Kim Corp. v. Central Markets, Inc.[27] A roller skating rink operator leased space from the owner of a building under a contract that required the operator to obtain liability insurance against the risk of accidents. Owner probably wanted to make sure that accident victims would receive ample compensation so that they would not be tempted to sue it as well as the operator of the rink; in addition, Owner would want to make sure that Operator stayed in business so it could pay the rent. In any event, Operator could not obtain insurance after the liability insurance crisis struck in the 1980s (insurers withdrew insurance from the market after developments in tort litigation, including rising awards, played havoc with their algorithms). Owner tried to evict Operator, and Operator responded by arguing that it should be released from its obligation to obtain insurance because obtaining adequate insurance had become impossible.

Note initially that Operator wants to enforce Owner's obligation to lease the premises but Operator also wants to avoid its own obligation to buy liability insurance. Operator is not arguing that because it is impossible to perform its side of the bargain, the contract should be rescinded; that would mean that Operator would lose the right to the lease. Operator

---

[27] 519 N.E.2d 295 (N.Y. 1987).

instead argues that only one of its obligations is impossible to perform, and only that obligation is discharged by the impossibility doctrine.

The cheaper insurer analysis might suggest that Operator should bear the risk because Operator is in the best position to buy the insurance. This might be true: liability insurers might prefer to deal with the operator of the rink rather than with the landlord. But, of course, the insurance market failed. And between the two of them, Owner seems better positioned to bear the risk of this market failure than Operator does. A liability insurance crisis does not hit an owner, who can put properties to different uses, as hard as it hits someone who invested in roller skating. The best that Operator could do is sublease to someone else, but this would put Operator in the unfamiliar position of landlord.

Still, the bottom line in this case is that if roller skating is no longer an economically feasible activity (because people are not willing to pay enough to engage in this activity to enable revenues to cover the costs of injury), then it makes little sense to force a landlord to tolerate roller skating on its premises. This landlord wisely protected itself by stipulating by contract that Operator must cover all the expenses generated by its activity; there is no reason to gainsay this judgment.

Let us now consider a frustration case. In Chase Precast Corp. v. John J. Paonessa Co.,[28] a subcontractor agreed to supply a general contractor with median barriers for a highway project. After a public outcry about the ugly median barriers, the Department of Public Works agreed to stop installing them, and instructed the general accordingly. Under its contract with the department, the general was compensated for the barriers that it installed, but could not demand compensation for the barriers that it had not yet installed, even if it had purchased them. The general turned around and told the subcontractor to stop delivering the median barriers. The sub did so but sued for breach of contract. The general-sub contract lacked the cancellation provision in the general-department contract.

The court applied the frustration doctrine, holding that the public outcry was the supervening event, the non-occurrence of which was a basic assumption of the contract, to use the words of the Restatement (Second) §265. It is interesting that the general and the department appeared to anticipate this event, or one like it, and provided for it in their contract. This suggests that the event was not unforeseeable, and accordingly that the sub-general contract should be enforced. The court declined to make this inference. Even if the parties had not anticipated the public outcry, would they have allocated the risk to the sub? As is often the case, it is not really clear. The sub was in a better position to sell unsold barriers to general contractors working on other projects. But the general was in a

---

[28] 566 N.E.2d 603 (Mass. 1991).

better position to anticipate the public outcry and, in any event, could probably have just resold the median barriers to other general contractors working on other projects.

A few other issues arise in impracticability/frustration cases. First, courts in the past used to treat the impossibility doctrine as, in effect, an interpretive device. In Taylor v. Caldwell, for example, the court held that the contract contained an "implied condition" that the music hall would still be standing at the time of performance. If the music hall is not standing, then the condition is not satisfied, and hence the music hall owner has no obligation to provide the hall. Technically, the court does not need to rescind the contract because the contract, as interpreted, provides that the music hall owner's obligation vanishes, and thus the performers cannot sue the owner for violating that obligation. Today, courts usually avoid the condition language, and simply hold that a contract is rescinded if performance is impracticable. Not much turns on this difference.

But the differing language suggests two distinct ways of understanding the impracticability and frustration doctrines. The "conditions" language suggests that the doctrines create interpretive presumptions that the parties may bargain around. Courts assume that parties do not want to force each other to do the impossible (or, actually, to pay damages when it is impossible or impractical to perform) and so fill this contractual gap with an implied term that releases them under appropriate circumstances. The modern language suggests that the doctrines are more akin to "policing" doctrines like the duress doctrine or the mistake doctrine. Indeed, the impossibility doctrine resembles the mistake doctrine, as both account for failures of information — in the case of mistake, about the present, and in the case of impracticability, about the future. Where parties contract under incomplete information, maybe courts should more readily step in when their expectations are disappointed.

For both views, unforeseeability is key because it suggests that the reason the parties neglected to assign the risk is that they did not anticipate it. If the parties did not anticipate an asteroid strike or fire or labor dispute, then unconditional language requiring performance might not reflect their actual intention. By contrast, if the parties did anticipate the event, unconditional language implies that they assigned the risk to whichever party is adversely affected by it — that party must perform regardless. If one concludes that the parties did not anticipate the risk, one must still take the second step and determine whether they would have assigned the risk to the promisor or the promisee if they had anticipated it. This leads one back to the cheaper insurer argument, discussed above. Rational, cost-minimizing parties will assign the risk to whichever party can bear it most cheaply.

When courts rescind a contract under the impracticability or frustration doctrine, they must untangle the parties' relationship. Suppose, for example, that Contractor has partly constructed a building on Owner's land to the point where further performance becomes impossible. Contractor can stop work, but does it get compensation for the work it has done? Even if Buyer places no value on a partially constructed building? Or does Buyer get to keep the structure without having to pay anything? Or what if Buyer has made some progress payments? Courts generally apply principles of restitution to ensure that promisors are paid for their efforts and that promisees do not get anything for free. If Contractor does $100 of work before the contract is rescinded, and has not been paid, Contractor receives $100 in damages. If Owner pays $200 in advance, and no work is done, then Owner gets $200 in damages. If Contractor does $100 of work, and Owner pays $50 in an installment payment, then Contractor gets $50 in damages. There are complications — courts disagree about whether Owner must pay Contractor if Contractor incurs some reliance expenses but has not yet conferred a benefit — but they would take us afield.

§7.6   Good Faith

Courts frequently say that parties must act in good faith, but they rarely tell us what good faith means. In most cases, the concept of good faith overlaps with other rules and does no independent analytic work. For example, misrepresentation of the quality of a good would be considered bad faith, but the cause of action would be for fraud and, while a court might condemn the seller for her bad faith in passing, the plaintiff's case would rise or fall on whether the elements of fraud are satisfied.

In some cases, however, the idea of good faith does more analytic work. These are cases where performance, rather than contract formation, is in question. We saw some of these cases in Section 5.4. Feld v. Henry S. Levy & Sons[29] involved an output contract under which a baker was required to supply its entire output of bread crumbs to the buyer. The baker's output plummeted to zero when it dismantled the machinery that made bread crumbs in order to make space for other operations. Buyer argued that the baker violated its obligation to supply its total output, while the baker argued that it complied with that obligation by supplying its total output of zero. The court held that the baker acted in bad faith in an unsatisfactory opinion that acknowledged that if baker's costs rose enough, it could reduce output, but it did not explain how much those costs needed to rise.

A more precise account of good faith can be found in Market Street Associates v. Frey.[30] J.C. Penney needed to raise money, so it entered into a sale-leaseback with G.E. Capital. A sale-leaseback is a kind of loan where

---

[29] 335 N.E.2d 320 (N.Y. 1975).
[30] 941 F.2d 588 (7th Cir. 1991).

an owner of property (here J.C. Penney) sells that property to the lender in return for cash, and then rents that property from the lender/buyer. The owner never vacates the property and can still operate its stores. But the initial sale yields cash (akin to the loan payment), which the owner then (in effect) repays through a series of rental payments. The problem for Penney was that because it no longer owned the property, it could not pledge it as collateral for any new loans should it need additional capital to improve its buildings or construct new ones. To address this problem, the contract provided that if Penney needed more capital, G.E. Capital would have to negotiate in good faith, and if negotiations failed, Penney would have the right to buy the land back at the original price plus 6 percent per year.

The last clause, known as Paragraph 25, is interesting. If the parties could foresee future market conditions, then they would have agreed on a particular interest rate for the future loan. But they could not. So they could do no better than agree to negotiate. But this alone was not good enough for Penney, because if G.E. Capital held out for an unreasonably high rate, Penney would not be able to borrow money for operations and improvements. Thus, G.E. Capital gave Penny the option to buy the property back at a price that reflected the parties' best prediction of the future value of the land. Of course, this prediction was just that, and the actual market price of the land would inevitably favor one party or the other.

A few years passed, and Penney transferred the property to Market Street Associates. Sure enough, MSA realized that it needed to raise more capital. It tried going to a bank but no bank would loan without security, so MSA approached G.E. Capital for a loan. After some back-and-forth, G.E. Capital refused, and MSA exercised its option and got the property back for $1 million. At this point, G.E. Capital realized that it had been had — the price presumably had appreciated to much more than that (G.E. Capital had offered to sell it earlier for $3 million) — and refused to part with the land.

The district court held that MSA acted in bad faith, and while the appellate court reversed and remanded, it agreed that MSA might have acted in bad faith. Orenstein, an executive at MSA, sent a pair of letters to Erb, his counterpart at G.E. Capital. In these letters, Orenstein asked for a loan, thus opening negotiations for an infusion of capital. Orenstein did not mention the lease in the first letter, and although he mentioned it in the second letter, he did not mention Paragraph 25. When Erb refused to advance a loan (the loan MSA sought was too small), Orenstein responded by informing Erb that MSA would seek a loan elsewhere. Thereupon MSA sought to exercise its option to buy the property. It was the failure to mention Paragraph 25 that gave rise to the inference of bad faith. Orenstein may well have hoped and believed that Erb would not bother to read the lease, and thus not realize that failure to negotiate would give MSA the right to exercise the option.

Why is such behavior bad faith? One could argue that MSA was entitled to expect G.E. Capital to read a contract that it kept in its own files, and to realize the consequence of terminating negotiations. However, the appellate court noted that the cost for MSA of reminding Erb of Paragraph 25 was zero; Orenstein could have added a reference to the letter. The cost for G.E. Capital was quite high. If parties like MSA were permitted to engage in such "trickery," then parties like G.E. Capital would have to engage in expensive self-protective measures — adding another layer of bureaucracy, for example, to ensure that lower-level executives do not fail to read contracts. Contracts would be cheaper if parties could not exploit each other's inattention.

The argument can be put in hypothetical-bargain terms. As a general matter, if parties could anticipate that one or both could take advantage of the inattention of the other, where one could instead simply remind the other party of the relevant contract language, they would want to bar this conduct. If they did not, then each party would have to spend more money to protect itself — just as homeowners must spend money on locks to protect themselves from thieves, as the court noted.

One could reach the same result by engaging in aggressive contract interpretation. The contract did not say that MSA had to remind G.E. Capital of Paragraph 25 when it came time to negotiate a new loan. But one can always invent such an "implied term," based on the same hypothetical-bargain reasoning that we saw above. The court opted for the good faith approach, but it probably does not matter. The bottom line is that attempts to take advantage of the other party's failure to reread the contract — and no doubt many similar "sharp" practices — may be regarded as contract breaches.

Chapter *8*

Remedies

§8.1   In General

When a promisor breaches a contract, the promisee is entitled to a remedy. There are two basic types of remedies: damages and injunctions. Damages are a money payment from the breacher to the victim of breach. Injunctions are judicial orders that require the breacher to take an action (such as performance of the promise) or refrain from taking an action (such as an action inconsistent with the promise).

We can subdivide each type of remedy. There are several measures of damages; they can best be understood with the help of a numerical illustration. Seller and Buyer enter a contract under which Buyer agrees to pay $6 for a widget that costs $2 for Seller to produce. If Buyer invests $3 in reliance on the promise, the product is worth $12 to him; otherwise it is worth $8. After the parties enter the contract, Buyer invests $3 in reliance. However, before Buyer pays the price to Seller, Seller breaches so that she can sell the widget to a new buyer, Buyer 2, who offers to pay $8 for it. Consider the following remedies:

Expectation damages. Seller must put Buyer in the position he would have been if Seller had performed. If Seller had performed, Buyer would have received a widget worth $12 to him (because he made the $3 investment) and would have paid $6. Accordingly, damages are $12 – $6 = $6.

Reliance damages. Seller must put Buyer back in the status quo, the state of affairs before Buyer had incurred reliance costs of $3. Accordingly, damages are $3.

Nominal damages. Seller must pay a symbolic amount of money, say, $1, to Buyer. Damages are $1.

Punitive damages. Seller must pay a large amount of money to Buyer. The amount would typically be determined by a jury on the basis of the outrageousness of Seller's conduct. Let us stipulate that punitive damages in this case are $100.

Restitution/disgorgement. Seller must pay Buyer the profit from the sale to Buyer 2. Damages are $8 – $2 = $6.

Expectation damages is the standard measure of damages; the other types of damages are awarded only in special circumstances that we will explore below.

Victims of breach can also obtain injunctions. *Specific performance* refers to a judicial order directed at the breacher to do whatever he promised. For example, if the promisor promises to sell her house and fails to do so, specific performance means that the court orders the promisor to sell the house. If she continues to resist, the court could order her to pay fines or go to jail. A *negative injunction* means an order not to do something. In contracts cases, the most common example occurs when an employee fails to perform for the employer. A negative injunction would forbid the employee from working for a competitor.

When a person breaks a contract, the default remedy is damages. Specific performance is limited to real estate contracts and sales of unique goods. Negative injunctions may be issued in certain types of employment contracts. When damages are awarded, they are typically awarded on the basis of the expectation measure. Punitive damages are awarded only if the breach is also a tort that entitles the victim to punitive damages (for example, an egregious medical malpractice case in which the doctor violates a contract as well as committing a tort). Nominal damages are available when other remedies cannot be calculated because the loss is indeterminate: they are a symbolic method of declaring that a breach did occur.

§8.2   Expectation Damages

Suppose that Seller promises to deliver a widget to Buyer. The contract price is $100, and payment will be on delivery. At the time of the contract

Seller will value the widget at less than $100 (why else sell it?), and Buyer will value the widget at more than $100. Let's say that Seller values the widget at $90 and Buyer values the widget at $110.

Suppose first that Seller's valuation of widgets changes after she signs the contract. This might happen because the market price of widgets rises to, say, $120. Seller would rather sell the widget to someone else for $120 than she would to Buyer for $100. Or Seller might simply decide that she would rather keep the widget. The market value doesn't change, but Seller is proud of her fine craftsmanship, prouder than she had expected to be when she undertook the contract. Seller would like to breach, but whether Seller breaches depends on what Buyer's remedy will be.

Suppose next that Buyer's valuation of widgets changes after he signs the contract. This might happen because the market price of widgets falls to, say, $80. Buyer would rather buy the widget from someone else for $80 than from Seller for $100. Or Buyer might simply decide that he no longer needs the widget. Perhaps he had planned to expand his factory, and needed another widget to do so, but has since dropped these plans in response to changes in the economy.

These two possibilities are mirror images, so for simplicity I will discuss only the first. Generally speaking, the victim of a breach is entitled to expectation damages. *Expectation damages are equivalent to the amount of money necessary to put the promisee in the position he would have been if the promisor had not breached.*[1] In other words, expectation damages are a way of reproducing the outcome that would have resulted if the promisor had performed, though in terms of money.

If Seller breaches, then Seller has deprived Buyer of the ability to pay $100 for a widget that Buyer values at $120 — in other words, Seller has deprived Buyer of $20. Thus, expectation damages are $20. Notice that expectation damages are so low because we assume that payment is due on delivery, and thus that Buyer has not had to pay. Suppose instead that Buyer had paid the $100 up front. Then expectation damages would be $120. Or suppose that Buyer had paid $50 up front and promised to pay $50 upon delivery. Then expectation damages would be $70. Expectation damages are whatever it takes to make Buyer better off by $20 compared to his position just prior to signing the contract.

---

[1] See Restatement (Second) of Contracts §347 (1981):

Subject to the limitations stated in §§350-353, the injured party has a right to damages based on his expectation interest as measured by

(a) the loss in the value to him of the other party's performance caused by its failure or deficiency, plus
(b) any other loss, including incidental or consequential loss, caused by the breach, less
(c) any cost or other loss that he has avoided by not having to perform.

Now you might respond that Buyer's valuation of the widget was only $110 when he signed the contract. Why should he receive $20 rather than $10? The answer is that now that the market has shifted, the widget is worth (at least) $120 to Buyer. If Seller had performed, Buyer would have a widget worth $120, not $110. But suppose that Buyer's idiosyncratic valuation increases as well, so that Buyer values the widget at $130. Shouldn't Buyer receive damages of $30? The answer is no, because Buyer can use his damages of $20, along with the unpaid $100, to buy a new widget for $120 but worth $130 to him. If Buyer received damages of $30, he could use $120 to buy a new widget and have $10 left over. So he would end up with $140 rather than $130, which is overcompensation.

The classic case on expectation damages is Hawkins v. McGee.[2] A doctor performs a skin graft operation on the plaintiff, unwisely promising him a "100 percent perfect hand." The operation was supposed to remove a scar but instead produced a hairy, unusable hand. The plaintiff sues and wins on liability. Normally, doctors do not promise perfection and patients understand that there is a chance of failure, but in this case there was evidence that the doctor had used exaggerated language to induce the plaintiff to submit to an experimental treatment, and that was enough for the jury and the court.

The trial judge instructed the jury to award damages sufficient to compensate the plaintiff for the injury to the hand, along with pain and suffering. But, as the appellate court pointed out, damages calculated on this basis would not put the plaintiff in the position he would have been in if the contract had been successful and he had been given a perfect hand. The damages would merely put the plaintiff back to the status quo at the time of contracting. The trial court should have instructed the jury to award damages sufficient to compensate the plaintiff for the difference between a hairy hand and a perfect hand.

This difference between tort and contract is important to understand. If a tortfeasor punches someone in the nose, tort damages put the victim back in the status quo — where he was before he suffered an injury to his nose, plus pain and suffering. Money should cover the medical expenses, plus the pain and suffering — in the sense that the victim is indifferent between the pain and suffering and the cash he is due. By contrast, if a patient hires a doctor to perform an operation, the operation fails, and the failure is deemed a breach of contract, she does not receive compensation for the pain and suffering that normally accompanies an operation of that sort. The pain and suffering is part of the original deal — the patient expected to incur it, and consented to a deal where it would occur. The

[2] 146 A. 641 (N.H. 1929).

patient would receive contract damages — enough to put her in the position she would have been in had the contract been a success, and that includes damages only for pain and suffering that she would *not* have incurred if the operation had been successful.

The accompanying diagram illustrates the different approaches of the trial and appellate courts. The trial judge used a tort measure of damages, or what is called reliance damages in contract law, which we will discuss below.

The diagram shows simply that the difference in well-being is greater between a person who has a perfect hand and a person who has a hairy hand, than between a person who has his original hand and a person with a hairy hand. Thus, expectation damages (which would, in theory, make the victim indifferent between having a hairy hand and having a perfect hand) are greater than reliance damages (which would make the victim indifferent between having a hairy hand and having his original hand).

§8.3   The Mechanics of Calculating Expectation Damages

Breaches can occur at different times during a contractual relationship, and the time of the breach has consequences for contract damages. When calculating damages, keep firmly in mind that the victim of breach must end up where he would have been if the contract had been performed — but it can take some thought to figure out what this means in a particular case.

Imagine that Seller and Buyer agree on a contract for the sale of a widget for $6. Buyer expects to resell it for $8, for a profit of $2. In fact, if the contract had gone through, that is what would have happened; instead, Seller breaches. Consider the following cases.

Seller breaches before Buyer has paid the price. Then the damages are $2. If Seller had not breached, Buyer would have achieved a profit of $2.

Seller breaches after Buyer has paid the price. Then the damages are $8. Buyer has paid $6. To be made whole, he needs the $6 back plus an additional $2 so that he makes his profit.

One can imagine other situations. For example, the contract provides that Buyer pay $3 at the time the contract is signed and $3 upon delivery. Seller breaches in between these two events. Damages are $5. To be made whole, Buyer needs the $3 back that he paid, plus the $2 in lost profits.

Or consider the reverse. Imagine that Buyer breaches. Suppose Seller's cost is $5, so Seller expected a profit of $1. If Buyer breaches before Seller builds the widget, Seller's damages are $1. If Buyer breaches after Seller builds the widget, Seller's damages are $6. In the second case, it is assumed that no one else wanted the widget. If Seller can sell it to someone else for, say, $5, then Seller's damages are $1.

Sometimes, the calculation of damages is tricky, but there is an easy way to avoid confusion. Consider this example, taken from the Restatement:[3]

> Contractor agrees to construct a structure for Owner for $5000, but breaches after constructing a foundation and Owner has paid $2800. It would cost $4000 to complete the structure.

What damages does Owner get? The answer is $1800, which the Restatement describes as "the cost of completion less the part of the price unpaid." Try to figure out why $1800 is the right answer, then read the next paragraph.

The key to understanding this problem is to imagine how much Owner, the victim of breach, must pay to get the work finished (the remainder of Contractor's obligation), and subtract the amount that Owner must still pay (the remainder of Owner's obligation). The first amount — the remainder of Contractor's obligation — is obviously $4000. That is how much Owner must pay to get someone else to complete the work. The second amount — the remainder of Owner's obligation — is $2200. That amount is how much Owner would have to pay the original Contractor if Contractor had completed the project. It is simply the purchase price ($5000) minus the amount that the Contractor has already paid ($2800). Now subtract $2200 (Owner's remaining obligation) from $4000 (Contractor's remaining obligation), and you get $1800.

Here is another way to see it. If Owner hires a new contractor to finish the job, Owner must pay that new Contractor $4000. At the end of the work, Owner has paid out a total of $6800 ($2800 to Contractor 1, $4000 to Contractor 2), and has received the structure that was promised. But the original contract price was only $5000. Owner is down $1800 relative to what he was promised (a structure for $5000). To put him in the position he would have been in if the contract had been performed, Contractor must pay Owner that $1800 difference.

At a more abstract level, it helps to recall this simple formula:

$$\text{Contract price} = \text{cost} + \text{profit}$$

The party that expects to perform (the seller, the contractor, the worker) calculates a contract price that covers her costs and leaves her something

---

[3] Restatement (Second) of Contracts §346 illus. 4 (1981).

left over, which I will call the "profit." Technically, the profit covers a cost as well: the opportunity cost.[4] But leave that aside. If Seller errs and offers a price less than her cost, then her profit is negative, as in the example above. As we saw earlier, if Buyer breaches before Seller incurs the cost, damages are just the profit. If Buyer breaches after Seller incurs the cost, damages are the cost plus the profit.

When breach occurs partway through performance, we rewrite our formula as follows:

$$\text{Contract price} = \text{incurred cost} + \text{avoided cost}[5] + \text{profit}$$

Now, the damages must cover only the incurred cost plus the profit. We can rearrange the equation to obtain a method for calculating damages:

$$\text{Contract price} - \text{avoided cost} = \text{incurred cost} + \text{profit}$$

Courts sometimes calculate damages by looking at the left side of the equation. The reason is that profit is not a thing that one can easily measure — it's what's left over after costs have been incurred and payments have been made. So one can calculate damages (incurred cost + profit) just by taking the contract price and subtracting avoided costs, which can be measured by looking at how much Seller has saved on materials and labor that it expected to but did not have to purchase.

Finally, consider the more complicated case where Seller has partly performed and Buyer has partly paid — the Restatement example we discussed above:

$$\text{Paid contract price} + \text{unpaid contract price} = \text{incurred cost} + \text{avoided cost} + \text{profit}$$

Again, we can rearrange:

$$\text{Unpaid contract price} - \text{avoided cost} = \text{incurred cost} + \text{profit} - \text{paid contract price}$$

So if Buyer breaches, Seller can demand the unpaid contract price minus the avoided cost. By now, the analysis should be intuitive. If Buyer had performed, Seller would have obtained the unpaid contract price but Seller would also have incurred the avoided costs. Given that Buyer has not performed, Seller is entitled to the unpaid contract price minus those avoided costs.

What if Seller breaches rather than Buyer? Buyer's "profit" is his valuation of the structure minus the price. But in these construction contract cases, Buyer typically gets a substitute — that is, the structure built by

---

[4] See Section 8.7.
[5] Also called "cost of completion," as in the Restatement example above.

someone else. Thus, the "profit" is best understood as how much Buyer saves (if anything) by using Contractor rather than someone else. To make Buyer whole, the law must give Buyer the substitute performance at the original price in the contract. If Contractor has done nothing, Buyer just enters a contract with another Contractor and obtains as damages the difference between the new price and the contract price. (If they are the same, damages are zero.) If Contractor has partly performed, and Buyer has fully paid, then Buyer obtains from Contractor the cost of completion — that is, whatever price the new contractor charged to finish the job. If Buyer has paid nothing, then Buyer obtains from Contractor the cost of completion minus the original contract price. If Buyer has partly paid, then Buyer obtains the cost of completion minus the unpaid portion of the price.

We can summarize using the following formula:

Price of substitute performance = price of original performance + "profit"

Again, the "profit" is just what Buyer gains from using Contractor rather than someone else. If the price of the substitute performance is greater than the price of the original performance, the "profit" is greater than zero, and damages are set to equal to it. If Buyer finds another Contractor at the same price or less, Buyer does not get any damages; the Contractor has made him better off (or no worse off) by breaching.

In the case of partial performance and partial payment, the formula needs to be modified:

Cost of finishing work = unpaid installments + "profit"

As we saw above, Buyer is entitled to have the work finished at whatever price he agreed to. If the work is partially done and Buyer has partially paid, then completing the work should cost Buyer as much as he is required to pay the original contractor under the original contract. If the new contractor charges more than the original contractor — in effect, charges for the remainder of the work — then Buyer must be compensated for the difference; this is the "profit" that he lost as a result of the breach. To calculate the "profit" and hence the damages, subtract unpaid installments from both sides of the equation.

§8.4 The Efficient Breach Theory

Assume Seller can produce a widget at a cost of $2. Buyer values the widget at $10. They agree on a price of $6. There are two possible future states of the world. In one, Buyer 2 values the widget at $8, and in the other, Buyer 2 values the widget at $16. (We assume that Buyer 2 offers to pay her valuation, so that the price if Seller sells to Buyer 2 is the same as Buyer 2's valuation, $8 or $16.) Efficiency requires that the widget go to Buyer 2 if and only if Buyer 2 values the widget at $16. The reason is that if Buyer 2 values the widget at $16, he values it more than Buyer 1 (who values it at $10). If Buyer 2 values the widget at $8, he values it less than Buyer 1, in which case Buyer 1 should get the widget. We define efficiency here to mean that the widget ends up in the hands of the party who values it the most.

Which (if any) of our measures of damages gets us to the efficient result? To answer this question, we will compare only three of them — nominal damages, expectation damages, and punitive damages. As it turns out, the analysis of reliance damages is similar to that of nominal damages, and the analysis of specific performance is similar to that of punitive damages, so our discussion is more general than it appears. We will show that expectation damages alone produce the efficient outcome.

I set out the analysis below.

Buyer 2's valuation	Seller's payoff	Nominal: $d = 1$	Punitive: $d = 100$	Expectation: $d = v_1 - p$	Efficient outcome
8	Performance: $p - c$	$6 - 2 = 4$	$6 - 2 = 4$	$6 - 2 = 4$	
8	Breach: $p_2 - c - d$	$8 - 2 - 1 = 5$	$8 - 2 - 100 = -94$	$8 - 2 - 4 = 2$	
8	Choice	Breach	Performance	Performance	Performance
16	Performance: $p - c$	$6 - 2 = 4$	$6 - 2 = 4$	$6 - 2 = 4$	
16	Breach: $p_2 - c - d$	$16 - 2 - 1 = 13$	$16 - 2 - 100 = -86$	$16 - 2 - 4 = 10$	
16	Choice	Breach	Performance	Breach	Breach

The second column lists Seller's payoff, which depends on what Seller chooses to do — perform or breach. The first three rows consider the state of the world where Buyer 2 values the widget at $8, and the second three rows consider the state of the world where Buyer 2 values the widget at $16.

Consider the first three rows. If Seller performs, she receives a payoff of $p - c$, which is $6 (the price) minus $2 (her cost), which equals $4. This is always true regardless of what the measure of damages is. The measure of damages matters only when Seller chooses to breach. If Seller pays nominal damages of $1, then she receives a payoff of $5 (Buyer 2's payment of the price of $8, minus Seller's cost of $2, minus nominal damages of $1). Because the payoff from performance ($4) is less than payoff from breach ($5), Seller will breach. If Seller pays punitive damages of $100, then she receives a payoff of –$94, so she will perform (–$94 is a lot less than $4).

For expectation damages, the calculation is a little more complex. As before, if Seller breaches she receives $8 from Buyer 2 and incurs costs of $2, which equals $6. In addition, she must pay damages. Expectation damages equals Buyer 1's valuation (v) minus the price (p), so $10 – $6 = $4. To determine Seller's payoff from breach, we subtract the damages of $4 from the $6 above, and the result is $2. Because $2 < $4, Seller performs.

These calculations show that when Buyer 2's valuation is $8, Seller will perform under punitive damages and expectation damages, but not under nominal damages. Because performance is efficient (last column), in this state of the world punitive damages and expectation damages are more efficient than nominal damages.

Now we must perform the calculations for the bottom three rows. The exercise is roughly the same. For performance, the payoff is always $6 – $2 = $4. For breach, Seller now obtains a higher payoff of $16, so the payoffs are just $8 higher than before. Seller's choice does not change for nominal and punitive damages; Seller still breaches in the first case and performs in the second case. But under expectation damages, Seller now breaches — efficiently as the last column tells us. Expectation damages is the only measure for which Seller's decision is efficient in both states of the world.

To understand why, look at the two highlighted boxes. The damages in both cases are $4. What does that figure remind you of? It is the "profit" or surplus that Buyer 1 receives from the transaction. *Expectation damages produce the efficient outcome because they force Seller to bear exactly the cost that she imposes on Buyer by breaching:* $4. This is what economists call internalizing the externality. The same logic causes tort law to force the polluter to pay its victim an amount equal to the victim's loss. This rule ensures that the polluter will pollute only if her gain is greater than the victim's loss, which is socially efficient.

This is the efficient breach theory. It owes its fame to the simple way in which it solves a garden-variety mystery — why expectation damages should be the standard measure of damages. Unfortunately, the theory has a number of flaws. First, it does not take into account the possibility of ex post renegotiation. If Buyer 1 and Seller can renegotiate when Buyer 2 appears, the efficient outcome will occur regardless of the measure of damages. For nominal damages, Buyer 1 will pay Seller not to breach when Buyer 1 has the higher valuation. For punitive damages, Seller will pay Buyer 1 to release her from the contract when Buyer 2 has the higher valuation. If ex post negotiation is cheap (it may not be), the measure of damages does not matter for the breach decision.

Second, the theory addresses the perform/breach decision but not other decisions that are just as important. Consider Seller's (or Buyer's) decision to make reliance investments in advance of performance. We want both parties to make the decision to make a reliance investment when the joint benefits exceed the costs. But because the investing party may produce benefits that are enjoyed by the other party, it may not have adequate incentives to invest. It turns out that expectation damages (and reliance damages) cause the investing party to overinvest because they cause her not to take into account the possibility that the trade should not go through. There are other types of decisions that matter as well: to enter a contract in the first place, to disclose information about one's valuation, to renegotiate, and so on. The models quickly become complicated, and it is impossible to say what measure of damages does best in taking into account all these margins of behavior.

So efficient breach theory does not prove that expectation damages are the optimal measure of damages. But it is interesting, and it illustrates how one engages in economic analysis of remedies. And it helps one see what the relevant factors are when one evaluates different types of remedies.

§8.5 Cost of Performance versus Diminution in Value

Expectation damages can be calculated in two ways. Suppose that Seller agrees to build a house on a plot of land owned by Buyer. Seller builds the house but it does not conform to specifications. Buyer is unhappy, sues for breach of contract, and wins. He is entitled to expectation damages. Consider two possible ways of calculating expectation damages.

Under the diminution-in-value method, expectation damages equal the difference between the value of the property as built and the value that the property would have had if it had been built properly. For example, the land with the house on it would be worth $200,000 if the house had been built properly, but because it was built improperly, the land with the house on it is worth only $150,000. Damages would be $50,000.

Under the cost-of-performance method, expectation damages equal the cost of obtaining a substitute performance. Suppose it would cost $40,000 to tear down the improperly built portions of the house and rebuild them properly. Damages would simply be $40,000.

Which measure should be used? The Restatement, section 348(2), provides:

> If a breach results in defective or unfinished construction and the loss in value to the injured party is not provided with sufficient certainty, he may recover damages based on:

(a) the diminution in the market price of the property caused by the breach, or

(b) the reasonable cost of completing performance or of remedying the defects if that cost is not clearly disproportionate to the probable loss in value to him.

The rule allows the victim to choose as long as the cost of performance is not "clearly disproportionate," and applying the infallible principle that more money is better than less money, we know that Buyer would choose the award of $50,000.

You should understand why both measures are valid ways to calculate expectation damages. The sum of $50,000 makes the buyer whole because he gets what he bargained for — something worth $200,000 (a $150,000 house plus $50,000 in cash). The sum of $40,000 makes the buyer whole because he gets what he bargained for — a house worth $200,000. But of course these are not the same, and we will explain why below.

In the case of Groves v. John Wunder Co.,[6] Groves sold to John Wunder the right to use its land and extract gravel from it. Wunder paid $105,000 and, in addition, promised to return the land at a level grade at the end of the seven-year term. However, when Buyer left the premises, the land was not graded, and Groves sued for damages.

Groves sought $60,000, the cost of performance — hiring a firm with bulldozers and other earthmoving equipment to grade the land. Wunder countered that Groves should receive approximately $12,000, the diminution-in-value measure — the difference between the market price of the land as promised ($12,000) and the market price of the land as delivered ($0). Note that both measures make Groves whole, albeit in different senses. With $60,000, Groves can pay someone to grade the land, with the result he ends up with the level piece of land he was promised. With $12,000, Groves has the value of the land he was promised; if he wants, he could buy another piece of land similar to the land that he expected — graded, industrial-zoned land near Minneapolis.

The majority opinion initially argued that Wunder should pay the higher amount because he acted "willfully." As we will discuss shortly,[7] this argument is not a good one. All breaches are willful to some extent. The bulk of the opinion argued that Wunder should pay $60,000 because he breached the contract and should make Groves whole. But that argument prompts the question how to make Groves whole. The court argues that Groves bargained for a flat piece of land, not the monetary value of a flat piece of land. But how does the court know that?

Here is a clue. Imagine that Groves receives $60,000; how will he use this money? Will he use it to grade the land? The answer is surely no.

[6] 286 N.W. 235 (Minn. 1939).
[7] See Section 8.9, on willful breaches.

Groves is a profit-making businessman, and no such person would spend $60,000 on a project that yields a return of $12,000, for a net loss of $48,000. Groves might use $12,000 to buy a flat piece of land, or he might use it in some other way. Would the parties have agreed that John Wunder must similarly make such a bad investment?

If the parties had anticipated the drop in property value (which they surely did not — the Great Depression intervened between the execution and termination of the contract), they would have agreed that John Wunder would not convert $60,000 to $12,000. In return for saving $60,000 multiplied by the probability of a sudden drop in the value of the land, Wunder would have agreed to pass some of the savings back to Groves. So John Wunder would have paid somewhat more for the lease, in return for the option not to grade the land if its value declined beyond a threshold. Of course, the parties did not enter such an agreement, but here we see the diminution-in-value rule serving as a default rule that minimizes the costs of contracting.

Why, then, would courts ever order damages equal to cost of performance? The answer is that sometimes the victim of breach really does care about a particular performance, and is not satisfied with market values. The ugly fountain case is frequently cited.[8] Buyer hires a contractor to build an ugly fountain in Buyer's backyard. The design appeals to Buyer's dubious taste, but not to anyone else's. Contractor decides to breach — perhaps because the cost of materials increases — and Buyer sues for damages. Contractor cites the diminution-in-value measure, and argues that Buyer should receive zero damages because the property has a higher market value without the fountain than it would if the fountain had been built.

Buyer would be awarded cost-of-performance damages. Buyer sought the ugly fountain, not the market value equivalent. By contrast, Groves sought the market value equivalent of graded land, not the land itself. How do we know? Parties rarely say what they really want out of the contract, but we assume that business people and profit-making firms seek money, while consumers may have more idiosyncratic goals.[9]

Unfortunately, the Restatement does not make this simple distinction. Instead, it says that Buyer gets cost-of-performance, at his option, unless the cost-of-performance measure is "disproportionate to the probable loss of value." This phrase does not provide much guidance. Is $60,000 "disproportionate" to $12,000? It may be the case that courts generally give the victim the choice of remedy unless the cost-of-performance measure is significantly higher than the diminution-in-value measure, but the better rule is that victim does not receive cost-of-performance damages unless

---

[8] Restatement (Second) of Contracts §344 cmt. b, illus. 4 (1981).

[9] For this reason, commentators tend to argue that Peeveyhouse v. Garland Coal & Mining Co, 382 P.2d 109 (Okla. 1962), was wrongly decided because the victims of breach lived on their farm and may have derived aesthetic enjoyment from it.

she sought a particular idiosyncratic end (usually, the construction of something that would have personal value for her) rather than money.

§8.6 Lost-Volume Damages

Suppose that Buyer agrees to buy a boat from Seller for $12,000.[10] A few days before delivery, Buyer changes his mind and refuses to go through with the deal. Seller sues for breach of contract, but in the meantime finds another buyer who agrees to buy the boat for the same price, $12,000. Buyer, the defendant in the breach of contract suit, is liable for breach of contract, but he argues that damages should be $0 because Seller did not lose anything. She sold the boat for the same price, so she is in the same position she would have been in if Buyer had not breached.

The problem with this argument is that Seller would have made even more money if Buyer had not breached — Seller would have sold two boats rather than one. If Buyer had not breached, Seller would have made twice the profit.[11] Buyer's breach deprived Seller of "volume" — that is, reduced the quantity of sales — and so this scenario is known as the lost-volume problem.

To put Seller in the position she would have been if Buyer had not breached, Seller should receive profits on two boats rather than profits on one boat. Of course, she did receive the profit on the second sale, so expectation damages should be whatever the profit would have been on the first sale. Suppose, for example, that Seller operates simply by conveying Buyer's order to the wholesaler, who charges Seller the wholesale price of $11,000. Seller's profit would have been $1000, so damages are $1000 rather than, as Buyer argued, $0.

Sellers do not always suffer volume losses from breach. In our example, we assume that Seller can always order another boat from the manufacturer and pass it along to the next buyer. But this is not always the case. Suppose Buyer orders the last boat in Seller's warehouse and Seller could not order additional boats except at great expense. After Buyer's breach, Seller resells that boat at the same price. If Buyer had not breached, Seller would have had to turn down the next buyer because no more boats were in stock or could have been ordered. Now the breach does not deprive Seller of lost-volume profits, and so Buyer would not be required to pay extra damages beyond the difference between market price and contract price of the boat in question.

---

[10] Cf. Neri v. Retail Marine Corp., 285 N.E.2d 311 (N.Y. 1972).

[11] Actually, probably less than twice, because normally marginal benefits decline and marginal costs increase with volume. See R.E. Davis Chem. Corp. v. Diasonics, Inc., 826 F.2d 678, 683-684 (7th Cir. 1987).

In an analogous case, Seller breached a contract to deliver 88,700 pounds of coal by delivering only 8200 pounds.[12] Buyer sues, arguing that he should receive expectation damages equal to the cost of buying 8200 pounds of coal at the market price. Seller responds that the market price per pound of coal at the retail level (which applies to 8200 pounds) is greater than the market price per pound of coal at the wholesale level (which applies to the original amount), and that Seller should have to pay the lesser amount. The court agrees, because Buyer keeps a large stock of coal on hand, and replaced the shortfall by making additional purchases of tens of thousands of pounds at the wholesale rate.

The simple lesson here is that the principle of putting the victim of breach in the position he would have been in if the contract had been performed is not always obvious in its application. We have not examined all the complexities of the lost-volume problem, but if one keeps in mind the idea that the victim must be fully compensated (and not overcompensated), one will usually find one's way through these thickets.

§8.7 Reliance Damages

Recall our example from the chapter on expectation damages: the sale price of the widget is $100, Seller's cost is $90, and Buyer's valuation is $110. Let us now add the following assumption: after the contract is signed, Buyer incurs a cost of $5 in reliance on the promise. For example, in order to obtain maximum value from the widget, prior to delivery Buyer must adjust the assembly line in his factory. This costs $5. Suppose that the widget is worth $98 to Buyer if he does not incur the cost of $5, and it is worth $110 if he does. Seller breaches because her valuation of the widget rises from $90 to $120.

Buyer's expectation damages are $10. The reliance cost does not change the analysis. Buyer has already paid the $5. If Seller had delivered, Buyer would pay $100 for something worth $110 to him, given the reliance costs already incurred. The difference is $10. (Of course, if Buyer had not incurred the $5 reliance costs prior to breach, the analysis would be different. Seller's breach saves Buyer both the $100 price and the $5 reliance cost, while depriving Buyer of something worth $110, so Buyer's expectation damages would be $5.)

Reliance damages are the amount of money that is necessary to put the promisee back in the position he was in at the moment the contract was signed.[13] At the moment the contract was signed, Buyer had not incurred

---

[12] Ill. Cent. R. Co. v. Crail, 281 U. S. 57 (1930).
[13] See Restatement (Second) of Contracts §§344(b), 349 (1981).

the reliance cost. So to return him to that position, Seller pays Buyer reliance damages of $5.

Reliance damages compensate the promisee for out-of-pocket costs. Expectation damages compensate the promisee both for these costs and for any lost profits as well. It is possible that profits will be negative, but, if so, expectation damages put a ceiling on the amount that one can recover through reliance damages. Suppose, for example, that Buyer invests $50 in anticipation of the widget. This is a dumb idea; Buyer will end up paying $100 + $50 for a widget worth $110, but this sort of thing happens from time to time. Buyer's claim for $50 in reliance damages will be denied, because if Buyer had asked for expectation damages, he could have recovered only $10. The best Buyer can do in this case is to recover $10.[14] This rule ensures that Buyer cannot make Seller bear the cost of Buyer's dumb investment.

A complication: Opportunity costs. Suppose Buyer is a middleman with little capital. He buys widgets and resells them. Suppose after making a deal with Seller, he must borrow $100 at 10 percent in order to pay for a widget; he incurs a reliance cost of $5 in anticipation of delivery, say, to lease some storage space; then he finds a new buyer and resells the widget for $120. Buyer expects a profit of $5: $120 minus the $100 price minus the $5 lease minus the $10 interest (if the transaction takes a year). Suppose that Seller breaches by failing to deliver after Buyer incurs the reliance costs. It should be clear that Buyer's reliance costs include both the $10 in interest and the $5 for the lease. Interest is just the cost of obtaining the use of money, so it should be covered by reliance damages just as the cost of the lease must be covered. So reliance damages would be $15. Note that expectation damages would be $20 (the value minus the cost, which would cover Buyer's reliance expenses and the lost profit of $5).

Now suppose that Buyer already has $100, and doesn't need to borrow it. Buyer can keep the money in a bank and earn 10 percent interest. When Buyer takes the money out of the bank to pay for the widget up front, Buyer loses the opportunity of making $10 on that money over a year. When Seller breaches, Buyer's reliance costs include the $10 in forgone interest. The $10 is what economists call "opportunity cost." That is to say, in reliance on Seller's promise Buyer gave up the opportunity to earn $10 by putting the money in the bank. Because reliance damages compensate for costs, they should equal $15, that is, the lost $10 opportunity as well as the $5 paid on the lease. Expectation damages, under our current assumptions, should still be $20.

One more complication. Suppose that Buyer has the $100 in his pocket, and has the choice between investing it in some other venture and investing it in the venture in question. The other venture might be to pay another

---

[14] See L. Albert & Son v. Armstrong Rubber Co., 178 F.2d 182 (2d Cir. 1949).

seller, Seller 2, for the widget, rather than to pay Seller. Seller 2 charges $100 for the widget or perhaps (more realistically) a touch more; that is why Buyer chooses to deal with Seller. Now we know that Buyer expects to earn a $20 return on his deal with Seller. Rather than invest the $100 in this deal, Buyer could invest it with the bank (and earn $10) or invest it with Seller 2 and earn $20 or slightly less. If there is a market with lots of sellers, then we expect that Buyer can get more or less the same deal with some other seller, like Seller 2, as he can with Seller, so it seems reasonable to assume that the forgone return is $20 or close to it. In reliance on the promise by Seller to sell a widget for $100, Buyer gives up the opportunity to rely on a promise by Seller 2 to sell a widget for $100 and earn a return of $20 or a tad less. But we must remember the $5 for the lease; so the real lost opportunity is $15. But to determine reliance damages we add back in the $5 for the lease (which has been paid) to the $15 lost opportunity, and we get $20. But that means that Buyer's reliance damages and Buyer's expectation damages are the same. What is going on?

The answer is that expectation damages are a kind of reliance damages. If one includes opportunity costs as a form of "cost" — and there is every reason to do so — reliance damages give the promisee the same "profits" that are guaranteed by expectation damages.

It should be clear that the conceptual division between "expectation and reliance interests," which is reflected in the doctrinal division between "expectation and reliance damages," is misleading.[15] Although the reliance interest really is the same as the expectation interest, people mean by reliance "all the promisee's costs except for his opportunity costs." One way of making sense of this confusion is to note that the promisee always has the burden of proof. If he can't prove his lost profits (and thus be entitled to expectation damages), he must be content with compensation for provable costs (and thus be entitled to reliance damages). But it means the same thing to say that the promisor is entitled to as much money as is sufficient to cover costs caused by breach, including opportunity costs and any other costs. And where victims of breach are entitled only to reliance damages as a matter of law — as is usually the case with promissory estoppel — a clever advocate can make the case that his client should receive lost profits because in relying on the promise he gave up opportunities to make profits elsewhere.

Post-contractual reliance. This point about opportunity costs also applies when the promisee seeks reliance damages to cover costs he incurred *after* the contract was entered. At first sight, this looks odd. If reliance damages puts one back to the status quo, and the status quo existed before one entered a contract, why would one be entitled to damages for reliance costs incurred after the contract?

---

[15] See Richard Craswell, Against Fuller and Purdue, 67 U. Chi. L. Rev. 99 (2000).

Consider, for example, Chicago Coliseum Club v. Dempsey.[16] A boxing promoter enters a contract with a boxer, Jack Dempsey, under which Dempsey would fight another boxer named Harry Wills. Dempsey breached, and the promoter sued for damages. Expectation damages were denied because gate receipts, and therefore the promoter's lost profits, were speculative. But the promoter was entitled to reliance damages, such as the fee it paid to an architect for plans for the venue. The promoter also asked for damages covering the cost of the Wills contract, which the court denied because the Wills contract was entered prior to the contract with Dempsey. As the court noted, the promoter "speculated as to the result of his efforts to procure the Dempsey contract";[17] it could have avoided this loss by entering the contract with Wills later, or making the two contracts contingent on each other.

Yet in Anglia Television Ltd. v. Reed,[18] a British court held the opposite. In that case, the actor Robert Reed, of *Brady Bunch* fame, agreed to appear in a British television program, and later breached. Before entering the contract, the television company hired a director and other personnel. Again, expectation damages were not available because lost profits were speculative, and the television company sought reliance damages covering the expenses incurred prior to the contract. The best explanation for awarding reliance damages covering pre-contractual expenses is that if Reed had refused to enter the contract, the television could have hired another actor. The program would have been made and revenues received that would have covered the expenses. The pre-contractual status quo includes the power to hire some other actor; to return the television company to the status quo, the monetary equivalent of that power must be given. This is again the concept of opportunity costs: the television company lost the opportunity to hire someone else. The logic applies to the *Dempsey* case, although one might distinguish that case on the ground that the promoter might not have been able to recover the cost of hiring Wills by finding some other boxer if Dempsey said no. It is possible that people only wanted to see Wills versus Dempsey, and would not have been willing to pay to see, say, Wills v. Mr. Bean.

§8.8   Restitution Damages

Restitution damages compensate the promisee for any benefit conferred on the promisor.[19] This is a messy area of the law that fits messily with

---

[16] 265 Ill. App. 542 (Ill. App. Ct. 1st Dist. 1932).
[17] Id. at 551.
[18] [1971] 3 All E.R. 690 (Court of Appeal, 1971).
[19] See Restatement §371 (1981):

the other doctrines of contract law. Indeed, restitution and its accompanying notions (quasi-contract, implied in law contract, quantum meruit, and so on) come from a part of law outside of contract law, the law of unjust enrichment. In the classic unjust enrichment case, a physician helps an unconscious patient, then sues for a fee after the patient refuses to pay. The physician conferred a benefit on the patient, and is entitled to restitution. There is no contract (or tort) here. Restitution becomes relevant for contract law when unjust enrichment occurs in the context of contractual relations.

Restitution problems in contract law arise in four patterns. First, the promisor breaches a contract, and the promisee simply prefers restitution to some other remedy, such as expectation damages. For example, I make a down payment toward the purchase of a car, and the seller of the car breaches after its market price rises. I am entitled to expectation damages, which will be greater than my down payment, but I may be perfectly happy to get my down payment back.[20] Maybe expectation damages are too hard to prove, so I ask for restitution instead. The money I gave to the seller is a benefit conferred on him, and I am entitled to the value of that benefit.

Second, a contract is void because of duress, incompetence, mistake, impossibility, violation of the consideration doctrine or the Statute of Frauds, or some other reason, but in the meantime one party conferred a benefit on the other. For example, I pay in advance for the car, and then the day before delivery, the seller breaches. When I sue for expectation damages, the seller observes that the contract was never put in writing and therefore argues that it is not valid. The judge agrees, and the contract is not enforced. But I have lost my down payment. I cannot get my down payment back by suing for breach of contract because there is no contract to sue on. Instead, I make an unjust enrichment claim and ask for restitution, which the court would grant.[21]

Third, the *promisor* breaches and sues for damages. The classic case is Britton v. Turner,[22] where the owner of a farm hired plaintiff to work for a year at a wage of $120. The plaintiff left work after nine and a half months,

---

If a sum of money is awarded to protect a party's restitution interest, it may as justice requires be measured by either

(a) the reasonable value to the other party of what he received in terms of what it would have cost him to obtain it from a person in the claimant's position, or

(b) the extent to which the other party's property has been increased in value or his other interests advanced.

[20] See Bush v. Canfield, 2 Conn. 485 (1818) (returning Bush's $5000 down payment on 2000 barrels of flour that was never delivered).

[21] See Boone v. Coe, 154 S.W. 900 (Ky. 1913), where, however, restitution was not ordered because a benefit had not been conferred.

[22] 6 N.H. 481 (1834).

and the employer refused to hand over the wage or a portion of it. The court held that plaintiff could sue for restitution for the benefit conferred on the employer. Normally, we do not think that the wrongdoer (the contract breacher) is entitled to damages, but the court believed that it would be unjust to allow the employer to benefit from the worker's labor. Here again we see the tension between contractual principles — you are free to agree to a deal where you risk getting nothing — and certain notions of fairness. There is no economic reason to forbid the employee to take this risk, and it is easy to think of reasons why the deal might have made sense to the parties. For example, suppose the worker is trained during the first part of the year, and then only does productive work during the second part. By leaving, he can get a higher wage from a competing farm owner who benefits from the training paid for by the first farm owner. Indeed, the court seemed to recognize this point, declaring that its holding was just a default rule that parties can contract around. And they do. Modern pensions, for example, vest after the worker has spent a period of time working for the employer.

Britton was an unusual case; but the rule in *Britton* has long been followed in construction contract cases. Suppose that the building constructed by a contractor under contract deviates in a small way from the specifications in the contract. The building's deviation is like the employee leaving early. Owners may try to withhold payment (normally, the last progress payment) but contractors can sue for restitution and usually win. Courts permit parties to contract around this rule, at least in theory.[23] My impression, however, is that parties rarely do. Owners and contractors know that a perfect building is virtually impossible, and it is hard to imagine a contractor agreeing to forfeit payment if performance is less than perfect. The default rule tracks this understanding.[24]

Fourth, a contract is valid, the promisor breaches, and the promisee is not entitled to expectation or reliance damages because his profit would have been negative, so he asks for restitution instead. Suppose that Contractor agrees to erect a crane for $100.[25] Contractor expects its cost to be $80. Halfway through the project, Contractor has incurred costs of $70, has received $50 in progress payments, and expects to incur another $70 in costs in order to complete the project. Because of error or unanticipated adversity, Contractor has entered a "losing contract," meaning a contract that produces a loss rather than a gain — here a loss of $40 ($100 − $140) rather than the expected gain of $20 ($100 − $80).[26]

---

[23] Jacob & Youngs v. Kent, 129 N.E. 889 (N.Y. 1921).

[24] See, e.g., Pinches v. Swedish Evangelical Lutheran Church, 10 A. 264 (Conn. 1887).

[25] United States v. Algernon Blair, Inc., 479 F.2d 638 (4th Cir. 1973).

[26] More precisely, Contractor expects to lose on the remainder of the contract — the remaining progress payments add up to a sum less than the remaining costs. If for some

At this halfway point, Buyer breaches. It is puzzling why Buyer would breach, given that he receives a project that normally costs $140 for a price of $100, but it is possible that Buyer simply does not value the project any more — again because of changes in conditions — or makes a mistake. In any event, Contractor now must decide what to do. It has incurred costs of $70 and received $50 in progress payments, so it is down $20.

As the wronged party, Contractor can sue for breach of contract and demand a remedy. The odd feature of losing contracts, however, is that expectation damages are zero. Contractor is down $20; if Buyer had not breached, Contractor would have had to complete the project, and been down $40. The breach thus makes the Contractor better off, not worse off. Expectation damages cannot be negative, but they can be zero, and that is all Contractor would receive.

Instead of seeking expectation damages, Contractor asks for restitution on the theory that it has conferred a benefit on Buyer by half-erecting the crane. Clearly, a benefit has been conferred: Buyer is closer to his goal of enjoying the use of a crane. To determine restitution, the court must attach a value to this benefit. A conventional way of doing so is to determine the market price of the halfway performance — how much it would cost to hire a contractor to erect the crane halfway. This amount is $70 in our example. Contractor is entitled to this amount as restitution damages.[27]

The rule makes little sense and has some negative consequences. Consider the perspective of Buyer. When considering whether to breach, he should compare the benefits of breaching and the benefits of not breaching. If he breaches, then he must pay Contractor $70, and in addition he must pay someone else $70 to finish the product. As a result, he obtains use of the crane at a cost of $140. If he does not breach, then Contractor must finish the project, and Buyer must pay Contractor the original price of $100. As a result, Buyer obtains use of the crane at a cost of $100. Clearly, Buyer will not breach the contract — even though breaching makes Contractor better off than complying with the contract and demanding performance.

For another example of this phenomenon, consider a contract between a lawyer and a client.[28] The lawyer charges $100 per hour for representing the client in a divorce, or a flat fee of $10,000. The client chooses the flat fee option. The lawyer works for 200 hours, and then the client fires him. The divorce is not yet complete, and the client hires a new lawyer to finish representing him.

---

reason Contractor received a lot of money in advance, the contract as a whole could be beneficial for Contractor.

[27] This fact pattern is actually quite close to the first; but it is important to see that because of the losing contract, the contractor has a stronger incentive to seek restitution.

[28] Cf. Oliver v. Campbell, 273 P.2d 15 (Cal. 1954).

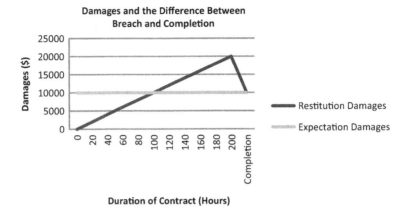

Damages and the Difference Between Breach and Completion

Duration of Contract (Hours)

The lawyer sues for breach of contract and wins. The question is what the damages will be. Expectation damages are $10,000 — the amount of money that the lawyer has been promised (minus cost savings through mitigation). But the lawyer could also ask for restitution damages. What is the benefit conferred? The client has received the benefit of 200 hours of representation, which probably has a market value of $100 per hour — the amount the lawyer would have charged on an hourly basis. Restitution damages are thus $20,000. Just as in our prior case, the lawyer earns more than she would have earned if the client had not breached, and the client could have avoided this extra payment — to the detriment of the lawyer — by not breaching. The accompanying graph makes clear the peculiar incentives that this rule creates. Client's restitution damages increase monotonically over the period of performance until the very end, when they plunge to $10,000.

The perplexing results in these cases are due to the mixing of two different legal theories — contract and unjust enrichment. Contract law directs courts to enforce parties' agreements; unjust enrichment directs courts to reverse "unjust" transfers of value from benefactors to beneficiaries. Each system works well enough in its domain; trouble arises when they overlap. In the lawyer-client case, the lawyer had conferred substantial benefits on the client, but the two parties had also agreed that the hourly rate would not be the measure of these benefits for complete performance. If breach does not occur, then the lawyer receives the agreed-upon amount of $10,000 rather than an amount calculated on an hourly basis. The difficulty arises because the parties did not say how much the lawyer would receive if the client fired her partway through performance.

Normally, this doesn't matter. When the contract is not a losing contract, the victim will demand expectation damages. If the lawyer had worked for only ten hours, she would sue for the contract price of $10,000 rather than the restitution value of $1000. The client will be deterred from breaching unless the benefit from breaching exceeds this cost. This might be the case if he finds a better lawyer, for example.

In addition, when the contract is a losing contract and the beneficiary does not breach, the problem does not arise. If the client does not fire the lawyer, the lawyer will not have an opportunity to ask for restitution damages. Courts do not award restitution damages when performance is completed because then the contract "controls." But why doesn't it control before then?

The problem arises only when the contract is a losing contract for one party *and* the other party breaches. This is unusual, especially given the incentives provided by the law not to breach a contract that is losing for the other party, so the practical effects of this doctrinal wrinkle are limited.

§8.9 Willful Breaches and Heightened Damages

In Groves v. John Wunder Co.,[29] the court held that the breacher should pay cost-of-performance damages rather than diminution-in-value damages because the former were higher, and the breacher should be punished for his "willful" breach: the breacher could have graded the land but simply chose not to. In Jacob & Youngs v. Kent,[30] the court held that the breacher should not pay cost-of-performance damages because the breach was inadvertent: the breacher had installed the wrong pipe through an oversight; the action was not willful.

Yet all breaches involve willfulness. The contractor in *Jacob & Youngs* could have torn down the building and started over with the correct pipe. It could have, but it chose not to. That choice was just as willful as the choice of the breacher in *Groves*. So what explains the differences in damages?

We can make some progress by introducing some distinctions. In some contract cases, the breach can be attributable to an earlier event. The earlier event occurs, and as a result of it, the cost of performance goes up. In *Jacob & Youngs*, the earlier event was the installation of the wrong pipe. Once the contractor installed the wrong pipe, the cost of performance shot up, as it would involve the demolition and reconstruction of the building. If the further work takes the contractor past the deadline, then the increased cost includes the payment of damages for delay. The court believed the failure to install the pipe was inadvertent, not even negligent; even if the later breach was willful, it was ultimately the result of an event that was not the contractor's fault.

---

[29] 286 N.W. 235 (Minn. 1939), discussed in Section 8.5.
[30] 129 N.E. 889 (N.Y. 1921); discussed in Section 7.3.

By contrast, the breach in *John Wunder* seems more objectionable, from a moral standpoint, at least at first sight. Wunder realized that the land was not worth very much if graded, and a lot less than the parties had anticipated (the Great Depression intervened and land prices collapsed). Still, grading the land would have been no more expensive than if land prices had not collapsed. So there might be something gratuitous about Wunder's breach, as compared with the contractor's in *Jacob & Youngs*.

But in many cases, the helplessness of the breacher is of no concern to anyone. When an insurance company insures a house against fire, it must pay compensation if the house burns down. The insurer could not have prevented the fire; the "event" — the fire — is inadvertent. Yet a failure to pay would be considered as willful as any other breach.

With some exceptions, courts do not pay much attention to the willfulness of the breach — or the fault or lack of fault of the breacher.[31] There are two reasons for this rule. First, unlike in tort, parties can stipulate in advance what will count as breach; and so if the contractor does not want to have to pay for an inadvertent mistake, he can insist on a provision in the contract that protects him. Second, the victim of breach must pay for heightened damages in the form of a higher ex ante price. If expectation damages fully compensate the victim, then extra damages for breach will be supracompensatory, driving up the promisor's costs, which she will pass on to contracting parties. Yet from the victim's perspective, a loss is a loss, and it should not matter whether the loss was caused by inadvertence, negligence, or willful action.

§8.10   Limitations on Damages

The foreseeability (or *Hadley*) rule, the mitigation rule, and the speculative loss rule all place limits on the amount of damages that a promisee can obtain. Usually, they are discussed as limits on expectations damages, though they appear to limit reliance damages as well, and there is every reason to think that they should.

Foreseeability

When Seller breaches a contract and fails to deliver goods, Buyer is expected to obtain substitutes on the market and sue for the difference

---

[31] Cf. George M. Cohen, The Fault Lines in Contract Damages, 80 Va. L. Rev. 1232 (1994). For a recent symposium on the role of fault in contract law, which turns out to be complex, see Omri Ben-Shahar & Ariel Porat, Foreword: Fault in American Contract Law, 107 Mich. L. Rev. 1341 (2009).

between the market price and the contract price. What if Buyer does not buy substitutes? Consider a Buyer who plans to use the goods as inputs in a production process; when Seller breaches, Buyer shuts down his factory because he can no longer produce the goods. He then sues Seller for lost profits, an amount considerably greater than the difference between the contract price and the market price. To obtain these lost profits, Buyer asks for "consequential damages," as distinguished from the difference between contract price and market price. Of course, the rule is symmetrical: if Buyer breaches, Seller should find another buyer rather than, say, destroy the goods and ask for consequential damages.

Yet there are situations where the victim of breach is entitled to consequential damages. The rule is stated in the old case of Hadley v. Baxendale.[32] In that case, a miller hired a carrier to deliver a broken crankshaft to the repair shop. The carrier was delayed, and the mill was shut down for the period of the delay. The miller sued for lost profits during the delay. The court held that the miller could not obtain damages from the delay. The carrier had reason to expect that the miller had an extra crankshaft and so that a delay would not result in an extended shutdown of the factory.

An initial source of confusion concerns what "consequential damages" means. The term suggests that it is something tacked onto other damages, but that is not accurate. A better way to think about consequential damages is by noting that in any business context, there will be a range of losses resulting from breach of contract. If a carrier fails to deliver the goods, or delivers them only after a delay, the loss could be literally zero, or it could be moderate, or very high. The average or modal loss will be lower than the losses at the high end of the distribution. The court in *Hadley* implicitly held that the victim of breach will be entitled to the average or normal loss unless he has good reason to believe that the loss will be unusually high — and one good reason would be that the victim told the breacher at the time of contracting that the victim attaches an especially high value to performance.

---

[32] Derived from the case Hadley v. Baxendale, 9 Ex. 341 (1854). See also Restatement (Second) of Contracts §351 (1981):

(1) Damages are not recoverable for loss that the party in breach did not have reason to foresee as a probable result of the breach when the contract was made.

(2) Loss may be foreseeable as a probable result of a breach because it follows from the breach

(a) in the ordinary course of events, or

(b) as a result of special circumstances, beyond the ordinary course of events, that the party in breach had reason to know.

(3) A court may limit damages for foreseeable loss by excluding recovery for loss of profits, by allowing recovery only for loss incurred in reliance, or otherwise if it concludes that in the circumstances justice so requires in order to avoid disproportionate compensation.

The term used nowadays is reasonable foreseeability. The normal loss is reasonably foreseeable; the unusually high loss is not. The choice of words is unfortunate, however. Foreseeability is one of those notions that is hard to keep within bounds. Very high losses are obviously foreseeable; maybe they are even reasonably foreseeable. So why make any distinction at all?

To answer this question, one must recall that nothing is free in contract law, and so if the victim of breach is entitled to "high" (consequential) damages, then, ex ante, he is required to pay for it. Sellers are repeat players; think of Federal Express. If Federal Express must pay the actual loss of buyers regardless of how high it is, then Federal Express will charge buyers an extra amount that covers this loss. If Federal Express must pay the loss of buyers only when the loss is the average loss or below, then the extra amount it charges will be lower. The question is whether buyers want to pay more ex ante in return for greater protection or insurance ex post.

One answer is that buyers want to be fully compensated and will pay for it. But, as we saw, buyers are diverse; some expect high losses and others expect low losses. Indeed, some buyers will buy insurance from third parties, and thus do not want to pay for any insurance at all. In any event, roughly speaking, higher-value buyers, as we will call them, should pay a higher price and receive higher damages; lower-value buyers should pay a lower price and receive lower damages. In return for the higher price and to avoid the higher liability, Seller will take extra precautions with respect to the higher-value performance; otherwise, Seller will take fewer precautions, which is efficient because the performance is worth less to the (lower-value) buyer.

If the parties enter complete contracts, then it does not matter what the rule is. Indeed, today carriers do enter highly detailed contracts: essentially, they limit liability for delay or destruction of the package (say, to $100) and then charge a separate fee for insurance against higher losses. If you don't pay the fee, you don't get consequential damages. The *Hadley* rule is a default rule: it comes into play only when the parties do not say what happens if the loss is above average.

The traditional explanation for the *Hadley* rule is that it gives higher-value buyers an incentive to disclose their otherwise hidden valuation to the seller (and vice versa: seller to buyer). Without the rule, the higher-value buyer does not want to reveal this information. If the seller breaches, she must pay the full loss to the buyer. If she knows in advance that the buyer is higher-value, she will pass along this cost and charge the higher-value buyer a high price. The *Hadley* rule provides that the higher-value buyer receives full compensation only if he reveals his high valuation, and thus he will do so, even though he must pay the higher price. And because Seller knows that Buyer is higher-value, Seller will take appropriate precautions in performance.

The argument is clever but it has a problem. Suppose that the rule is unlimited liability. It is true that the higher-value buyer has no reason to disclose his (high) valuation to Seller; but it is also the case that the *lower-value buyer* now has a reason to disclose his (low) valuation to Seller. The reason is that if Seller does not know which customer is higher-value and which is lower-value, Seller must charge an average price that fully compensates her for expected liability where some buyers are higher-value and some are lower-value. The lower-value buyer can obtain a lower price by disclosing his low valuation (more precisely, by agreeing to limited liability in the contract), because Seller will pass along the lower expected liability to him in the form of a lower price. Meanwhile, the higher-value buyers remain silent, but Seller can infer from their silence that they are higher-value — because all the lower-value buyers speak up — and can charge all the higher-value buyers a higher price.

So it is not entirely clear that the *Hadley* rule is superior to a rule of unlimited liability. The full analysis requires one to take into account a lot of hard-to-evaluate facts: the distribution of higher- and lower-value types in the population, the cost of disclosure, the cost of excessive or inadequate precautions, and so forth.

The recurring problem in *Hadley* cases is determining what is reasonably foreseeable. In *Hadley* itself, the carrier could surely have foreseen the possibility that the mill would be shut down, with a loss of profits, during any delay. But the court believed that the carrier would reasonably expect the mill to have an extra shaft, so that a shutdown would not take place.[33] The cost of delay would be zero. We can contrast *Hadley* with *Victoria Laundry*, where the installation of an enormous boiler for a commercial laundry facility was delayed.[34] The court awarded consequential damages covering lost profits because in that case the seller, an engineering firm that specialized in this transaction (unlike the carrier, who probably knew nothing about mill operations), should have realized that the laundry could not operate during the delay. It could not have had a spare boiler somewhere.

A related problem is determining when communication gives adequate notice of the idiosyncratic loss. In *Globe Refining*,[35] Justice Holmes took a hard line. A buyer might inform a seller that the loss would be high, but

---

[33] Although the reporter of the case reported that the miller disclosed to the carrier that the factory was shut down, the actual opinion appears not to assume that this is the case, or otherwise attaches no importance to it, perhaps because the disclosure may have seemed too casual or otherwise not adequate.

[34] Victoria Laundry (Windsor) Ltd. v. Newman Indus., Ltd., [1949] 2 K.B. 528. For a similar case, see Hector Martinez Co. v. Southern Pacific Transportation Co., 606 F.2d 106 (5th Cir. 1979) (holding that the rent paid for heavy equipment borrowed because of delay in delivery of equipment shipped is recoverable as a foreseeable loss).

[35] Globe Refining Co. v. Landa Cotton Oil Co., 190 U.S. 540 (1903).

the seller need not accept an obligation to take on that loss. What is necessary is to infer whether the parties agreed that the buyer would pay the seller to accept the loss — or a "tacit agreement," as Holmes put it. The argument makes sense. If Buyer casually mentions to Seller that he plans to use the widget to make a lot of money, Seller is not necessarily put on notice that Buyer expects Seller to pay an unusually high level of damages if breach occurs. After all, Buyer might have some contingency plans — a substitute lined up somewhere — if breach occurs. However, courts have backed away from the tacit agreement test, and indeed in practice the *Hadley* rule today does not seem to put much of a limit on liability at all. The victim of breach must always cover if she can; and if she can but does not, she will not receive consequential damages for lost profits. But otherwise courts seem pretty liberal about awarding consequential damages. The inevitable result is that virtually every contract has a clause that limits liability and/or excludes consequential damages.

One further lesson is that the *Hadley* rule implies that victims of breach are not always fully compensated. A victim of breach will be fully compensated only if (1) he has a "normal" (foreseeable) loss, or (2) he disclosed that his loss would be unusually high at the time of contracting. If one of these conditions is not met, then the higher-value victim ends up getting the expectation damages that would be sufficient to compensate the normal victim. As we saw above, the reason may be to encourage the victim to disclose information that minimizes the loss from breach. The important lesson is that contract law puts duties on both parties — breacher and victim — and not just on the breacher.

Mitigation

The mitigation doctrine says that if a promisee fails to take steps to reduce a loss after breach, the promisee cannot recover for the avoidable loss.[36] For example, suppose that the seller breaches a contract by refusing to deliver goods. The contract price of the goods is $100 and the market price is $150. The *unavoidable* loss is $50. Now suppose that instead of buying replacements on the market for $150 and suing for the difference, the buyer shuts down his factory, for a loss of $1000. One can argue that the breach led to a total loss of $1000, but $950 of that loss was avoidable, and therefore the buyer cannot recover for it. It was avoidable because the buyer could have kept his factory open if he had purchased

---

[36] See Restatement (Second) of Contracts §350 (1981):

(1) Except as stated in Subsection (2), damages are not recoverable for loss that the injured party could have avoided without undue risk, burden or humiliation.

(2) The injured party is not precluded from recovery by the rule stated in Subsection (1) to the extent that he has made reasonable but unsuccessful efforts to avoid loss.

on the market, that is, "covered" (on which more follows). So the mitigation doctrine discourages the buyer from letting costs run up after a seller's breach causes some initial loss.[37]

The duty to mitigate can give rise to confusion about whether a victim of breach can recover for overhead costs. All businesses have fixed costs (for example, salaries for permanent employees and rent) and variable costs (for example, materials and assistance needed on a project-by-project basis). Consider a contractor who sues for breach. She seeks the contract price (say, $10,000) minus avoided (or avoidable) costs (say, $2000), which equals $8000. The theory is that $8000 compensates her for lost profits and unavoidable (that is, overhead) costs. The defendant argues that contractor should not recover for overhead costs; she would have incurred them even if the contract had never been entered in the first place. So overhead costs should be subtracted. Courts hold in favor of the contractor.[38] Expectation damages should put you in the position you would have been in if the contract had been performed. The contract price reflects a bargain that gives the victim not only profits but sufficient money to cover a share of overhead expenses, as well as the variable costs which by hypothesis are not incurred.

Note the tension between these cases and cases like *Dempsey*,[39] where the victim is entitled only to reliance damages, and overhead costs cannot be recovered. The basis for this difference is not clear. Reliance damages should send the victim back to the status quo, when overhead costs had not yet been incurred. But for the contract, the victim might have recovered the overhead costs through a transaction with a different party.

What if the breach allows the victim to obtain more business elsewhere? Shouldn't this amount be subtracted from damages? If performance really would have prevented the victim from providing profitable services to someone else, the answer is yes. Consider a portrait painter who takes on a new job when the original promisor breached. If the promisor had not breached, the painter could not have taken this new job, and so a portion of the profits from that job should be subtracted from damages. But this is not usually the case for businesses, which can usually expand output to meet demand.[40]

Additional issues arise when employees are the victims of breach of contract. Employees must also mitigate — which means obtaining an identical job, if one is available, in which case damages are reduced by the

---

[37] See also Rockingham County v. Luten Bridge Co., 35 F.2d 301 (4th Cir. 1929).

[38] See Leingang v. City of Mandan Weed Bd., 468 N.W.2d 397 (N.D. 1991). See also J.O. Hooker & Sons v. Roberts Cabinet Co., 683 So. 2d 369 (1996) (determining that a subcontractor's costs for renting storage space for building materials were not to be paid as contract damages because they were a fixed cost).

[39] See Section 8.7.

[40] See Kearsarge Computer, Inc. v. Acme Staple Co., 366 A.2d 467 (N.H. 1976):41. Parker v. Twentieth Century Fox Film Corp., 474 P.2d 689 (Cal. 1970).

employee's salary at the new job. But what if the identical job is not available? Courts hold that the employee need not accept jobs that are worse.[41]
So the employee's duty to mitigate is more limited than that of a contractor or buyer or seller. The likely reason for this difference is that employees accumulate experience and expertise when they work, which helps
them get better jobs, and promotions and wage increases in the future. In
addition, many employees choose their jobs just because they like them.
If they were required to take worse jobs by the duty to mitigate, they would
certainly be undercompensated, unless somehow the "worseness" could
be monetized and converted into damages.

Workers who are fired often receive various benefits from third
parties — insurance, social security, and the like. When they sue for damages, the employer will argue that those payments should be subtracted
from damages for lost wages (applying the "collateral source rule"). Courts
have divided over the argument. The third-party source of funds creates a
wedge between what the breacher pays and what the victim receives.
Should the breacher pay the full amount, with the result that the victim is
overcompensated? Or should the breacher pay the reduced amount, with
the result that the victim is adequately compensated? Normally, we think
that the victim should not be overcompensated; this suggests that the
third-party payments should be deducted from the damages. But the problem is that if the employer does not expect to pay full damages, it will
breach excessively, and the taxpayer or other third-party source will pick
up the cost.

The mitigation doctrine and the *Hadley* doctrine are similar. The *Hadley*
doctrine encourages the promisee to reduce losses caused by any future
breaches by the promisor, by giving the promisor relevant information in
advance. The mitigation doctrine encourages the promisee to reduce
losses caused by a past breach by a promisor, by covering or taking other
steps to limit damage. The lesson here is that although one has a tendency
to treat the breaching promisor as the bad guy, who ought to pay for all
the loss caused by his conduct, this is not the approach of the law. The
traditional common law of tort law is similar: the negligent driver seems
like the bad guy, but if the pedestrian is also negligent (contributory negligence), the pedestrian will recover nothing.

A note on "cover." We mentioned above that a party must "cover" when
the other party breaches. "Cover" means obtaining a substitute performance. If Buyer breaches by repudiating his promise to buy widgets from
Seller, Seller covers by finding another buyer and selling the widgets to
that buyer. Damages, then, are the difference between the contract price
(with original Buyer) and market price (with new buyer). If the market
price is greater than or equal to the contract price, Seller receives zero
damages — because the breach makes Seller better off. Similarly, if Seller

breaches her promise to deliver widgets to Buyer, Buyer covers by finding another seller and buying the widgets from that seller. Damages are the difference between the contract price (with original Seller) and market price (with new seller). If the market price is less than or equal to the contract price, Buyer receives zero damages — because the breach makes Buyer better off.

The duty to cover follows from the mitigation rule. If the victim fails to cover, then usually something awful happens. Suppose Buyer operates a factory, and Seller breaches her promise to deliver coal. Rather than covering — buying substitute coal at the market price — Buyer shuts down the factory and profits are lost. The duty to mitigate here is just the duty to cover. Or suppose that Seller is the victim of breach, but rather than cover, she just throws the widgets in a trash dump. Again, Seller should have mitigated so that the loss from the breach was only the difference between contract and market price, rather than the value of the widgets.

The duty to cover can raise some complex problems when the market offers more than one way to buy or sell a good. In Missouri Furnace v. Cochrane,[42] the promisor breached a long-term contract to deliver coal on a monthly basis. The victim of breach had a choice: it could buy coal by entering a new spot-market contract every month; or it could buy coal by entering a new long-term contract that provided for monthly delivery. (There were other options as well; for example, the victim could enter a series of medium-term contracts, or a combination of longer-term contracts and shorter-term contracts.) The price for a long-term contract and the price for a bunch of short-term contracts are not the same. If the price fluctuates, the long-term contract will include a risk premium: the seller is insuring the buyer against fluctuations (that is, high prices) and will demand a premium to compensate her for taking on the risk (that she will have to deliver at a low contract price coal that she can obtain only at high cost because, for example, her workers go on strike). The buyer might reasonably believe that since the original contract was long-term, the substitute may also be long-term, but it is also possible that a long-term contract will be more expensive than a series of short-term contracts. The court held that the buyer violated its duty to mitigate by entering the long-term contract. As it turned out, prices fell, so the breacher would have to pay higher damages than if the buyer had entered a series of short-term contracts. This decision was harsh: the buyer could not anticipate that the price would fall; and if the buyer had entered short-term contracts and prices had risen, maybe the court would have said that the buyer should have entered a long-term contract. Nowadays, courts give the victim

---

[42] 8 F. 463 (W.D. Pa. 1881).

of breach more discretion to choose among reasonable alternative ways to cover.[43]

Speculative Loss

A promisor cannot recover damages for losses that are "speculative," that is, difficult to prove.[44] The rule against the recovery of speculative losses might seem to follow from the burden of proof requirements created by the rules of civil procedure: if a plaintiff cannot prove a loss, then she cannot recover damages for it.

Still, courts are sometimes willing to infer losses and to award damages. The issue is often raised in cases where entrepreneurs seek to establish businesses but fail to do so as a result of a breach of contract. An entrepreneur plans to open a specialty clothing shop in a mall. He enters contracts to buy stock, hires employees, pays for advertising — but at the last moment, his landlord violates the lease and does not allow him to set up his shop. He sues the landlord for damages. Traditional expectation damages would be just the difference between the contract price and the market price of the leased space, which could well be zero. The entrepreneur might be able to obtain reliance damages covering expenditures. But what he really wants is to obtain damages for lost profits.

Profits may be extremely difficult to calculate, however. The store has not proven itself; it does not yet have a clientele. The entrepreneur therefore cannot establish that he would have had enough customers to cover his costs. The landlord's breach may have cost him profits, but it is just as likely that it saved him from losses and bankruptcy. Expectation damages cannot be calculated.

Some courts enforce the so-called new business rule more strictly than others. A good lawyer would make a case for damages by drawing on the experiences of comparable institutions. Perhaps a similar shop was set up in a nearby location and did very well. If so, then the lawyer can argue that the court should assume that the entrepreneur would make similar

---

[43] U.C.C. §§2-713(1)(a)-(b) ("[I]f the seller wrongfully fails to deliver or repudiates or the buyer rightfully rejects or justifiably revokes acceptance ... the measure of damages in the case of wrongful failure to deliver by the seller or rightful rejection or justifiable revocation of acceptance by the buyer is the difference between the market price at the time for tender under the contract and the contract price together with any incidental or consequential damages ... but less expenses saved in consequence of the seller's breach; and ... the measure of damages for repudiation by the seller is the difference between the market price at the expiration of a commercially reasonable time after the buyer learned of the repudiation. . . . . .").

[44] See Restatement (Second) of Contracts §352 (1981) ("Damages are not recoverable for loss beyond an amount that the evidence permits to be established with reasonable certainty.").

profits. Of course, the existence of a similar store could mean precisely the opposite — that the market is not big enough for two stores with the same specialty and therefore the entrepreneur's effort against an entrenched incumbent would have failed.

When the business is not new, the speculative loss doctrine can still be a problem for plaintiffs, but at least in such a case the entrepreneur can draw on his business's record. Suppose that the landlord breaches the contract several years into the lease, and the entrepreneur presents records of profits during those years. A characteristic dispute will arise over whether those profits can be used to project future profits. The entrepreneur will argue that they can be used to project future profits; the defendant will argue that they cannot. It will be helpful if the entrepreneur can provide evidence about comparable businesses. If the industry is profitable in general, and the firm's past profits are in line with those of the industry, the court will feel more confident about awarding damages for lost profits. The more idiosyncratic the firm's performance, the less likely it is that the court will award damages for lost profits.

In *Mindgames*[45] and *Dempsey*,[46] the courts held that the loss was too speculative to award damages. In *Mindgames*, the plaintiff invented a new board game and hired defendant to promote it. Defendant did not adequately promote the game and plaintiff sued for damages. In *Dempsey*, the plaintiff hired Jack Dempsey, the heavyweight boxing champion, to fight with Harry Wills. Dempsey breached. The problem in both cases was that the plaintiff could not provide an adequate basis for determining the loss. A board game might sell millions of copies or just a few dozen; it is impossible to predict the public's taste. A boxing match could be successful or it could fail (because of bad weather, competing events, or some other development). These types of determinations are fact-intensive. Plaintiffs in these cases try to show a track record suggesting that because the plaintiff made money off similar ideas or events in the past, it is likely to do so again in the future. Or they point to similar projects or business that earned revenues. Courts vary in their willingness to project loss on the basis of such evidence.

The court in *Mindgames* notes that the new business rule is a "rule" rather than a "standard." Rules are more predictable but can create injustices. As the court points out, the new business rule seems problematic because sometimes the future profits of new businesses are predictable, and the rule forbids an award even in those circumstances. Yet like all rules, the new business rule makes it clear to the parties in advance what the consequences of breach will be. It is hard to predict how a court will calculate future profits if the only guide is that they cannot be excessively "speculative." Given the ubiquity of limited liability provisions in contracts,

[45] MindGames, Inc. v. Western Pub. Co., 218 F.3d 652 (7th Cir. 2000).
[46] Dempsey v. Chicago Coliseum Club, 162 N.E. 237 (Ind. App. 1928).

one suspects that parties generally would prefer not to gamble on judicial calculation of lost profits for new businesses. Remember that if the entrepreneur is entitled to damages for lost profits based on judicial speculation, he must pay for them in advance in the form of a higher price.

The assumption that contracting parties do not want to gamble on litigation outcomes underlies the related rule that victims of breach cannot obtain damages for emotional distress unless the contract has "elements of personality."[47] Routine employment contracts, sales of goods, sales of real estate, mergers, and the like do not have elements of personality. Contracts to provide medical treatment or therapy or special treatment of a corpse may. Nowadays, these disputes are typically decided in tort litigation. Valentine v. General American Credit, Inc.[48] — a case where an employee sued her employer for firing her in violation of the employment contract — raises the question why an employee cannot obtain damages for emotional distress given that *Hadley* permits damages for foreseeable losses, and surely emotional distress is a foreseeable consequence of the breach of an employment contract. The answer is that courts do not believe that parties would bargain for coverage of idiosyncratic and hard-to-predict losses. The employer would have to reduce wages to cover the expected loss, and employees may well regard this trade-off as not worthwhile (but who knows?). Employers are very likely to refuse in any event because they probably prefer to screen out workers who are emotionally fragile (though it would be nice to have someone so deeply committed to the job).

§8.11 Specific Performance

Doctrine tells us that the normal remedy for breach of contract is damages — usually, expectation damages — and that injunctive relief is available only for enforcement of (1) real estate transactions[49] and (2) consumer goods that are "unique."[50]

---

[47] Valentine v. Gen. Amer. Credit, Inc., 362 N.W.2d 628, 630 (Mich. 1984).

[48] Id.

[49] Loveless v. Diehl, 364 S.W.2d 317 (Ark. 1963) (determining that specific performance for sales of land is permitted if there is a writing and consideration, and the agreement is fair and just).

[50] See Restatement (Second) of Contracts §359 (1981):

(1) Specific performance or an injunction will not be ordered if damages would be adequate to protect the expectation interest of the injured party.

(2) The adequacy of the damage remedy for failure to render one part of the performance due does not preclude specific performance or injunction as to the contract as a whole.

The standard reasoning for this state of affairs goes like this. Damages are the presumptive remedy because they are easier to enforce than performance itself, and sometimes it is efficient for the promisor to breach anyway. But to award damages, the court must calculate the value of the performance. This is difficult when there is no market for the promised good or service. There is no market for paintings by old masters, rare baseball cards, and other unique goods, so when a promisor fails to deliver such a unique good, a damages remedy is likely to be arbitrary.[51] Because the market in real estate is thin, it is proper to make specific performance the norm. But there is a countervailing policy when we move to contracts for services. Compelling an opera singer to perform is akin to slavery, and anyway how is a court to judge when the opera singer has performed in satisfaction of the contract? Better to compel performance by ordering the singer not to sing at any competing houses.[52] That remedy — a negative injunction — does not treat the opera singer as a slave and is easier for the court to enforce.

Do these reasons persuade you? Let us begin with the claim that damages are easier to enforce than performance. Suppose that Buyer wins a breach of contract suit against Seller and is awarded damages of $10,000. Seller is under no obligation to hand over this money to Buyer. If Seller refuses, then Buyer must obtain an order from the court authorizing the sheriff to seize Seller's property to satisfy the debt. If Seller continues to resist, the sheriff will use force. Now suppose that Buyer obtains an award of specific performance requiring Seller to hand over a widget. If Seller refuses to hand over the widget, then Buyer must again obtain the assistance of the sheriff. The sheriff might have to use force, but he had to use force when the remedy was damages. Seller might conceal or destroy the widget, but then Buyer will have either a claim for its value, which is the same as expectation damages, or a more serious tort claim for conversion, and the court may hold Seller in contempt. In short, whether the Seller is cooperative or hostile, the court's use of force and other resources is the same.

The argument applies as well when the promised performance is a service rather than an object. Suppose that Seller promised to sing at Buyer's nightclub. The court can compel performance in ordinary circumstances by threatening the Seller with a fine or term in jail. It is true that Seller, if

---

(3) Specific performance or an injunction will not be refused merely because there is a remedy for breach other than damages, but such a remedy may be considered in exercising discretion under the rule stated in §357.

[51] See, e.g., Van Wagner Adver. Corp. v. S&M Enters., 492 N.E.2d 756 (N.Y. 1986), where the court denied specific performance because the market value of lost billboard space could be calculated; but see Cumbest v. Harris, 363 So. 2d 294 (Miss. 1978) (granting a specific performance request for specialized stereo equipment).

[52] See Lumley v. Wagner, 42 Eng. Rep. 687 (1852).

hostile, could retaliate against Buyer by singing badly. But this is a run-of-the-mill contract problem. If Seller had, rather than refused to perform, simply performed badly, and Buyer sued for damages, the Court would face the same problem of determining whether the mediocre performance constituted a breach of the contract.[53]

Performances are almost always hard to value. If courts can enforce specific performance just as easily as they can expectation damages, they might as well rely on specific performance — except in cases where specific performance is no longer possible (for example, because the goods have been destroyed). But it is said that when the cost of performance is greater than the value of performance, the promisor should have the right to perform and pay damages — the theory of efficient breach.

The efficient breach concept exerts a powerful hold on the minds of many commentators, but it does not justify a presumption in favor of damages. When parties are sophisticated and well informed, they will anticipate that cases will arise in which performance of the contract is not efficient. They can provide for this contingency directly in the contract — simply by giving each party the option not to perform and instead pay the other party's loss. Parties will not always do this. When they anticipate that valuation will be easy, they can include the option; when not, they will not include the option and instead rely on specific performance of the promises. The point is that if specific performance is the remedy, the parties are free to stipulate to an option to perform or pay, or not to create an option. If damages are the remedy, then the law forces the parties to use an option. Why should the law in this way interfere with their freedom of contract?

Even when parties neglect to include options, inefficient performance will not necessarily occur. The parties can renegotiate instead. If, for example, Seller's cost of performance is $100, Buyer values performance at $50, and the price is $40, Seller will pay up to $60 to avoid performance, and Buyer will demand at least $10 to release her from performance. A deal is within reach. Renegotiation is not a panacea. Bargaining can fail, and even when it does not fail, it can have perverse effects on ex ante incentives. But the availability of renegotiation further limits whatever advantage that expectation damages have over specific performance.

I should make a few more observations about specific performance. It is an equitable remedy, meaning that originally it was ordered only by courts of equity. Historical practice, though greatly eroded, probably explains why specific performance remains exceptional rather than the norm. The attempt to rationalize the law goes only so far. If our baseline is expectation damages, it may make sense to order specific performance

---

[53] There are separate considerations that may justify avoiding a harsh remedy — we discuss them in Section 8.9 — but these considerations apply whether the remedy is damages or injunction.

for "unique," that is, hard-to-value goods. But there is no reason to think that real estate is hard to value in this sense; it is no harder to value than many commodities and services.

§8.12   Negative Injunctions

Courts do not award specific performance in contracts involving personal services but they do sometimes issue negative injunctions — orders that prohibit the breacher from engaging in certain actions. In Lumley v. Wagner,[54] a singer hired by Benjamin Lumley, operator of Her Majesty's Theatre, breached by not showing up and working elsewhere. Damages could not be calculated because of the uniqueness of the service. For a remedy, the court ordered the defendant not to sing at the competing venue. Thus, if she wanted to work and be paid, she could do so only by performing the contract with the plaintiff.

Why do courts issue negative but not affirmative injunctions in personal services contracts? One reason courts give for not issuing affirmative injunctions is that they may run afoul of the Thirteenth Amendment, which bans slavery. That seems like an extreme statement: one can avoid "enslavement" by not entering the contract in the first place. Ordinary damages remedies have a similar coercive effect: one can always pay expectation damages rather than perform, but if paying expectation damages means not being able to eat, one is coerced into performing.

Another common reason for not awarding specific performance in personal services contracts is that specific performance is difficult for courts to monitor. Imagine that the defendant in *Lumley* agrees to sing but sings badly, or not as well as usual, in order to get back at the plaintiff. Would the judge have to attend the performances to ensure that the singing is up to snuff? Or take testimony from local music critics? This might seem more trouble than it is worth. A negative injunction would be easier to enforce. The defendant complies with it by not singing elsewhere. However, if she complies with the injunction by singing at the plaintiff's venue, while taking revenge by singing badly, we are back where we started.

§8.13   Liquidated Damages and Penalties

Parties often place a liquidated damages clause in their contracts, which states the damages that the promisor must pay in case of breach. Courts

---

[54] 42 E.R. 687 (Q.B. 1852).

strike down such clauses as "penalties" when they are "unreasonably high."[55] This could mean that the liquidated damages are much higher than the actual damages, or the liquidated damages are much higher than anticipated damages, or both, depending on the court.

The penalty doctrine raises some difficult questions. A liquidated damages clause is a term like any other term in the contract. A sales contract provides that the seller must deliver widgets in return for a price of $X. Courts would not dream of regulating the price, of holding that $X is too high or too low. The legal consequences of this contract are that the seller must either deliver the widgets or pay damages, such as the price of cover. Call this amount $D. Now we can reinterpret the contract as an option: Seller must deliver the widget and receive $X or not deliver the widget and pay $D.

A liquidated damages provision sets $D in advance. Why should courts object to such an agreement? The amount, $D, is now just another aspect of the price. Suppose the parties entered into an agreement that explicitly laid out the option: Seller must either deliver or pay $D. Courts would enforce such an option contract under the general principle of freedom of contract. If instead the parties say that Seller must deliver but pay $D if she breaches, the provision setting $D is now considered liquidated damages subject to review under the penalty doctrine.

Why do parties stipulate damages? One reason is that parties fear that the court will not be able to accurately determine damages itself. In Yockey v. Horn,[56] two parties settled a dispute and provided for $50,000 damages in case one of the two parties voluntarily testified against the other in any other litigation. In the absence of such a clause, a court would have trouble determining damages; the harm is exceedingly diffuse — the victim of breach might suffer a loss of reputation if a former partner testifies against him — but real. This is the type of case in which courts are more sympathetic about liquidated damages, and are most likely to enforce them, as long as they seem "reasonable."

In other cases, courts strike down liquidated damages clauses because they believe that the actual damages can be determined relatively easily, so there is no reason to rely on the parties' estimates.[57] The problem with these cases is that the optimal "price" that parties set for breach is not

---

[55] See Restatement (Second) of Contracts §356 (1981):

(1) Damages for breach by either party may be liquidated in the agreement but only at an amount that is reasonable in the light of the anticipated or actual loss caused by the breach and the difficulties of proof of loss. A term fixing unreasonably large liquidated damages is unenforceable on grounds of public policy as a penalty.

(2) A term in a bond providing for an amount of money as a penalty for non-occurrence of the condition of the bond is unenforceable on grounds of public policy to the extent that the amount exceeds the loss caused by such non-occurrence.

[56] 880 F.2d 945 (7th Cir. 1989).
[57] See, e.g., H.J. McGrath Co. v. Wisner, 55 A.2d 793 (Md. 1947).

necessarily the same as expectation damages. The price might reflect other factors that parties care about, such as their desire to give the parties the right incentives to mitigate, renegotiate, and so forth.

When courts strike down liquidated damages clauses, they often point out that the event that gave rise to the breach was out of the ordinary, and thus not likely anticipated by the parties and not incorporated into their calculation of liquidated damages. Owner hires Contractor to build a funeral monument and is anxious that Contractor complete the monument on time. The parties agree that the purchase price will be reduced by $10 for every day that the project is late. If the project is one day late, Contractor loses $10. If the project is one hundred days late, Contractor loses $1000. The Contractor might have agreed to the liquidated damages to prevent Owner from hiring a contractor with a better reputation for timeliness. The liquidated damages amount in this case serves as a signal from Contractor that it believes itself capable of finishing the project on time. It is not hard to understand why such an agreement could be in the joint interests of the parties. But courts frequently strike down such liquidated damages provisions, calling them impermissible "spurs" or penalties rather than efforts to ensure compensation for actual loss.[58]

If the problem with this type of contract is that the liquidated damages provision assumed a different set of circumstances from those that actually occurred — a moderate delay caused by the contractor's negligence rather than an extreme delay caused by events outside his control, for example — then the better approach is a doctrine that strikes down liquidated damages clauses only in those extreme cases. Courts sometimes achieve this result by aggressively interpreting the contract. Here, one could argue that the parties understood the liquidated damages clause to be capped at some point. Moreover, it is not obvious what is wrong with a "spur." The point of a contract is to give the promisor an incentive to perform. Regular contract damages are in this way a spur to enforcement; supracompensatory damages provide an even stronger spur, which might be justified, as noted before, when the performing party lacks a reputation for timeliness. Indeed, courts do not object to bonuses, which are just another kind of spur. If the parties were to redesign the contract above to provide for a lower price and a later completion date, plus a "bonus" of $10 for every day early, a court would enforce it.

However, there is a recurrent theme in the cases that casts judges' uneasiness about liquidated damages in a more favorable light. Liquidated damages provisions often apply to all breaches in an undifferentiated fashion, regardless of whether the breach is serious or slight. In Wilt v. Waterfield,[59] for example, the court refused to enforce the liquidated damages because they applied whether the breach was refusing to transfer title or

---

[58] See Muldoon v. Lynch, 6 P. 417 (Cal. 1885).
[59] 273 S.W.2d (Mo. 1954).

failing to hold the other party's check until a specified date. It is hard to think of a reason why the parties would want a breacher to pay $1900 if the victim's check was cashed a day early.

Still, these considerations hardly solve the puzzle about why courts are skeptical about liquidated damages clauses. Courts do not lavish this kind of attention on any of the other types of clauses that appear in contracts, however sloppy or ill considered they might appear.

Another odd fact is that while courts frequently strike down excessively high liquidated damages, they rarely strike down liquidated damages as excessively low. These cases are sometimes hard to distinguish from cases involving limited liability clauses. The distinction is that limited liability clauses put a ceiling on the victim's damages, but the award will be less than the ceiling if the actual loss is less than the ceiling; liquidated damages clauses determine the actual award regardless of the loss. Parties do not make this distinction very carefully, and it does not seem to matter much to the courts, either. In both cases, courts generally enforce. The recurring example is the case involving a burglar alarm system that fails to stop a burglary because of the negligence of the alarm company. Courts usually enforce limited liability or low liquidated damages clauses.[60] In some cases, they have held that the limits do not apply to losses caused by negligence,[61] but these cases almost always involve clauses that do not mention negligence; if alarm companies insert a clause limiting liability in case of negligence as well, courts will enforce the clause.

It is easy to understand why parties want to limit liability. If the buyer of the alarm service wants insurance, he can buy it from an insurance company. We are accustomed to this type of transaction in many areas of life — for example, paying a delivery company to deliver a package. The company disclaims liability — unless the buyer wants to pay extra for insurance. Because some buyers do not want insurance, sellers give buyers an option to buy the insurance from the company, and for that a limited liability clause is necessary. We discussed these issues in connection with the *Hadley* rule.[62]

§8.14   Covenants Not to Compete

Covenants not to compete (CNCs) can be found in employment contracts. The usual way in which they work is that the employer hires a

---

[60] See, e.g., Fretwell v. Prot. Alarm Co., 764 P.2d 149 (Okla. 1988).
[61] See Samson Sales, Inc. v. Honeywell, Inc., 465 N.E.2d 392 (Ohio 1984).
[62] See Section 8.10.

worker (usually a manager or somebody with special skills). The CNC stipulates that if the employment relationship ends, the worker may not obtain a similar position with another employer that competes with the first employer, or start a business that competes with the first employer. Competition is defined along three dimensions. The CNC has a duration (a few months or years or indefinitely), a geographic reach (a few or many miles, a single city or state, or the world), and an industry definition (for example, sales of lumber). It is a safe bet that a CNC that lasts for a few months or even one or two years that covers a city or perhaps a state, and that defines the industry narrowly will be upheld. But courts often strike down CNCs that are more restrictive.

The first thing to understand about CNCs is that they are a substitute for legal remedies when legal remedies are inadequate. An employer hires a worker and makes an investment in him. The employer might, for example, train the worker or let him in on the tricks of the trade or disclose secrets to him, such as customer lists or formulas for manufacturing products or management techniques.[63] Media companies often insist that their celebrity employees sign CNCs because the companies fear that after they spend a lot of money promoting the employees and turning them into household names, they will move to a competitor.[64] In all these cases, the employer can obtain a return on its investment only if the worker stays on the job long enough and does not take the secrets to competitors or set up his own competing business. If legal remedies were adequate, the employer could deter such bad behavior simply by suing workers who leave the job prematurely or misuse secrets, and obtain compensation for any loss of investment or proprietary information. But as is so often the case, these standard remedies are inadequate. It may be impossible to prove that a high-tech worker who left Google and began working for Microsoft conveyed secret information to his new employer, even if Microsoft starts selling products that look suspiciously like Google's. And if Google can prove that the worker was responsible, the worker may not have enough wealth to compensate Google for the loss. Similarly, if the employer trains or promotes the employee, it can be hard to prove the value added taken by the employee to the new employer, or to recover the monetary value of it from the employee in a lawsuit.

A CNC provides an alternative remedy: the worker cannot take a job with Microsoft in the first place, and so will have no opportunity to convey Google's secrets to it. Denied this opportunity, the worker will never

---

[63] See, e.g., Data Mgmt., Inc. v. Greene, 757 P.2d 62 (Alaska 1988).
[64] ABC v. Wolf, 420 N.E.2d 363 (N.Y. 1981).

leave Google. Thus, Google benefits from whatever training it gives to the worker and also minimizes the risk that the worker will convey secrets to competitors.[65]

CNCs might seem unobjectionable. They are freely chosen by employers and workers — and usually sophisticated workers because CNCs are not necessary for ordinary workers. If workers do not want to close off future employment opportunities, they do not have to agree to a CNC in the first place and can look elsewhere for work. Yet courts regard CNCs with a great deal of suspicion, and for that reason will enforce them only when they are "reasonable."

What accounts for this suspicion? Courts fear that CNCs reduce competition, which results in higher prices for consumers. Imagine that a town has a single lumber retailer. The boss hires a manager and discloses his customer list and other secrets. A few years later, the manager quits and starts his own business. The former boss sues to enforce a CNC.[66] If the court issues an injunction, the town will be stuck with one rather than two lumber retailers, which means less competition and higher prices in the retail lumber industry.

This explanation is only superficially attractive. Most markets are competitive, and when they are not, the usual solution is intervention by antitrust authorities, which can break up firms. In other cases, governments may regulate rates. Trying to regulate market power through contract law is rarely advisable. In our example, it is hard to believe that a lumber retailer can have a monopoly; other stores, such as hardware stores, can also sell wood. Even if it does have a monopoly, the boss of the single lumber retailer would be unlikely to risk his monopoly by hiring someone who can take his secrets and set up a competing firm. Instead, he will run his store himself or minimize the information made available to employees, which will raise prices further for customers, since his costs will be higher.

Another reason courts might refuse to enforce broad CNCs is that they require workers with valuable skills not to take jobs in firms that cannot fully exploit their skills. This seems unfair and wasteful. But if workers agree to a CNC with full understanding, it is hard to see where the unfairness lies. As for wastefulness, if the CNCs deter workers from quitting in the first place, no waste will occur. More wastefulness occurs if employers do not invest in their workers because the employers cannot recover the return on the investment. In addition, when unemployment is

---

[65] The worker can sell trade secrets to another firm, but this is criminal behavior.
[66] See Fullerton Lumber Co. v. Torborg, 70 N.W. 2d 585 (Wis. 1955).

wasteful, then the worker, the old employer, and the new employer have a strong incentive to renegotiate. The new employer and/or the worker will pay the old employer to release him from the CNC.

As noted above, courts do not enforce "unreasonable" CNCs. What this means varies state by state. Narrowly drawn CNCs are almost always enforced; broader CNCs are sometimes but not always enforced. When a firm in question has global reach — consider a major pharmaceutical company like Merck or a software company like Microsoft — a court might enforce a global CNC, so that the worker cannot be hired by a competitor in Germany or Japan. This is most likely to be the case for high-level executives. Courts will take into account how quickly secret information will degrade. If secrets obtained prior to an employee's termination are still valuable two months later, but worthless two years later, a CNC of two years will not be enforced. Marketing strategies are an example of information that degrades rapidly. By contrast, Coca-Cola's secret formula will fuel soft drink consumption until the Last Judgment, when that drink will surely be served.

§8.15   Conditions and Forfeiture, Again

The argument about CNCs can be generalized, and this brings us around again to the points made in the discussion of the penalty doctrine. Contract remedies are often weak — in the sense that they cannot deter opportunistic behavior — because the victim of the breach cannot obtain cash or other valuable goods from the breacher, or because the information that would be necessary to produce an adequate remedy is not available. Liquidated damages address the second problem by giving the victim the right to a stipulated pool of cash if a breach takes place. CNCs address both problems by giving the victim the right to prevent the breacher from exploiting a valuable opportunity such as an offer of a new job. CNCs are just a form of condition: the worker's right to obtain a new job in the same industry is conditional on not breaching in the first place.

Conditions are used by parties to minimize the risk that one particular party will breach and be judgment-proof.[67] The owner of land hires a contractor to build a house. The contract conditions the contractor's right to payment on delivery of the completed house to the owner. If the contractor is not, or not likely, judgment-proof — in the expansive sense that either it does not have money to pay damages or the owner cannot prove that the contractor failed to deliver a satisfactory product even when defects

---

[67] See Section 7.3.

exist — the condition is unnecessary. If the house has a problem such as a leaky roof, the owner simply obtains damages that make him whole.

The problem is that a house that does not meet all specifications may disappoint the owner in ways that cannot be calculated in damages, or that the contractor does not have money to pay. Suppose, for example, that the owner pays in advance, and there is no condition in the contract. When problems arise with the finished product, she sues the contractor. But the owner cannot prove that the problems actually reduce the market value of the house or otherwise cause discomfort, and the contractor does not have any money anyway, having spent it all. The owner does not obtain an adequate remedy; the contractor gets off scot-free.

The condition solves this problem. Because payment is conditional on the house meeting specifications, the owner has no obligation to pay the contractor. To obtain payment, the contractor will work very hard to get things right.

But conditions create problems of their own. If a contractor does not get paid until the house is completed, the contractor may have trouble financing the house construction. It may be able to borrow from the bank, but a bank would worry that the contractor will not be able to pay back the loan because it fails to comply with some tiny aspect of the contract. Indeed, there is a risk that now the owner will act opportunistically, claiming that some tiny deviation from the contract renders performance unsatisfactory, the condition unmet.

The standard contract balances these considerations. The owner pays in installments. When phase 1 of the contract is completed (say, the laying of the foundation), the owner pays a portion of the contract price. When phase 2 is completed, the owner pays another portion. Each installment will cover most or all of the contractor's costs up to that point, and sometimes more, though typically the contract is designed to ensure that the contractor is not fully compensated for partial performance; thus, the last payment is significant. Paying by installment reduces the cost of financing for the contractor (it can take out smaller loans for shorter periods) and reduces the risk to the contractor that it will incur significant expenditures without being paid. At the same time, installment payments give the owner some leverage to punish contractors who deviate from specifications.

Still, opportunism is possible on both sides, and courts have stepped in to limit it. Consider the case of Jacob & Youngs v. Kent.[68] The contractor completed the building but installed the wrong piping. However, the piping that it did install was no worse than the piping it was supposed to install.

---

[68] 129 N.E. 889 (N.Y. 1921).

The owner refused to pay because the building deviated from the plans. The court gave the contractor the right to restitution for its expenditures, subject to a set-off for the owner. The effect of this was to eliminate the advantage of the condition: the owner could not refuse to pay unless he could independently prove that he had been harmed. However, the court blunted this effect by holding that the contractor could not obtain restitution if it acted in bad faith or the contract was sufficiently explicit about the condition.

This problem also crops up in insurance contracts. In Howard v. Federal Crop Insurance Corp.,[69] a farmer sued his insurer after his tobacco crop was destroyed by a rainstorm. The contract provided that "[t]he tobacco stalks on any acreage of tobacco . . . with respect to which a loss is claimed shall not be destroyed until [the insurer] makes an inspection." The insurer refused to pay because the farmer violated this clause, arguing that the insurer's duty to pay was conditional on the farmer not destroying the tobacco stalks. The farmer argued that the clause did not establish a condition — it did not use the word "condition," unlike an earlier clause.

There are good reasons for construing the clause as a condition. If the tobacco stalks are destroyed, the insurer may not be able to ascertain that the tobacco crop was destroyed by rain. Perhaps the farmer surreptitiously replaced the crop or the crop was destroyed by another event not covered by the insurance contract. If the clause is deemed a promise (rather than a condition), the insurer can sue the farmer for violating it, but damages would be impossible to determine. A court would not be able to verify that the insurer has been damaged unless it can determine whether the crop was destroyed by an event not covered by the insurance contract; but because the farmer destroyed the stalks, the evidence is gone. However, the court held otherwise. There is a presumption against forfeitures; therefore, a court should not interpret a clause that is only ambiguously conditional as though it were in fact conditional.

The *Jacob & Youngs* and *Howard* cases illustrate the judicial concern about forfeitures. This concern is identical to the concern about liquidated damages that amount to penalties, and CNCs that prevent people from working. In all the cases, the breacher suffers an economic loss that seems out of proportion to the harm that it caused. Yet it is important to remember that parties can rationally agree to these outcomes. They create knife-edge incentives to perform that can be necessary when courts are unable to determine optimal damages, which is often the case.

---

[69] 540 F.2d 695 (4th Cir. 1976).

§8.16   Summary

The diagram below might help organize your thinking about remedies. Note that it is a simplification of the law.

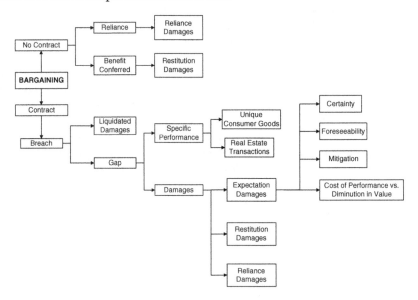

Chapter 9

Contiguous Bodies of Law

§9.1   Tort, Fraud, and Estoppel

Let us begin with tort. It is possible to recharacterize a breach of contract as a tort.[1] A tort occurs when a person violates a duty, resulting in harm. People owe a general duty of care to all strangers, and also particular duties to particular persons; for example, parents have a duty to protect their children. Let a promise create by law a duty to perform the promise, and the breach can be thought of as a tort. If we want to stick as close to contract law as possible, we will require that liability be strict: a person who takes care but nonetheless violates a promise is liable.

What follows from this recharacterization? Not much, it turns out, although there was for a time a great deal of scholarly excitement about it, especially because in many foreign legal systems the distinction between contract and tort is not as crisp as it is in the common law. Observe first of all that judges still need to do the hard work of determining whether a promise was made and acted on, and how it should be interpreted. Thus, most of contract law doctrine would be preserved, though now considered a branch of tort law.[2] A few scholars have argued that if breaches of contracts are really torts, then expectations damages are not justified; reliance damages are appropriate. But, as we have seen in Chapter 8, there are conceptual difficulties with this argument, and from the perspective of social policy nothing is gained by replacing expectation damages with reliance damages.

More interesting is the way that tort law impinges on contract doctrine as it is currently understood. As we have seen, one might evade the parol

---

[1] See, e.g., Grant Gilmore, The Death of Contract (1974).

[2] What is true is that tort and contract law reflect the same economic principles. See Robert Cooter, Unity in Tort, Contract, and Property: The Model of Precaution, 73 Cal. L. Rev. 1 (1985).

evidence rule by recharacterizing a promise and its breach as a fraudulent scheme.[3] One must show that the promisor intended not to keep his promise, and that the promisee relied on the promise. Here is a way that a partial redescription of a contract as a tort can do some doctrinal work for a litigant anxious to introduce parol evidence. The problem, though, is that proving intention and reliance can be difficult, and it is this reed alone — thin or not — that prevents contract law from collapsing into tort law.

More significant is the gradual takeover by tort law of medical malpractice and products liability cases. Each type of takeover is quite different from the other. Doctors often promise to make patients better, and when they fail, patients can sue for breach of contract. These promises are often specific enough to justify liability under the normal principles of contract, but judges believe that (1) doctors overstate the chances of recovery for therapeutic reasons; (2) patients often hear what they want to hear, and testify accordingly; and (3) juries feel more sympathy for the mutilated patient than for the wealthy doctor, and accordingly find promises where they do not exist. Courts responded to these problems by barring contract liability in the absence of particularly clear promises or other bad behavior, and sometimes have refused to permit expectation damages otherwise. Patients end up suing doctors in tort, for malpractice, in which case liability is not strict (as under contract, once a promise is found), but judged according to the standards of the medical community, with the doctor negligent if he falls below them.[4]

The opposite has happened with products liability. The victim of the exploding toaster used to sue in contract, claiming violation of an implied warranty. The cause of action was always complicated by the existence of an intermediary — the retail outlet — between the manufacturer and the victim. In past times, the victim could not sue the manufacturer because of the absence of privity, a contractual relationship between victim and manufacturer, and the retailer would not be wealthy enough to pay damages or would protect itself with warranty disclaimers. Even after the privity barrier was overcome, the manufacturer could use the same disclaimers to avoid liability. Courts assumed that consumers could not bargain for protections, and over time increasingly held manufacturers liable in tort, until for all intents and purposes strict products liability prevailed. Tort, rather than contract, became the cause of action because the parties' contractual negotiations — or the consumer's signing of a form contract — no longer seemed to express joint intention, or so the courts thought, and so most contract doctrine could be ignored.

---

[3] See Section 6.8.
[4] See Bardessono v. Michels, 478 P.2d 480, 485 (Cal. 1970).

In medical malpractice, courts weakened liability from contract to tort with a negligence standard; in products liability, courts strengthened liability from contracts (with disclaimers) to tort with strict liability (and no disclaimers allowed). Ironically, the motivation was in both cases a conviction that the buyer is unable to bargain in his own interest — and this makes sense, to some extent, for an external standard must then be imposed — but one must ask why courts were more generous to doctors than manufacturers. Economic analysis of tort law teaches that the choice of rules makes no difference to the level of care — cost-justified care will be taken in both cases — but that there will be a price adjustment, so that products will become relatively more expensive, and less frequently purchased, while medical care will not. The justification for this difference in treatment is unclear.

§9.2   Quasi-Contract and Restitution

I have mentioned the law of unjust enrichment, which exists "outside" contract law. It addresses a different set of problems that, however, sometimes overlap with the sorts of problems addressed by contract law.

First, some terminology. As we discussed in Sections 3.12 and 8.8, there are a number of quasi-synonyms that refer to this body of law or actions that arise under it. These include unjust enrichment, restitution, quasi-contract, implied contract, implied-in-law contract,[5] and quantum meruit. The remedy is called "restitution," which, as we have already seen, is also a remedy for breach of contract.[6] If you win a breach of contract claim, you have the option to seek restitution. If you win an unjust enrichment claim, you have no choice but to seek restitution (generally speaking).

A plaintiff has an unjust enrichment claim when she has conferred a benefit on the defendant as long as she has not done so in an officious or gratuitous way.[7] Such claims arise in diverse settings. I accidentally deposit some cash in your bank account and you refuse to return it to me: I have a claim for unjust enrichment. A physician helps an unconscious patient who refuses to pay for the service: the physician has a claim for unjust enrichment.[8] So does a contractor who improves your land after

---

[5] As opposed to implied-in-fact, which we discussed in Section 3.12.

[6] The word "restitution," then, is used in two ways: to refer to the theory of liability (unjust enrichment) and to refer to a remedy available in contract law as well as in unjust enrichment law (the value of the benefit conferred).

[7] See Restatement (Second) of Contracts §370 (1981).

[8] See, e.g., Contam v. Wisdom, 104 S.W. 164 (Ark. 1907) (awarding a doctor fees for the services provided to a car wreck victim at the scene of the crash).

honestly and reasonably believing that the land belongs to someone else, who hired her.

There are, of course, limitations and exceptions to these general principles. The most important are the exceptions for gratuitous and officious actions. If a neighbor deliberately mows your lawn and then asks for compensation, you have no obligation to pay him. He has volunteered; he hasn't made a mistake. He didn't expect you to pay him — or, at least, he shouldn't have expected you to pay him, unlike the doctor who treats the unconscious patient. The law does not create an obligation here because it is better for people to bargain than to impose on each other. You may not want your lawn to be mowed; or you may prefer to do it yourself and not pay; or you may prefer to hire an old friend who needs some money; or you may prefer to wait until after your next paycheck. All of these reasons and a thousand others suggest that people do better if they first make agreements.

An unjust enrichment claim does not require a promise. The doctor obtains a remedy from the unconscious patient even though the patient does not (and cannot) make a promise to pay him in return for medical aid. That is why unjust enrichment exists "outside of" contract law, which is focused on promises. Unjust enrichment law is in this way like tort law: it is just another body of law that focuses on a distinct set of problems. But the areas of law overlap, permitting people to make multiple claims arising out of a single set of circumstances. For example, if a person buys a toaster and it explodes, that person can sue both for breach of contract (the seller implicitly promised that the toaster would function properly) and tort (the exploding toaster caused an injury).

What is the justification for the law of unjust enrichment? It is hard to generalize because the law is complex and seems to have evolved to address different problems. But the explanation for some of the doctrines is straightforward. We do not let you keep cash mistakenly transferred to your bank account because the prospect of such windfalls will not improve anyone's behavior, while the risk of losing cash in this way could only cause people to take expensive self-protective measures. While tort imposes a duty of care, unjust enrichment imposes a duty not to take advantage of people who fail to take care but harm themselves rather than others. We give the doctor who helps an unconscious person the right to his fee because we want doctors to help people who are unconscious. The doctor cannot collect when he helps a conscious person because in that case the doctor should bargain first. This example reflects a general principle: the law encourages people to bargain before transferring services because that is the way to ascertain that each side actually benefits from the exchange. If the law rewarded volunteers, then people could impose goods and services on others and then claim a fee — when the supposed beneficiary may not in fact want the goods or services, or may prefer to buy them from someone else. But when contracting is not possible — a party is unconscious, for example — the law encourages people to perform services in the interest of others as long as they possess the relevant skills. So a doctor may recover for helping an unconscious victim; a layman cannot.

We saw in Chapter 8 the ways in which restitution remedies differ from, and overlap with, ordinary contractual remedies such as expectation damages. The tensions in the cases we discuss reflect the fact that the two bodies of law — contract and unjust enrichment — have different goals, and courts are not always sure how to reconcile them.

The law of unjust enrichment does help illuminate a puzzle that we discussed in Section 5.1: why courts do not enforce intra-family contracts. A little history is helpful here.[9] In the nineteenth century, a number of judicial opinions addressed lawsuits by adult children against the estates of their deceased parents. The children argued that the estate should pay them for the cost of providing care. In the typical case, an adult child (or other relative) lives at home with his parent, and performs various kinds of work that benefit the parent — cultivating fields, maintaining the house, shopping, nursing, and so on. The parent dies and leaves little or nothing to the child in his will. The child sues, arguing that he has conferred numerous benefits on the parent and ought to be compensated under the principle of unjust enrichment.

If the child could just point to a contract, the case would not be hard. The child can sue on a contract to provide care in return for consideration. But family members have rarely entered contracts of this sort. Thus, the child must fall back on the argument that he provided the care with the expectation of being paid, and that the parent expected to pay the child. This puts the child in the awkward position of arguing that he did not provide the care out of love or generosity. To argue the opposite would be to imply that the child was a volunteer and did not expect to be paid.

The problem faced by the courts is that family members often do provide care to each other without expectation of being paid. Parents care for their children, and rarely submit a bill to them when they reach the age of majority, let alone threaten to sue them for unjust enrichment. Likewise, adult children and their parents often provide benefits to each other without expecting or believing that they ought to be paid — in part, because each side expects reciprocal transfers of in-kind benefits, with, for example, the adult child occasionally performing some repairs on the parents' house and the parents occasionally babysitting the grandchildren. At the same time, it is conceivable and no doubt has happened quite often that at some point the burdens and benefits become one-sided. The parent becomes an invalid; the adult child must devote long hours to care for

---

[9] See Hendrik Hartog, Quantum Meruit and Old Age Care in American Family Life (Fulton Lecture on Legal History, University of Chicago, 2011).

the parent and loses other opportunities to make money. Here, the adult child no doubt acts out of mixed motives — love or duty, on the one hand, and an expectation to be paid or to inherit the homestead, on the other.

Mixed motives cases such as these pose formidable obstacles. And although the parent-child cases have disappeared, no doubt thanks to social security and changes in family norms, a late-twentieth-century development took up the slack. These cases involved a couple who lived together for a number of years, having children but never marrying. The woman keeps the home; the man earns the money. Subsequently, the man abandons the woman and the woman sues for damages.[10]

Students usually find questionable and even insulting the argument that the woman should not recover in quantum meruit because she volunteered household services. But the nineteenth-century background should make clear why courts would come to this conclusion. People who live together perform services for each other but do not expect to receive payment. Thus, they are volunteers in the sense of the doctrine. No payment was expected because presumably each partner expected to get as much out of the relationship (or more) than he or she put into it. If they do not specify rights and obligations in advance in a clearly drafted contract, courts can hardly be expected to untangle the relationship and determine who contributed how much relative to the other.

The real problem in these cases is that, in these families (which are decreasingly common today), the woman's contribution is front-loaded. She works part time and raises the children while the man attends medical school — she, in effect, makes an investment and expects to receive a future payout in the form of a higher joint income when the man is a doctor and she can enjoy a portion of his salary. The man violates this deal by leaving early. He enjoys the fruits of her investment, she only bears the costs. Most courts believed that the woman can best protect herself by insisting on marriage, which gives her the right to alimony. Other courts held otherwise.

§9.3   Consumer Protection

Another body of law at the margins of contract law is consumer protection law. The common law does not treat consumers — that is, ordinary people who buy goods and services from established merchants — much different from other contract parties such as sophisticated businesses that make purchases and sales. But consumers of various sorts have

---

[10] See Morone v. Morone, 413 N.E.2d 1154 (N.Y. 1988) (refusing to recognize an implied contract); Marvin v. Marvin, 557 P.2d 106 (Cal. 1976) (recognizing an implied contract).

often been protected by doctrines outside contract law proper — some of very old pedigree.

For example, if you take out a mortgage on your house, you may not pledge the entire value of the house as collateral if the value exceeds the debt. The difference between the value of the house and the debt on it is called "equity," a term that comes from the equity courts that protected the homeowner's equity of redemption starting many centuries ago. For example, if you borrow $380,000 to buy a $400,000 house, you have $20,000 of equity, and if subsequently the house appreciates to $410,000 while you have paid off $10,000 of your debt, your equity has increased to $40,000. If you then miss a payment, and the bank forecloses, the bank will auction off your house for $410,000, keep $370,000 for itself, and give you $40,000 in cash.

Mortgage contracts are designed to ensure that you get your equity, but it is possible to imagine a mortgage contract under which you forfeit your equity if you default. The bank is, in effect, overpaid (it receives more than the outstanding debt), but it should pass this benefit on to customers in the form of lower interest rates. Such a deal might be attractive for certain people — people who think they won't default — but it is unlawful.

The upshot is that people must pay higher interest rates, but if they face financial difficulties and lose their house, they will be able to fall back on the equity cushion — unless, of course, they continually refinance their house or borrow against the equity in subsequent loans.

There is a related set of laws in the United States called exemption laws. These state statutes provide that creditors cannot seize certain assets — homes, cars, clothes, furniture, even guns — to satisfy debts, albeit subject in most cases to limits. The homeowner exemption in many states ranges in the tens of thousands (in a few states, it is unlimited). This means that if a debtor owes a creditor $100,000, the debtor has $30,000 in equity in his house, and the homeowner exemption is $40,000, then the creditor cannot force a sale of the house. Exemption laws ensure that people with property don't lose all of it if they default on a loan, and so can continue to support themselves. The price is that creditors will not be willing to lend as much money , or will lend at a higher rate of interest.

Usury laws put ceilings on the amount of interest that creditors can charge. If a person wants to borrow some money, a creditor will demand interest that covers the time value of money (a dollar today is worth more than a dollar in the future) and the opportunity cost of money (a dollar could be invested in some other way and earn a return). If the creditor is absolutely certain that the borrower will pay back principal and interest, then the creditor will charge a low rate of interest. But many borrowers are bad risks: they are likely to lose their jobs, don't have assets that can be collected, or may be hard to find. In these cases, creditors will lend only if borrowers pay a high rate of interest. If usury laws put a ceiling on the interest rate, then creditors will not lend to high-risk borrowers.

We see the same sort of trade-off as we saw in the unconscionability cases. Usury and exemption laws protect people from entering bad deals or protect them from bad luck, and will reduce the cost of credit for some people, but they also reduce the amount of credit available to people who want to borrow, depriving them of durable goods that they might want and need, and of opportunities to pursue investments. Economists have long been skeptical about consumer protection laws because they are in tension with the basic idea that contracts make people better off. If people are rational, then they should refrain from buying products they do not understand, or they should demand greater information from sellers; sellers should volunteer that information in order to make the sale. As we saw in Chapter 4, it is possible that mandated disclosure could solve certain market failures, but the evidence suggests that the law has a limited impact on the buying habits of consumers. Legal scholars have searched for insight from the psychology literature, but that work is in its infancy.[11]

The modern consumer protection movement began in the 1970s, and has produced a range of laws that further regulate transactions between consumers and merchants. An important example is the federal Truth in Lending Act, which requires creditors to provide the terms of credit according to a formula that is supposed to make it easier for borrowers to understand the price they are paying for credit. One recurrent problem in credit transactions is that the interest rate can be described in various ways (by week, by month, by year; by dollar amount or by percentage) and can be hidden in various fees. Borrowers have trouble calculating the actual cost of credit from these terms and comparing across lenders. The Truth in Lending Act standardizes the information that creditors provide, but there is not much evidence that borrowers understand the terms any better. The fact is that credit transactions are by nature complex, and many if not most people lack the time, sophistication, and cognitive ability to understand these transactions fully.

Another interesting rule that can be found in many states is the right to withdraw.[12] When consumers buy goods at established merchants, the law often gives them the right to withdraw from the contract and return the goods within a certain period (for example, 30 days) from the time of sale. If the goods are used, then the consumer may have to pay a fee or restitution. This rule gives people the chance to experience the good so as to have better information as to whether it meets expectations. Many stores, of course, voluntarily allow people to return goods that they don't want.

---

[11] See, e.g., Oren Bar-Gill, The Behavioral Economics of Consumer Contracts, 92 Minn. L. Rev. 749 (2008).

[12] See Omri Ben-Shahar & Eric A. Posner, The Right to Withdraw in Contract Law, 40 J. Legal Stud. 115 (2011).

Sellers no doubt believe that people will be more likely to buy if they can return goods that they turn out not to want. But some goods lose value when taken out of the store (food, for example) or can be easily copied (intellectual property), and in these cases the right to withdraw is not extended, nor is it required by law.

Chapter *10*

Policy and Theory

Why should courts enforce contracts? This is a philosophical question, and the answer may seem so obvious that the question is not worth asking. But the question does matter, and not just because it is of academic interest. The normative basis for enforcing contracts matters because the theory behind the enforcement of contracts sheds light on how they should be enforced: what the level of damages should be, for example, or when performance should be excused.

I have assumed throughout this book that the normative basis of contract law is welfarist. Courts enforce contracts because contracts are vehicles through which people enhance their well-being. This statement prompts many questions that I will try to answer in this chapter. In doing so, I will discuss alternative theories of contract law.

§10.1   Reliance Theories

I start with the so-called reliance theory of contract law. This theory holds that courts should enforce contracts because of the reliance of promisees. The theory has been proposed by several prominent scholars, including Fuller[1] and Atiyah.[2]

---

[1] Lon L. Fuller & William R. Perdue, Jr., The Reliance Interest in Contract Damages, 46 Yale L.J. 52 (1936).
[2] See Patrick S. Atiyah, Essays on Contract (1988).

Let us first consider the theory as a description of contract law, then examine its normative appeal. The theory implies that when a person relies on a promise, he is entitled to recover damages if the promisor breaks the promise. Notice that the theory does not imply that a contract must exist; a promise is sufficient. This is why reliance theorists find themselves attracted to promissory estoppel. But promissory estoppel has not made contracting unnecessary. If I promise to sell my house to you, and you rely by selling your old house at a discount, the Statute of Frauds will bar recovery. And, of course, if your reliance is not reasonable — if you give away your house when you could have sold it at a reasonable price — no one thinks that you should recover. Reliance is not a sufficient condition for recovery.

Reliance is not a necessary condition for recovery, either. If I promise to deliver some widgets to you in response to your promise to give me money, then I break the promise a minute later, before you have had a chance to rely, I am liable for breach of contract. If prices change in the meantime, I could owe you a lot of money.

What's wrong with making reliance the basis of recovery? Reliance theorists argue that the reliance approach nicely shows how contracts and torts converge. You commit a breach of contract, just as you commit a tort, by inflicting a harm on another person.[3] Contract law is just a kind of tort law: the purpose is to prevent individuals from harming each other, whether by knocking into them (torts) or breaking promises (contracts). Let's get rid of the old-fashioned doctrinal distinctions between these areas of the law, and call the new field "contorts."[4]

Philosophers generally believe that the basis for tort recovery is corrective justice. If a person culpably harms another person, then the wrongdoer owes a remedy to the victim. So if breaching a contract is a culpable harm, and the harm is the lost reliance, then the breacher owes a remedy to the victim — arguably the reliance damages necessary to return her to the status quo.

However, there is a difference between tort and contract. It is hard to avoid a punch in the nose, but one can avoid the reliance costs resulting from breach of contract merely by not relying on the promise. The claim that the law should punish those who break promises implies that there is something valuable about promising in the first place. But what exactly? The idea of corrective justice, by itself, does not answer this question.

[3] See Oliver Wendell Holmes, The Path of the Law, 10 Harv. L. Rev. 457, 462 (1897).

[4] This happy pun is due to Grant Gilmore, see Grant Gilmore, The Death of Contract 90 (1974). And see Section 9.1, on the relationship between contract law and tort law.

§10.2   Rights Theories

Several scholars have taken a more philosophically sophisticated approach than the reliance theory without abandoning the latter theory's non-welfarist foundations. They argue that contract law is concerned with protecting the rights of individuals.

This approach appears in two flavors. One argument is that people have a natural or moral right to alienate their property. They do so by exchanging it for other things, and this inevitably involves making promises. If the law did not enforce promises, people would not be able to make binding promises, so an important aspect of their freedom would be lacking.[5]

The second argument is that the law concerns itself with protecting people from non-consensual takings of their property. Tort law is a prominent example. But if people consent to alienation, then the law should permit that alienation. Contract law enforces promises because by making a promise people consent to its enforcement by the law.[6]

Both theories are based on the premise that the law should respect individual autonomy. The autonomous person has the freedom to arrange his life in any way that he sees fit, as long as he does not violate the autonomy of others. If a person consents to the transfer of his own property through a promise, then legal enforcement of that promise is unobjectionable (argument 2). If the person makes a promise, then he seeks to bind himself, and legal enforcement of that promise can only enhance the person's autonomy (argument 1).

Unfortunately, autonomy is a vague concept, and it does not imply legal enforcement of promises. One problem is that legal enforcement takes away freedom as well as gives it. If I have made a legally enforceable promise, and then change my mind and want to retract it, I am not permitted to do so. The later self is bound by the earlier self's promise, so the later self's autonomy is diminished by the enhancement of the autonomy of the earlier self. This is a serious enough problem that in a wide range of contexts contracts are not enforceable — for example, a promise to enter slavery if one does not repay a loan.

And as a description of the law, neither theory does very well. Both theories imply that gratuitous promises should be enforced; but they generally are not. More important, neither theory provides a basis for distinguishing between different rules of contract law.[7] Specific performance, expectation damages, and reliance damages all bind the promisor by sanctioning him if he breaches. The rights theories do not explain why one remedy might be preferable to another.

---

[5] See Charles Fried, Contract as Promise: A Theory of Contractual Obligation (1982).

[6] See Randy E. Barnett, A Consent Theory of Contract, 86 Colum. L. Rev. 269 (1986).

[7] See Richard Craswell, Contract Law, Default Rules, and the Philosophy of Promising, 88 Mich. L. Rev. 489 (1989).

§10.3   Welfarist Theories

This brings us to welfarist theories. This family of theories holds that laws should be evaluated according to their effect on the welfare or well-being of citizens. The welfarist defense of contract law argues that contract law enables people to enhance their own well-being through bargains and exchanges. And the welfarist evaluation of contract law judges its doctrines by the extent to which they maximize well-being.[8]

What is welfare? Philosophers have proposed three approaches to thinking about this complex idea. Mental-state theorists believe that welfare or well-being refers to a mental state characterized by the feeling of happiness. Objective-list theorists believe that a person enjoys well-being if she satisfies certain objective criteria of happiness — for example, an adequate diet, literacy, companionship, and satisfying work. Desire-based theorists believe that a person is happy if she is able to satisfy her desires. In the latter group, we can distinguish those who believe that the relevant desires are those that the person happens to have, and those who believe that the relevant desires are those that would satisfy certain objective criteria, for example, that they be adequately informed.

Economists use the first version of the desire-based theory. They speak in terms of "preferences" rather than desires, but the idea is the same. The economic approach holds that an individual may be conceived to have "preferences" about the world, which technically means that she can rank various states of the world according to desirability. A utility function maps these outcomes to an index of utility. When the individual makes choices, these choices reflect his preference ranking, that is, they maximize his utility. Because an individual always has a certain set of endowments or a budget that restricts his ability to take actions, he maximizes his utility subject to the constraint that he has limited resources.

Individuals frequently trade, and they do so for the reasons given in Section 2.7. A person with a lot of oranges does not receive as much satisfaction from the marginal orange as he would from a first apple; if he can find a person with a lot of apples and no oranges, a jointly value-maximizing trade can be made. In a modern economy people work, receive wages, then use the cash to buy goods and services that they value. Trade in this way can result in higher utility for each party.

However, trade does not always maximize social welfare — defined as the aggregation of the utilities of all the individuals in a society. There are two main reasons. First, when people are poorly informed, coerced, and in other ways deflected from acting on their preferences, they may be made worse off by a trade. Second, even when a trade makes the two parties

---

[8]This assumption has guided economic analysis from the beginning; for a comprehensive defense of this approach, see Alan Schwartz & Robert E. Scott, Contract Theory and the Limits of Contract Law, 113 Yale L.J. 541 (2003).

better off, it can make a third party — a person not involved in the trade — worse off. Conspiracies to commit crimes, including restraints on trade, are examples.

Law can help solve these problems. To evaluate a law, one needs a way to measure its effect on the well-being of citizens. This is harder than it looks. There are conceptual, philosophical, and practical difficulties with what might seem the obvious route to go: sum up everyone's utilities in the status quo, and then estimate the effect of the law on this aggregate. The problem is that the economic approach to utility is ordinal, not cardinal: a person only has a preference ranking, so his utility function expresses only an ordering. A certain utility number is arbitrary in the sense that any number can be chosen as long as the ordering is preserved; but if you add up arbitrary numbers, you get an arbitrary number.

There have been a number of responses to this difficulty, but the literature is difficult and would take us afield. Let me just stipulate to two welfare or "efficiency" measures, both of which have problems that will be discussed in due course. A law passes the Pareto standard when it makes at least one person better off without making any other person worse off. A law passes the Kaldor-Hicks standard when it produces winners who are sufficiently better off that they could compensate the losers. The Pareto standard is relatively uncontroversial but weak: many desirable laws do not meet it. The Kaldor-Hicks standard is controversial but stronger: many undesirable laws do meet it.

An example will show why. A factory manufactures products at a cost of $10 per unit, but it also produces pollution that injures nearby residents to the extent of $4 per unit. If the factory installed new machinery at a cost of $1 per unit, the pollution would be reduced by $3 per unit. The factory has no incentive to install the new machinery because it does not enjoy the benefit of the pollution reduction although it incurs the cost. Should the law force the factory to install the new machinery? Under the Kaldor-Hicks standard, the answer is yes: the residents are made better off by $3 per unit, which is more than enough to compensate the factory for the $1 per unit loss. However, the outcome is not Pareto superior. The manufacturer is not actually compensated; the new law makes it worse off and the residents better off. The government could also tax residents by $2 per unit and give this money to the manufacturer. This outcome would be Pareto superior: the residents are better off by $1 per unit and the manufacturer is better off by $1 per unit.

I said that the Pareto criterion is uncontroversial but too strong. The reason is that it would block many laws that are generally considered desirable. Suppose it turns out to be impossible to compensate the manufacturer; most people would nonetheless agree that the pollution law is desirable. Or consider a law requiring everyone to get a vaccine against a dangerous disease. The vaccine will save millions of lives, but it will also, statistically, raise the risk of cancer for a small number of people. The government cannot identify and compensate those hurt by the vaccine, so the program is not Pareto superior. Nonetheless, the vaccine program is a good idea.

The Kaldor-Hicks criterion permits government projects that may be offensive. Consider a project that taxes people living in a poor neighborhood to create an environmental amenity for rich people living in a suburb. It is possible that the rich people will (being rich) be willing to pay a lot for the project, while the poor people (being poor) will be willing to pay very little for it and yet they must pay the tax. The Kaldor-Hicks criterion creates a bias for rich people because rich people have more money and therefore are willing to pay more for projects that benefit them.

Many of the arguments in this book have used the Pareto standard, though cheating slightly. Consider, for example, the argument that expectation damages are superior to reliance damages. One way to think of this argument is to imagine that a legislature must decide what remedy to codify. One would argue that expectation damages is Pareto superior to the reliance damages remedy. The reason is that if you switched from reliance damages to expectation damages, contracts would become more valuable. Compared to reliance damages, the promisor under expectation damages cannot engage in inefficient breaches, or extract more money from the promisee in order to agree to perform. The promisee is thus willing to pay more, ex ante, to enter the contract. Depending on the relative bargaining power of the parties, at least one and possibly both parties are better off. The promisee can rely more heavily and thus increase the value of the performance to himself; and the promisor might in return receive a higher payment for his services. However, changes in the law inevitably produce winners and losers, and one would need to take account of these effects when deciding whether to pass a new law.

§10.4   Problems with Welfarism

Not everyone agrees with welfarism. There are various standard criticisms:

- Welfarist arguments frequently violate strong moral intuitions that require, among other things, that people's autonomy be respected. Many people argue that it is wrong to break promises, whether or not breach is efficient.
- People's preferences are often foolish, poorly informed, and distorted by the circumstances under which they are brought up. Perhaps

people would be better off if they were prevented from entering the rat race and accumulating excess wealth and goods they do not need.

- Trades are not always socially desirable. Certain products — organs, gestational services[9] — should not be traded because trade in them offends widespread notions about how people should be treated.

It is an undeniable fact that policy is oriented toward promoting the well-being of society, but at the same time that this goal is subject to various moral and pragmatic constraints. It is good to remember that when policy makers design tax systems, social programs, environmental regulations, and other social constructs, they aim (in theory) to promote well-being, not to advance other normative goals that may be philosophically respectable. These other goals often serve as side constraints. Contract law is no different from these other areas of policy.

§10.5 Does Economics Explain Contract Law?

At a high level of generality, the answer is yes. Economics recommends freedom of contract, and by and large contract law respects freedom of contract. But many lower-level doctrinal rules of contract law conflict with economic prescriptions — the penalty doctrine is an example — and although scholars have attempted to rationalize these areas of law from an economic perspective, the rationalizations often seem strained. And then a great deal of contract law does not follow in any obvious way from economics, though it is possible that it is consistent with economic prescriptions. It is just not clear, for example, what economics tells us about the parol evidence rule or the offer/acceptance doctrines.[10] An early success for economics was the efficient breach theory, but, as I have explained, it is doubtful that the efficient breach theory provides an adequate justification for expectation damages.

Indeed, it would be surprising if contract doctrine consistently advanced efficiency. The judges who developed contract doctrine for the most part lacked economic training, and probably fell back on their everyday moral intuitions, which no doubt overlapped with economics only partially. In other areas of judge-made law — for example, antitrust law — judges did not show themselves to be economically sophisticated, and the doctrine made little sense until they started listening to economists. Some scholars have argued that the nature of the litigation process — in particular, the supposed benefits from litigating when rules are inefficient — would exert

---

[9] See In re Baby Girl M., 688 P.2d 918 (Cal. 1993) (en banc).

[10] See Eric A. Posner, Economic Analysis of Contract Law After Three Decades: Success or Failure?, 112 Yale L.J. 829 (2003).

evolutionary pressure in the direction of efficiency,[11] but these arguments are not persuasive.

But if you think that the government should promote the well-being of citizens, and that contract law is relevant to the well-being of citizens, as it surely is, then economic ideas provide useful tools for advancing the law, and for understanding it.

---

[11] See, e.g., George L. Priest, The Common Law Process and the Selection of Efficient Rules, 6 J. Legal Stud. 65 (1977); Paul H. Rubin, Why Is the Common Law Efficient?, 6 J. Legal Stud. 51 (1977).

Table of Cases

References to notes are indicated by n and the note number following page numbers.

Table of Cases

Table of Cases

Index

References to notes are indicated by n following page numbers.

Index

Index

CPSIA information can be obtained at www.ICGtesting.com
Printed in the USA
LVOW03s2159190914

404994LV00009B/26/P